A PASSION FOR PLANTS

A hanging basket is like a portable
garden. This combination of fuchsia
and variegated ivy would be ideal for
partial shade

A Passion For

PLANTS

Geoffrey Smith

DAVID & CHARLES

Newton Abbot   London

This year, the *Ipomoea* (morning glory),
grown more in hope than anticipation,
scrambled up from their own territory
below the terrace wall to mingle blue
flowers with the scarlet blossoms of the
Schizostylis. By carefully chipping
morning glory seed it is possible to
persuade good germination

Photographs by Kelvin H. Smith
Illustrations by Janet Hutsby

*British Library Cataloguing
in Publication Data*

Smith, Geoffrey *1928–*
  A passion for plants.
  1. Gardens. Ornamental plants
  I. Title
  635.9

  ISBN 0-7153-9427-4

Typeset by Typesetters (Brimingham) Ltd
Smethwick, West Midlands
and printed in West Germany
by Mohndruck GmbH
for David & Charles Publishers plc
Brunel House   Newton Abbot   Devon

Contents

But though so familiar, that spectral light in the silence has never lost its meaning; the violets are sweet year by year though never so many summers pass away; indeed, its meaning grows wider as time goes on. The roses are even dearer now with so many years, as it were, upon the petals.

Richard Jefferies with his ability to draw word pictures expresses an almost mystical communication with the natural world: a deep and abiding delight in green leaves, grass and sunshine, blue skies and sparkle of the brook. For as Jefferies insists it is the small things, the scent of damask roses or the enamelling purple thyme growing across moss-covered stones, which come back to mind in later years, still warm and fragrant because they have never quite been forgotten.

1
Why Be a Gardener?

Though we can exercise little control over what happens in the broader landscape around us, inside the garden boundaries our authority is near absolute. No matter how limited the space, there we can give free rein to all our creative, artistic skill and practical handicraft.

Gardening is such a personal experience of success and failure that no one can make a proper analysis of the satisfaction to be derived from growing plants without first becoming involved in the routine work of digging, seed sowing, and weeding. The best gardeners are those who love plants, whether their interest is fruit, vegetable, or flower. Such people can never pass a garden or allotment without peering into it in an effort to learn something more about the design of a border, or discover some new method of cultivating a particular plant. Without this kind of love for, and interest in, plants there can be no development of that instinctive understanding which breeds succulent fruit, fresh vegetables and beautiful flowers.

Quality produce is only part of the reward. There is the beauty and delight to be found in green leaves and sunshine: seeing the slow improvement through the work we do in preparing the soil; all the digging and manuring of the autumn past coming to fruition through the summer and autumn to come. There is the slow yet inevitable passage of the seasons, so different in their very quality of timelessness from the frenetic rush of modern living.

Though it may one day be possible to buy a garden already made as seen at Chelsea or similar fashionable venue, what satisfaction is there to be derived from that? It is more in the nature of an experience enjoyed second-hand; in avoiding the pitfalls, the supermarket gardener misses out on the personal involvement where triumph balances disappointment to leave a credit of satisfaction. Each new observation throughout the course of a lifetime spent gardening simply increases the conviction that the knowledge gained over the years is only a fraction of a vast well of information still left to be tapped.

Gardening is for the larger part a routine of digging, planting, or sowing, followed by a sequence of watering, feeding, weeding and pruning. Interspersed with all this healthy toil there are moments of sublime quality, sometimes of beauty, and moments of a silent spiritual, mystical nature which are still a form of communicating. No one can predict these never-to-be forgotten interludes – they

A tired bunch of *Anemone* 'De Caen' flowers clutched in a child's hot hand is so expressive a symbol of Mothers' Day. I wonder how many people have felt a first stirring of interest in gardening as a result. Certainly, I remember my daughter's intense disappointment when the corms planted at least a week before the date in question failed to produce even a token flower. Useless to explain to a

five-year-old child the slow maturation process of seed or corm until the ultimate flower. Such knowledge is only gained by experience. *Anemone coronaria* 'De Caen' corms planted 2in (5cm) deep in fertile soil, as she now knows, will flower profusely and make the most reliable cut flowers

Sir Francis Bacon writing of gardens in 1625:

It is the purest of human pleasures; it is the greatest refreshment to the spirits of man without which buildings and palaces are but gross handyworks: and a man shall ever see that, when ages grow to civility and elegancy, men come to build stately sooner than to garden finely; as if gardening were the greater perfection.

The above was included in a book dealing with gardening phrases in common use which I had taken with me on a working tour of French rose gardens. I had just returned from spending a day in the Bagatelle near Paris; sun-soaked hours spent seeing roses and breathing roses in that lovely tranquil garden left me in a condition which I am convinced only gardeners experience outside of Paradise. The phrase, 'It is the purest of human pleasures', expressed my feelings so perfectly that I copied the passage down.

The 'Hidcote' lavender offers more than just a grey and blue, for a delectable scent must be added to this much loved shrub's credit

are only bought by experience and by being as much in the garden as time and weather will permit.

There have been enough of such encounters in my own gardening life to encourage an interest in growing plants which I can only describe as impassioned. I remember the first snowdrops in bloom amongst a drift of aconites as the bitterly cold, hardly endured winter of 1947 progressed from memory into legend. I had to pass the sheltered corner where the aconites and snowdrops were growing every morning, yet on only one occasion, as the morning sunshine polished the dew-fresh flowers and the swelling sound of a still unpractised dawn chorus banished the frozen stillness, did the beauty of the scene reveal itself.

There are so many late winter offerings of hope which are like salve to the gardening eye. That flush of purple which colours the silver birch twigs sometime during February is one of the eagerly awaited signs of resurgence of life. In my last garden I planted three witch hazel against the background of a five-stemmed silver birch so that the extra dimension of scent was added to the optimistic note of colour. Sure signs these that, though the indoor garden will still be a prime source of expression for several weeks yet, already the world outdoors is laying claim to our attention.

No calendar yet devised can predict exactly when I know beyond doubt that spring has finally pushed the garden gate wide open. There is the unmistakable scent of rain-moist earth and the sight of clods steaming under a warm sun. Then there are the quiet few minutes spent hand pollinating wide-open peach flowers in the greenhouse at mid-day, when temperatures rise and the rabbit's tail which functions as a bumble bee is stained yellow by the free running pollen. Damping down the trees after pollination fills the air with a fragrance familiar to me since early childhood. So many annually repeated tasks, part of a familiar pattern which can have changed little since that veteran of Virgil's made a kitchen garden by the Galaseus on derelict land – and lived there happy as a king.

Summer comes almost as a respite after the near frenetic onslaught of spring. Lengthening days permit a more leisurely approach to the daily round and common task. For though there is much to be done the work provides an excuse for being out in the garden surrounded by the still unsullied loveliness of flowers and the concentrated, silent energy of growing things. The scent from a handful of lavender flowers pushed down the front of my open shirt mingles with the distillation from the roses and the freshly mown grass, as much a part of summer's days as the repetitive calling of the cuckoo.

Early morning and the cool of mid evening are the most rewarding times to be abroad in the garden, especially when, as this morning, overnight rain has refreshed all the plants after a month-long drought. I was out in the garden before the sun had cleared the horizon, when the air was full of so many subtle odours – mock orange, lily, and the sweet pea, border pink perfume which is so absolutely summer's portion. White clouds rolling together across the sky, a blackbird foraging busily on the lawn, and the

The castor oil plant *Ricinus communis* is grown as an annual for use in summer bedding schemes, or as a centrepiece to a container. The form *R.gibsonii* illustrated is more compact with bronze foliage. A plant I treated with respect as a youngster for medicinal reasons – the flowers look ominously oil-filled

Scabiosa caucasica is a good example of knowledge gained from practical experience. In one garden where the soil was a free draining magnesium limestone-based loam, *Scabious* 'Clive Greaves' grew and blossomed so profusely as to provide me with a most useful cut-flower income supplement. My next garden made on glacial clay proved so totally unsuitable I gave up growing scabious and sorely missed the powder-blue flowers which had been so much a feature of summers past

merest whisper of a breeze stirring the leaves above my head served only to increase the all-pervading quiet. For a brief while I was held in an invisible web, at one with the complete garden world not just the plants: aware of the busy life going on amongst the grass blades, in the bushes, and through the air about me, all a part of nature's timeless process. A house martin skimmed low over the pool, two white butterflies fluttered around each other above the lawn, then a tractor turned into the lane and immediately it was a bustling, busy day.

Autumn is when the leaves on just one horsechestnut tree down the lane change from green to pale yellow. Dahlias flaunt their bright coloured flowers in the borders and the pungent scent of dew-wet chrysanthemums identifies the change of season. There is a noticeable switch in my attitude, a tomorrow-will-do approach to routine work, now a little untidiness is not only acceptable but obligatory. Amongst the joyous festival of colour and abundance of the autumn there are sudden pauses of quite inexplicable forlornness and despondency. Then the mood passes and the joyous humour of the season reasserts itself.

Winter has a reputation, not altogether deserved, for being all dull grey, brown, and lifeless. Those of us who garden know that the colour is there still, though more refined and subtle: hoar-frosted seed heads of teasel jewels polished by sunlight, fragile white loveliness of Christmas roses gathered to float in a bowl of

water on New Year's Day, twig tracery of trees framed against the orange scarlet of a January sunset, and the lambs-tail catkins on twisted hazel. There is contentment, too, in looking back over the freshly turned and manured earth as darkness falls at the end of a day spent digging – the ache of tired muscles a reassurance that the evening relaxation in front of a glowing fire has been duly earned. Grand landscape or miniature, each season has moments of breathtaking beauty which are like finger prints uniquely their own. Above and beyond all else there is that comforting knowledge of earth and plants at rest yet gathering strength for the joyous upsurge of growth that comes with spring: watching seeds sown in March grow through the ensuing months, or in the case of shrubs and trees, over the passage of years, to maturity – a tree possibly marking too precisely our own progression through life.

Some might argue, and rightly so, that all these experiences could be enjoyed walking in a garden someone else had toiled to make. For me this would be like sitting down to a banquet without having worked up appetite enough to do justice to the food provided, or following a man smoking a fine Havana cigar and catching just a whiff of fragrant smoke.

'Why be a gardener?' was the question posed at the start of this chapter. The answer, of course, is that nothing else offers the same degree of gratification.

There is always a place for the primrose, one of my favourite flowers

OPPOSITE
Sedum spectabile 'Brilliant' is well named, for the flowers are busy with butterflies in September

C. Day Lewis: 'That veteran of Virgil's I recall, Who made a kitchen garden by the Galaesus, On derelict land, and got the first of spring, From airs and buds, the first fruits in the fall, And lived at peace there, happy as a king.'

Aquilegias are easily grown, short-lived perennials which are not slow to self seed into odd corners to surprise me with their beauty

2

Adam's Profession to Till the Ground

Exactly when man changed from being merely a hunter to become a tiller of the soil and a grower of crops no one really knows. Even the most eminent authorities on the subject can do no more than make a considered guess. By general agreement the suggestion is that farming in some form has gone on in Britain for more than 4,000 years. Looking across my own garden, over a hoar-frosted molehill-encrusted lawn, to where winter aconite are burnished to even brighter yellow by the January sunshine, the sense of being one of many who have worked this plot of land is somehow reassuring.

No special talent is needed to become a gardener, only a love of, and interest in, the cultivation of plants. There is no question of eligibility by birth or degree, for gardening is the common factor which takes no account of class divisions. First prize for roses in the local show might as easily return to a cottage as to a baronial hall.

There are those who get fulfilment and derive satisfaction from the study of one specialist group of plants. The chrysanthemum grower who strives over eleven months to achieve one perfect flower is just as committed a son of Adam as the dilettante who, in the rich and diverse world of plants, takes pleasure if not in all, at least in the major portion of what is offered. The favourite flower for such a lover of nature's artistry is the one in bloom at the time. In the beginning then, embrace the whole broad spectrum of the plant world. Some will appeal more than others. Gradually, the garden will become not just an expression of individual creative design; it will be a declaration of our personal choice of tree, shrub, herbaceous perennial, annual, or bulb. Then we become, like the specialist, strivers after perfection in one flower, though not just once but ten, twenty, or a hundred times a year.

Initially the beginner is at the mercy of every self-professed expert. Each and every one with experience of growing plants will have a particular method of sowing seed, potting, planting, and feeding which is beyond doubt better than any other. That the gardener next door uses totally different means and yet succeeds in reaching a similar standard may at first seem like a contradiction of the term 'expert'. Yet this very lack of a precise formula, a blueprint with which to engineer a garden filled with perfect plants, is what makes the practice of gardening so fascinating.

And the Lord God planted a garden eastward in Eden; and out of the ground made the Lord God to grow every tree that is pleasant to the sight and good for food.

So, then, as the Bible tells us, it was in the beginning and has been ever since, for there is so much happiness and fulfilment to be discovered in the cultivation of a garden and the growing of plants, as all sons of Adam well know.

Always, when reading this passage in Genesis, I find cause for regret that the tree of knowledge was lost to cultivation. Instead of gaining experience in the sweat of our faces and through the slow passage of years, how easy it would be to acquire the wisdom of ages simply by picking and eating a fruit. Not so, for the real underlying pleasure through all the years of my gardening adventure has been the distant view, new experience and the slowly accumulated better understanding. To learn all about plants and gardening right at the outset would not have given me any sense of satisfaction at all.

Gardening is not an exact science. There is no handbook which, if slavishly adhered to, will guarantee success on every occasion. There are so many influential factors beyond our control. The soil we work with is teeming with life, so chemically complex that it defies complete understanding or analysis. Another factor which is beyond our regulation, at least in the open garden, and yet has the most important influence over the well-being of the plants we grow, is the weather. To see eagerly awaited flowers and tender young growth turned to black ruin by a May frost is an experience common to most of us who garden. Fortunately, there is always another year. A gale may lay two centuries of growth in a twisted tangle of branches. What does it matter? After all, the man who planted that tree never saw it in proud maturity, so we can, with similar faith in tomorrow, plant another to replace it.

Knowledge acquired through practical experience is certainly of value. There are those who maintain this is the only way, which is a little like saying that the only way to become a proficient gardener is to live on an island cut off from all outside influence. There are numerous books, first-hand accounts by writers with a lifetime's experience on every aspect of horticulture. Why ignore such a vast storehouse of knowledge, the accumulated wisdom of centuries? Enjoy and profit from conversation with those who speak from practical experience and have a seasoned familiarity with the subject. Theirs is the wine of advice; without this sharing of experience gardeners would live like members of some monastic order in a sterile silence. Enjoy a long, leisurely apprenticeship, for these formative years will prove in retrospect to be the most enjoyable and rewarding of all. Let there be time to absorb the principles and practice along with some of the history and romance as well. For gardeners and gardens now are what the past has made them. Everything attempted is in the nature of an exploration, for each experience is new, even though gardeners have been through a precisely similar initiation process ever since Eve acquired a liking for apples.

EARTH BEFORE IT IS GREEN – OR FERTILE

Soil is the basic material with which gardeners work. From even a cursory enquiry into the subject it will be obvious that soils vary in character. What then makes a soil? The rough classification of light, heavy, acid, alkaline, hardly answers the question. Soil is a mixture of rock broken down over centuries of time into fine particles of varying size, mixed with plant and animal remains. The nature of a surface soil depends on the type of rock from which it was formed: sandstone, chalk, limestone, granite, basalt, and millstone grit have all subscribed to the base soils of Britain. Climatic forces – glaciers most importantly – have blurred the clearly defined regions by carrying soil from one area to mix with that of another possibly hundreds of miles away. Having gardened on peat moss in Lancashire, light sand in Norfolk, Cornish flint,

Gardening to the beginner seems to be all an inconsistent mystery. Some plants want this, he or she is told, and some that; and the poor bewildered novice can see no more reason for the diversity of their wants than for the difference of their flower colour or shape of leaves. He or she regards the expert gardener as a kind of magician, as one who can make all plants thrive by the very way in which he handles them, and who knows by instinct what they want. Now it is quite true that the best gardeners do seem to have a way of their own with plants and that they will often succeed with a plant they know nothing about where an inferior gardener less ignorant would fail. But they are not born with this gift.

A comforting philosophy this, expressed in a newspaper article nearly one hundred years ago.

Gardeners, I am convinced, should be like children and observe with a less intense interest, for dispassionate observation is the secret of a long memory – so then for the gardener, poet or artist the secret of success is detached observation.

Lavatera olbia 'Rosea' is one of my 'must have' shrubs, for its flowering season lasts all summer. A hot, sun-baked corner of the garden will encourage a 6ft (5.5m) high bush to open a continuous succession of large, pink flowers, backed by greyish, downy foliage

Gradually the garden will become a declaration of personal choice

---

Knowledge is like current coin. A man may have some right to be proud of possessing it only if he has worked for the gold of it, and assayed it and stamped it, so that it may be received of all men as true or earned it fairly, being already assayed. (Ruskin)

---

glacial Yorkshire clay, and the limestone mixture of the Craven fault, I would offer the suggestion that there is no such thing as an average or even ordinary soil, for all are different, even in gardens which are next door to one another. As for the soil – well, failing four acres in the Vale of Evesham, I would settle for a clay soil which had been well worked with dressings of compost for seven years. Preferably such a soil should be on the acid side of neutral, and drain freely yet, in contradiction, retain moisture and in consequence plant nutrients. Such soils are easy to cultivate; with a good crumb structure they are what is known as early land, for they warm up quickly in spring. This is not a description of some Lotus land, for all soils, whether glutinously adhesive clay or blow-away sands, are capable of being brought into a comparable state of fertility.

Only a very few are fortunate enough to possess soils which are so naturally fertile as to need scarcely any work at all to keep them productive. And even they will never admit to having a good soil; there is always some serpent to mar the perfection of their little Eden. Apart from the fortunate few, most gardeners must seek ways of improving the soil they have: a conglomeration of rock fragments, vegetable and animal remains held together with water. Add to this a teeming population of micro-organisms and not so micro bugs, worms and beetles, all busily engaged in breaking down organic materials, feeding, being fed on, reproducing, dying and being reprocessed – a teeming factory of potential fertility waiting to serve their purpose. All the gardener needs to do is to provide the raw materials and congenial working conditions. Remember the slow recycling process is going on the whole time in hedgerows, woodlands and wasteland, making certain that the balance of what is removed from the soil is preserved by what is returned.

A good soil structure is of the utmost importance and the work done in achieving this most desirable end will be repaid a hundredfold. Fortunately, the sort of cultivation needed to clean any weed-infested plot and make it fit for planting will, given a few minor additions, improve the fertility at the same time. There are chemicals available which will clear the soil of weeds with no more effort than is required to apply them. Once cleared of unwanted debris, that same soil can be made productive with yet another formulation from the chemist's equivalent of a compost heap or manure stack. They may, indeed, work, bringing the Utopian condition of a labour-free garden within reach of all. I have a morbid fear of reducing my garden to a sterile thing, inhabited by myself and those plants allowed to flourish there, with no black-birds tugging for worms on the back lawn for, of course, to make less work it has been dewormed, and no butterflies, those by-blows of summer, for perish the thought, they produce caterpillars. So, never having proved any of the magic formulas, it is with spade, compost heap and the expenditure of effort and perspiration that my garden is made and maintained.

Seeing the quality of the soil we work improve each year as a result of our efforts satisfies the peasant instinct latent in all who garden. That the time spent in the garden amongst the plants will lead to a better understanding of all those things which, when correctly applied, produce the best results is an encouraging bonus. There is a harmony and sense of purpose to be found in a well maintained garden which soothes the eye and refreshes the spirit. But, just in case we get carried away on a wave of euphoria, there is a deal of hard work in the process and patience will be needed. Unlike diamonds, a garden may not be forever, but always work as though it will.

On any soil, labour to improve fertility will be wasted unless excess moisture drains away quickly. My own experience with the problem of impeded drainage came during my formative gardening years when working a heavy clay soil which puddled like adobe mud in winter and baked brick hard in summer. A combination of ignorance and a strong back insisted that the way to solve the

There are 'difficult to grow' plants that are demanding for obvious reasons. Some iris need more sun than a British summer usually provides. In an excess of zeal I once built a frame especially for Juno iris and when, after much persuasion, they flowered found their beauty an illusion fostered by their intransigence.

Other plants never seem to flourish in captivity even in soil and situations not dissimilar to those of their native homes. Hardy terrestrial orchids, particularly Cypripedium, *have never accepted my hospitality, largely, I suspect, because they failed to recover from the shock of disturbance.*

The only chance of success with so many of the most capricious garden plants is to grow them from seed, and with such slowly maturing plants as orchids that would mean a degree of specialisation. Some plants, like the Madonna lily, respond to neglect as I found when several bulbs, after resolutely refusing to flower in carefully prepared soil, were unceremoniously dumped under a south-facing wall. The following July afforded such a display of these breathtakingly lovely white flowers as I had only previously encountered in their native home. Specialising in reverse might be a proper description of such a negative approach.

The soil is the seat of a number of slow chemical changes affecting the organic material it receives; residues of an animal or vegetable nature, when applied to the soil are converted into the dark coloured complex known as 'humus' which becomes slowly oxidised to carbonic acid, water, nitric acid, and other simple substances serving as food for plants. These changes at one time regarded as purely chemical, are now recognised as dependent upon the vital processes of certain minute organisms, universally distributed throughout cultivated soil, and subject to the same laws of nutrition, multiplication, life and death, as hold for the higher organisms.

A passage from The Soil *by Sir Daniel Hall which, as a student, I committed to memory. So much of modern techniques of crop production ignores the basic concept that the fertility of the soil is wholly bound up in the maintenance of this cycle of change.*

drainage problem was from above. All my labour was in vain until I saw what happened when a nearby field was mole-drained. The volume of water which poured out of the narrow tunnels left by the plough into a ditch along the field edge astonished me. It was not practical to bring a tractor complete with mole drains into my half-acre garden. The alternative of using land tiles laid to a soak-away was the most effective solution to the waterlogging. Once the surface moisture was removed, dressings or organic matter worked into the top 15in of soil brought about, season by season, a visible change for the better in soil structure and plant growth.

WASTE NOT, WANT NOT

Organic matter is, in fact, anything which will rot down under natural conditions. Spent hops, cotton seed waste, digested sludge, leather dust, peat, and farmyard manure are all grist to the compost heap's mill. Briefly, I contracted to take all the unsaleable waste from the local greengrocer. This included banana stalks which made the best compost of all.

All organic matter rots down to form humus, that black amorphous residue with the near magical ability to benefit all soils. Humus, by binding clay particles into a loose, larger crumb structure, opens up stagnant, lifeless, inert clods and transforms them into a friable tilth. This, in consequence, allows free passage of water and, equally important, of air, without which plant roots cannot survive, let alone grow.

Autumn is in practical terms the best time to dig over the soil and work in the organic matter, leaving the clods rough for the alternating wet-dry, freeze-thaw of winter weather to work on. Remove all deep-rooted and persistent perennial weeds at the same time. Let a single root of bindweed, bishop's curse, or couch grass remain to recolonise the newly planted borders or recently seeded lawn, and the ensuing work of trying to clear the intruders will take much of the pleasure and refreshment out of our future gardening activities. Such weeds are a malaise which spreads even as we sleep.

Then in late February apply a dressing of lime to the soil, though not if plants which will not grow in alkaline soils are the main source of interest. The improvement in the texture of clay soils after the lime application is quite remarkable. Due to a chemical reaction with the clay fraction, the individual particles cling together forming larger granules. So instead of a dense mass the soil forms a more open texture less liable to compaction, which makes it easier to cultivate. Lime also makes valuable nutrients available to the plant roots. The action of lime may appear to be the same as that of organic matter, but the one is no substitute for the other. Both are an integral part of what is termed good cultivation. Humus does much more than improve the structure in clay soils, for it acts as a reservoir to moisture and helps stabilise light soils by binding the finer particles together, while at the same time holding minerals, which are the plants' food source, against leaching out under excessive rain.

Plants grow by taking up the minerals dissolved in the soil's moisture through fine hairs located at the tip of each root. Then, by making use of energy derived from sunlight and the green colouring matter of the leaf which botanists identify by the name of chlorophyll, they convert simple chemical substances into complex proteins, sugars and starches – an over-simplified explanation of a process on which the whole of life on this earth is based.

The gardener's task is to ensure that there are sufficient of the main food sources in the soil, and not merely there but in a form or state which enables the plant to absorb and use them. Because these various sources of nutrient are invisible we can only ensure that there is a plentiful supply of major elements – nitrogen, phosphates and potash – by regular applications of compound fertiliser. Any subsequent deficiency can be identified by the reaction of the crops planted in the soil. Lush, luxuriant growth is an indication of abundant nitrogen; too much leads to soft growth which can be corrected by feeding with potash. Potash encourages flower production and intensifies petal and fruit colour; it also concentrates flavour in fruit and vegetables and improves their eating qualities. Phosphates are needed particularly by young seedlings for healthy root development.

Dressings of farm manure, compost, and other organic matter will, as they break down, release the elements of their own composition back into the soil, where they then become available to the plants growing there. This is important not so much for the major ingredients, nitrogen, potash, and phosphates, which are easily supplemented. Organic matter, particularly made from plant debris in the form of well conditioned compost, supplies valuable minor or trace elements without which the plant suffers an imbalance; a shortage of iron, for example, shows as a leaf yellowing in rhododendrons. All these elements, major and trace, can be supplemented by means of foliar feeding, or direct application to the soil, though not with the same precision as the organic manure, compost soil conditioner method which does the two jobs in one.

As mentioned earlier, a fertile soil contains a thriving population of insects, fungi, bacteria, and other life forms. Some, indeed most, are beneficial like the bacteria and fungi which feed on and break down organic matter. Others are decidedly harmful, as witness the fungus which causes root rots or the eel worm which attacks phlox or narcissus. The rest are unaligned neutrals which strive to maintain a balance between the saprophyte and pathogen by feeding on both with splendid impartiality. The soil is a complex, interacting world, yet so simple to maintain in a healthy, fertile condition with a well used spade and a never failing supply of organic matter.

Beauty in All Things if Men Had Eyes

With the soil dug and in prime weed-free condition, the most fascinating of all garden processes may begin. Certainly designs for

The obedient plant, *Physostegia virginiana* 'Vivid', which grows to 36in (91cm) high, was often used as an example of compliance and tractability by my father when I had been disobedient. If pushed to one side, the flowers remain there; which is more than can be said for the average seven-year-old. An easy-to-grow perennial which opens spikes of pink blooms during July and August

According to Goethe, 'Nature gives you
the impression as if there were nothing
contradictory in the world; and yet,
when you return back to the dwelling
place of man, be it lofty or low, wide or
narrow, there is ever somewhat to
contend with, to battle with, to smooth
and put to rights'.
In short, Goethe is offering a truth most
of those who grow plants are
immediately and constantly aware of; in
a garden there is always work waiting
to be done.

LEFT
Prunus sargentii is always the first to anticipate the change from summer to autumn

A garden in a wheelbarrow – easily adapted to any plant, and easily moved into full sun

the garden can be drawn up even as the builder lays the concrete foundations of the house. In practice the best place to make mistakes is on paper; they take less erasing there. On the drawing board extravagant, impractical ideas can be cleansed from the system, then flushed away.

In all matters pertaining to design, the wise practise restraint, not from lack of confidence, more from prudence engendered by hard-bought experience. An assumption that the original concept and design is the ultimate and best is frequently not the case, though several years may pass before the painful truth becomes undeniably apparent. To lessen the risk of perpetrating a major blunder, the whole area can be grassed down; this keeps all neat and tidy while the work of planning continues at a comfortable, leisurely pace. Once the lawn is established enough to walk on, the designs worked out on graph paper can be tried out *in situ*. By using canes, hosepipe, and sheets of black polythene it is possible to outline the various shapes of prospective shrub, herbaceous, or rose borders. Forms of pool or patio, even summer houses, can be sited to best advantage without a turf being cut or stone laid. Persuading various members of the family to walk around the garden holding a multi-hued umbrella may prove difficult. Patience is needed while attempting to ensure that the proposed tree which they are simulating with the raised umbrella is in the correct place. It's amazing how voices get a decibel or two louder when the effort to make them understand your left is their right is ignored or misunderstood. Asking various members of the family to help at this stage is a diplomatic way of ensuring their continuing practical assistance later on with routine work like lawn mowing and weeding. Be certain that permanent features – pools, rock garden, flagged paths, and greenhouses – are absolutely, without any

Hemerocallis 'Hyperion' came to me as a result of my being patient. The lovely canary-yellow flowers pushing up out of a tangle of weeds were my reward for ignoring advice to poison the lot and start with a weed-free plot. Fifteen years later that same plant still expresses a perennial gratitude with crops of yellow flowers which are so very sweetly scented

To design with purpose and express that intention clearly in the finished garden is in a way much more difficult than to make an arbitrary arrangement of grass, trees, shrubs and other flowering plants. The initial design is more difficult in execution because the main lines of the blueprint must be clearly drawn out and established before a spade is taken in hand, and there must be a purpose for each of them. In one respect it is easier because when once the main lines are determined the lesser details of planting will be clearly defined by them. In a garden well planned for use and pleasure there will be room for plants of all kinds arranged in many different ways.

The above from notes written by a Mr Trevor in 1908 which I copied out in 1954 as being perfectly applicable in the sixty-acre garden I was occupied with at the time.

Hypericum 'Rowallane' is one of those special semi-evergreen plants which fits into what I describe as the natural garden context. The rich, slightly cupped, golden-yellow flowers are beautifully sculpted. Especially complementary to campion, meadow cranesbill, and others of rustic character (though not reliably hardy) 'Rowallane' is well worth a trial

argument or shadow of doubt, in the ideal place. This is something that should be checked and queried in both practical and aesthetic terms. Anyone who has experienced that moment of near total despair when the suspicion that the perfectly landscaped, very expensive pool, complete with fountain, is in the wrong place becomes irrefutable fact, will understand why. Check and then double check is one of the garden designer's ten commandments. A gardener's mistakes, like those of the medical profession, can be buried. Unfortunately, in the garden they have a nasty habit of resurrecting themselves.

Even greater patience must be exercised by anyone taking over an established garden. Always assume that the previous owner was capable of doing no wrong and had impeccable taste until events prove otherwise. Live with the garden as it is and let the seasonal patterns reveal what is good, bad, or indifferent, for repentance is, indeed, the child of haste. Having studied the layout and decided what, if anything, should be kept and incorporated into the new design, then allow all your repressed, creative artistry free scope.

Caveat Emptor – Let the Buyer Beware

Choosing and buying the plants is the next phase in what to me is an absorbing progression. There are those so well informed and rigidly disciplined as to be able, with no further delay, to order all the plants needed, almost without reference to a nursery list. Never having arrived at so enviable a position, I make the planting of a new garden my excuse for a whole sequence of visits to nurseries, garden centres and, above all, other people's gardens which are open to the public. This is a marvellous way of learning about plants, their names, characteristics, vices and virtues, and there may be one or two landscape ideas worth adopting for your own plot of earth. Do not be tempted to buy just odd plants as they take your fancy; this is a very expensive way of stocking a garden as no discount will be given on small orders. Always keep in mind your own concept of what the garden will be like on completion – not bits and pieces but a unified, harmonious whole.

The results of your observations and note-taking during visits to other gardens should be, indeed almost certainly will be, a list of plants long enough to cause severe misgivings. Having lived with the garden over several months, you should have some idea of what will thrive, merely exist, or not be worth trying at all. That should shorten the list by a fraction or two. By this time it will be the gardener's biblical equivalent of the seventh day, namely winter, offering a respite from toil: the long, dark evenings, with the cold outside so bitter that no more valid reason could be found for staying indoors. Armed with a series of reference books supplemented by a selection of nursery catalogues, let the weather do its worst; your progress towards being the complete gardener continues. Work through the list checking the credentials of every plant on it. Note height, spread, and season of flowering. Question also the all-season interest: beautiful leaves, colourful stems, or even curious twig tracery, as in the twisted hazel or contorted willow, are all points to be noted alongside the appropriate name.

Take care the final list is of plants which will carry your interest right through the year. One of the arguments against the deadly sin of 'bit buying' is that of ending up with a one-season garden only. A valuable side-effect of all this browsing and analysis is that you will be familiarising yourself with a whole range of plants and their Latin names. One of the pre-requisites to enrolment in the Gardeners' Guild is the ability to recite whole strings of Latin names. By the time New Year's Day arrives the list of names should have been reduced, if not to the proper requisite, at least to manageable, proportions. Instructions in the shape of well filled order forms listing the 'must have' plants can then be dispatched to the various nurseries. The rest of the plants on the list itemised as 'nice to have' and 'need further information on' can be held in reserve. There are always trees, shrubs, herbaceous plants, annuals and others at present unknown which may, when discovered, make such an appeal they become immediately one of the 'must haves'.

Ruta graveolens 'Jackman's Blue' is a plant which charms with soft, pastel shades

PERSONALITY IS EVERYTHING

Just one or two personal thoughts on plant associations, the where and in what context each individual will best fulfil its potential. Plants are possessed of what I can only term, for want of a better word to describe it, personality. Some, like magnolia, only exert a powerful influence when they are in bloom. This is in marked contrast to a white-stemmed birch whose authority is evident at all seasons. I first became aware of how important an influence the dominant plants such as *Betula* have on the overall design when my work entailed visiting a series of gardens that in size, concept, and plant interest were totally different one from the other. In some there was a sense of balanced harmony that was a result, not of the overall design, but more of the way in which the various component plant groups had been arranged in relationship one with the other.

Possibly a description of one particular grouping which impressed me so much at the time will help illustrate the point I am trying to make. The centrepiece forming a focal point of the association was a *Betula costata* with graceful outline and creamy-white exfoliating bark. On the north side of the tree lady's mantle, *Alchemilla*, added a delightful lime-green tone to the deepening shade. *Smilacina racemosa* offered a change in outline with upright growth, the creamy-white scented flowers giving their own particular quality to the May scene. A dark evergreen *Mahonia japonica*, only slightly less assertive than the birch, provided the positive contrast to a pastel-shaded ensemble. In February when the *Mahonia* opened pale-yellow, sweetly scented racemes of flowers over handsome pinnate leaves, the winter aconite bloomed to cast a deep-yellow shadow under the primrose-tinted paleness of the shrub. Quite without shame I have reproduced this association with just two additions: snowdrops in the form of

The cottage garden ideal delivered us from so many extremes of landscape design by preserving itself intact for reasons of excellence. A large garden can no more be made to imitate a cottage garden than a large house can be passed off as a cottage. Just as the irregularity which is so pleasing and full of character in a cottage becomes incoherent and absurd in a large house, so the haphazard plantings of a cottage garden which are pleasing when they are made necessary by restricted space become merely chaotic when practised on a grander scale where there is no need for them. The cottage garden has provided a standard for the art of gardening which has redeemed that art from exotic perversities.

From a newspaper cutting dated 1908 found in a copy of Robinson's The Flower Garden.

Betula pendula 'Youngii' makes an
elegant focal point for a small garden
(*York Gate, Leeds*)

Specialists strive for perfection in a
single flower – a 'Peace' rose.

Galanthus 'S. Arnott', white against the birch stems' cream, and
primroses, for they are so expressive of spring time.

From that first awareness I have made a note of groupings which
expressed compatibility and discovered a store of information in the
process about plant individuality and how to make the most of all
this latent potential in the garden, of which more in Chapter 4, 'The
Artistry of Plant Association'.

The plants which are truly native to this country offer pastel-
shaded flowers. Lanes are bright with colour in their season, but it
is the blue of meadow cranesbill, the white of Queen Anne's lace,
with pale-pink wild roses, cream honeysuckle, and yellow flag iris.
Even purple foxglove flowers and the shocking-pink, self-
advertising campion are soft rather than strident shades. Now I use
the hotter reds and oranges of pelargonium and the modern rose
with care. Instead of large companies a group of three or five,
always odd numbers, are used to make a focal point or full stops
amongst the softer pastel shades. Bright colours, by catching the
eye, cause a modest-sized garden to appear even smaller. Soft,
pastel-shaded hues blended with subtle variations of foliage shape
and colour lead the eye in a gentle progression as the garden reveals
its charm. The eye is soothed and the spirit refreshed, as I am sure
some poet must have written ere now – or if no one has, then they
have never made a garden.

One of the most curious and at times contradictory quirks of
human nature is exhibited to a remarkable degree by those who

grow plants. The proverbial stubbornness of the mule is as nothing to the inflexibility of a gardener determined to grow rhododendrons and other calcifuge plants in a soil impregnated with lime. No effort or expense is spared even though the end result is a mere travesty of a plant struggling to survive. There have been many times when I have wished a plant could speak. To have a rhododendron's unqualified opinion of the individual who, by dowsing it with copious draughts of fertiliser enriched with trace elements and root-smothering mulches of peat, tries to persuade so determined a lime hater to grow and flower in a completely alien soil, would be most revealing. On second thoughts, the description might be too graphically precise to bear recording.

The great gardeners of this and other generations have built reputations by discovering first those plants which grow naturally and with the minimum of persuasion in the soil their garden was made from, and then, with the knowledge so gained, having the wisdom and singleness of purpose to concentrate on growing the sympathetic plants to perfection.

At least in the early formative years of the garden, let personal preference be disciplined within the limitations imposed by soil and, to some extent, climate. To try and grow delphiniums on an exposed hillside is to fly in the face of providence. In such a situation a wise gardener discovers a passionate interest in the study and cultivation of alpines.

Anyone moving into unfamiliar surroundings need only study the plants which are thriving in the gardens round about. Select those which most suit your personal inclination and are likely to serve your purpose best. Once the main framework of the garden landscape is established and, short of fire, flood and tempest, likely to remain, then and only then try the rare, exciting, imaginative, though possibly less reliable, plantings. For if the garden were to offer no more challenge to skill than the mechanical repetition of seasonal work, then painted concrete and statuary would serve the purpose just as well.

Keep the Devil Out

Suspect those who, like the Greeks of Troy, come bearing gifts. Though it would be churlish of me to suggest such a thing, refusing plants of any sort without a written pedigree is not a bad idea. Introducing a pernicious pest or disease on infected plant material into a previously healthy soil is very easy. Also, very often, unsolicited gifts of plants in large quantities mean one of two things. They are so invasive as to need constant restraint, or of a degree of mediocrity that persuades complete expulsion in favour of something more worthy of cultivation. Not all gifts, of course, fall into the categories described, so before refusing ask the question – What is it? Should the answer be 'Just a small root from one of my treasures, all I could spare for it is rather precious', then accept with alacrity, for the donor of such bounty is one of the true breed and bell metal for soundness.

Salvia pratensis I grow not because it is useful, like common sage, or even exceptionally handsome like 'Cambridge Blue', but simply because the bees are always busy about the crab-claw blue flowers

3

Order is Truth

Prior to the eighteenth century plants were recognised in the botanical world by names which were really a description of their salient features couched in Latin which is still the internationally accepted language of science. Rhubarb, the *Rheum rhaponticum* of botanists at the time when Parkinson was writing *Pardisi in Sole Paradisus Terrestris* in 1629, had a very different and longer name, *Hippolopathum maximum rotundifolium exoticum*. I am not sure how the Hippolopathum is broken down – hippo for horse, lophos, crested or patelles, disk-shaped? For the rest; maximum, largest; rotundifolium, with round leaves; exoticum, from a foreign country. A resounding title for something most people meet decently swathed in custard.

Gardeners in those distant days had need to be classical scholars and, surely, greeted with enthusiasm and relief a system as simple as that which Linnaeus produced. Born in 1707 in Sweden, Linnaeus began by drawing up an accurate description of the various plants. When comparing these descriptions with those used by botanists in the past and in other botanical institutions he discovered that one plant might have several different names – all of them, by the standards which applied at the time, perfectly valid. The botanists, studying in comparative isolation, had no way of knowing that similar work of classification was being done elsewhere. In these days of instant communication with almost every country in the world it is hard to appreciate how different it must have been in those insular times to avoid duplication and multiplication of scientific names. In practical terms, the long descriptive names were unwieldy; just writing them down required time and a working knowledge of Latin.

Linnaeus sifted all the information, comparing like with like and his own detailed descriptions. In the process he found that certain plants had flowers of similar construction and could, therefore, be grouped together under a single heading. From this painstaking and laborious beginning came the wonderful flower of Linnaeus's genius – the now universally accepted two-name system, with modifications to include sub-species, cultivars, and varieties.

There are two names which the beginner needs to identify until familiarity leads to a confident appraisal of all plant nomenclature. Take as an example dandelion, that most familiar of yellow flowers, the *Taraxacum officinale* of the botanist. The first name is, in oversimplified terms, the botanical equivalent of a surname in that it defines the plant's relationship with other plants. The second name

The name *Phalaris* illustrates both the antiquity of plant nomenclature and the simplicity of that which Linnaeus produced. *Phalaris* is from the Greek name for a grass of the genus Phalaris. *Phalaris arundinacea picta* is the green-and-gold striped 'gardeners' garters' – a useful ground cover in moist soil

officinale is the equivalent of a Christian name in that it singles out the common *dandelion* from other closely related species. In the system of plant nomenclature the generic surname or group name can only be given once. There can never be two groups of plants with the generic name of *Taraxacum*. The specific, or plant equivalent of the Christian name, can be used, fortunately for the sanity of gardeners, many times between different genera, as in *Taraxacum officinale* (dandelion), *Stachys officinale* (lamb's ears), *Valerian officinalis* (common valerian) and so on. Plants may be given a third name where there is some variation from the true species. A white dandelion would be identified as *Taraxacum officinale* 'Album'. Some specific names are repeated so often that remembering them is easy: *officinale, vulgaris, floribunda*, producing abundant flowers, *japonica* – Japanese, *odora* – fragrant, are examples of names met with frequently.

WHY NOT 'NO LATIN WE ARE BRITISH'?

Not all the plants we grow in our gardens are native to the British Isles. Common or popular names have been in use since primitive man first sought to differentiate between one plant and another by more than a grunt and gesture of the hand. Throughout the world countries and often individual tribes within a country would invent as required vernacular names for those plants in common usage. The majority with no value for food or medicine would not be identified by name. So peasants in western China would have their own vernacular name for a plant that even today would be totally meaningless to anyone in this country. Nor need we take such an extreme example of the confusion which can arise from using popular, non-scientific names to identify one plant from another. The bluebell of Scotland is, in fact, the harebell of England. There

Let it not be supposed that Carl Linne (Linnaeus) was the first botanist to make an attempt at setting out a simple system of plant classification. Pliny produced seven volumes dealing with the medicinal uses of plants nearly 2,000 years ago. Whether this was an attempt at classification I do not know. Certainly Parkinson of Paradisi in Sole Paradisus Terrestris *fame suggested 1,600 years or so later that plants might be grouped according to their herbal uses and values.*

In fact, it was the work of earlier botanists, Grew, Anatomy of Plants, *1682, and Vaillant with his studies on the reproductive processes of plants,*

which gave Linnaeus the inspiration to study the sex organs of plants. As a result of his findings he was eventually to base the whole system of his own formula for plant classification on the male stamens and female pistil, the sexual system rather than anything else.

The justification, according to Maxwell, of using dead languages for classifying plants and animals consists, first in the fact that they are dead and, therefore, subject to no change in form or meaning and, second, that they are the common property of all civilised nations. Greek and Latin, therefore, afford the most reliable means of ensuring precision. Most would answer Amen to that.

is not the same risk of mistake with the correct botanical name; the bluebell of Scotland is *Campanula rotundifolia* in England, China, and Scotland. A Yorkshire bluebell, *Hyacinthoides non-scripta* remains *Hyacinthoides* unlimited in its accuracy by regional, national, or international boundaries.

But why Latin when English would be equally suitable as the internationally accepted language for describing and naming of plants? I am not sure that blaming Theophrastus for the imposition of Latin as the universal language of science is quite justified. When he wrote his *Inquiry into Plants* and *Growth of Plants* 200 years before the birth of Christ, Theophrastus almost certainly wrote in Greek. Possibly Pliny began it all with his monumental work on botany written around 50AD. Rather than apportioning blame it is better to give credit for what is a most practical and efficient system to the fact that when the present structure of classification was evolving in the eighteenth century Latin was the universal language of science. Though it is doubtful if Pliny, elder or younger, would recognise the Latin used by botanists today, it is still a legacy dating back many centuries. Years ago when as a student I was struggling to improve a mark of three out of twenty for a plant identification examination, the lecturer in charge offered these words of comfort: 'The first hundred names are the hardest to learn.'

BELOW
Rhododendron forrestii, named after an indomitable plant hunter. The white daffodils serve to emphasise its waxen-textured red petals.

RIGHT
The simple beauty of white *Pyracantha* blossom with *Iris* 'Oriental Beauty'. Golden-foliaged Chamaecyparis, *Hebe* 'Quicksilver' and viola form a complementary foreground

Magnolia stellata, star-like and beautiful

WHAT'S IN A NAME? BEAUTY AND INFORMATION!

Having accepted that a wild flower from China or Tasmania has no common English name, what then, other than identification, is the purpose of scientific titles? Specific names of plants are in many instances a source of information. In some cases a specific name describes the country of origin, *Gladiolus byzantinus* indicates Turkey as that most attractive species' native home. *Genista aetnensis* localises the habitat even more accurately as the slopes of Mount Etna. *Dianthus sinensis* (*chinensis*) is distinguished as the Chinese or Indian pink. Immediately the difficulty of Latin names begins to resolve itself into a new, vibrant life.

Even more informative are those names which describe some obvious feature of the plant itself: macrophylla – large leaved as in *Elaeagnus macrophylla*, *Daphne odora* – sweet scented, or *Magnolia stellata* with star-like flowers.

Names which tell something of the condition in which a plant is found growing naturally, though at times misleading, are useful aids to the gardener. *Cypripedium calceolus* was one name which misled me for years for it has nothing to do with this beautiful native orchid growing in limesoil; *calceolus* in this case means a little slipper. Such minor pieces of misinformation notwithstanding, names identifying habitat have a poetic ring – *Daphne collina* growing on hills as, indeed, it does, or *Arnica montana*, more obviously descriptive. *Senecio maritima* pertaining to the sea, or *Geranium pratense* of meadows, all give a clue to the sort of conditions the plants need when transferred from the wild into cultivation. Try, then, with thoughts on *Potentilla rupestris* – of rocks,

William Robinson who wrote the classic English Flower Garden *was a strenuous advocate for the use of English names. To him saxifraga could be identified as rockfoil, clematis as virgin's bower and so on. 'The stock of bad Latin', Mr Robinson complains, which we owe to the botanists leads some people to cut capers with that language with fearful results; the terms issuing from the mouths of botanists are bad enough, when descending into those of gardeners they are grotesque indeed. In botany these technical terms may be essential but gardening is quite a different affair. Mr Robinson considered 'the names in our own tongue are as good as any, and we are not prevented from adding the Latin names when necessary'.*

Any nurseryman following Mr Robinson's precept would be pilloried by every media and press pundit in the land as retrogressive and reactionary. For me 'Welcome Home Husband Though Never So Drunk' instead of sedum acre *has a fine if ponderous, homely ring to it – though only to an Englishman.*

'Who have not viewed with rapture-smitten frame, the power of grace – the magic of a name.' No doubt Thomas Campbell when he penned these lines had a name more evocative and enchanting than Metasequoia glyptostroboides *in mind.*

On the same theme whenever I hear people grumbling, as they often do, about Latin and Greek names for plants, I am reminded of Sir Herbert Maxwell's story about a gardener called Wyber. A visitor to his garden once asked him how he managed to remember all the botanical names. 'Oh', he replied, 'I mind them easy enough. You see, I have what is called a memoria technica.' When asked how this worked Wyber gave this example. 'There's a tree now, the Cryptomeria japonica. When I'm teaching the bothie lads I tell them when looking at that tree to say – Creep to the mare and jump onto her.' Which is a sound enough aid to memory, as I have proved myself on numerous occasions with names which are hard to remember.

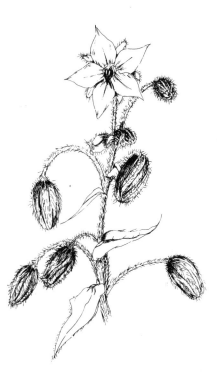

Borago officinalis – the name borage refers, so it is thought, to the hairiness of the leaves, while *officinalis* refers to the plant's medicinal properties. The blue flowers and leaves have a fragrance like fresh-cut cucumber

or a descriptive generical name like *Saxifraga*, the rock breaker, and the world of plant nomenclature becomes interesting, even exciting.

Others, which commemorate the name of the finder or honour a dignitary, may not supply culture information, yet they still mark significant milestones in garden history: *Rhododendron forrestii* for the great plant hunter George Forrest, *Primula bulleyana* named after the man who sponsored Forrest's expeditions to China. Most apt of all, *Linnaea borealis*, a modest little woodland flower, is the plant chosen by the great man himself as a worthy memorial to his name: *Linnaea* for Linnaeus, *borealis*, northern – a great deal of information and history contained in two words.

As for the pronunciation of the Latin names I am reminded of a doggerel which was pinned on the potting shed wall by my father after an argument on the subject of cyclamen.

How shall we sound its mystic name,
Of Greek descent and Persian fame?
Shall 'y' be long and 'a' be short,
Or will the 'y' and 'a' retort?
Shall 'y' be lightly hurried o'er,
Or should we emphasise it more?
Alas the botanists disagree,
For y's a doubtful quantity.
Some people use it now and then,
As if the word were sickly-men.

What matter the pronunciation so long as the meaning is clear and the plant under discussion identified? For 'Sicklymen' or 'Kicklaymen' is better understood world-wide than the popular Greek name *Kyklaninos* which means a circle. So give thanks for the genius of Linnaeus who simplified it all for us.

4

The Artistry of Plant Association

Gardens are like buildings in that they are capable of expressing a pleasing harmony, a balanced symmetry of design which is altogether gratifying. Walk around any garden which combines agreeable plant affiliation with attractive design and find out what an enjoyable experience it is, for beauty, indeed, sweeps out all that is trivial. The appeal is not in any way due to the extravagant use of colour to produce a garish or startling effect. Rather it relies on artistry, subtle gradations of leaf, shade and shape, with flowers as the embellishment and not the principal factor.

Fanciful though it may seem, plants do express a personality. There are those of such a demanding presence that all the planting within their area of influence must be complementary, not competitive. A field of buttercups relies on mass effect for its visual impact. Beautiful though the carpet of yellow is under a summer sun, it lacks the lyric quality of a *Magnolia campbellii* so carefully sited that its deep rose-pink flowers are seen framed against no other background than the blue and white of a March sky. Though it is not difficult in gardening, as in painting, to achieve the sort of impact which brings gasps of astonishment from all who see it, restraint and discipline produce a landscape which is much easier to live with. Was it not Browning who said 'If you get simple beauty and naught else you get about the best thing God invents'.

Harmony apart, bright colours such as orange, scarlet, electric blue, draw the eye immediately and must be used with restraint. There are times, however, when a vivid splash of colour embellishes rather than detracts from a beautiful view. One garden in particular springs readily to mind, and here the virtue of simplicity had been carried almost to the point of austerity. A broad sweep of lawn in front of the house carried the eye across to a weeping beech, *Fagus sylvatica* 'Purpurea Pendula' like a 20ft (6m) high mushroom growing out of the bright-green grass. A bed filled with scarlet-flowered 'Evelyn Fison' roses linked the beech to a magnificent blue cedar, *Cedrus atlantica* 'Glauca'. Without the emphatic contribution made by the scarlet-flowered rose, the beauty of the landscape would have been much reduced.

To plant and then maintain a garden which is satisfyingly interesting no matter what the season, is not quite so easy as it may at first appear. A glance at any nursery catalogue will certainly

A large book full of poetry and curious learning might be written about the association of flowers; and there are few of us, at least among those who care much for flowers, who can think of them apart from their associations. Thus we naturally associate the most beautiful of our native wildflowers with hills, vales and open countryside.

The above is one interpretation of association which is concerned more with connection in thought.
Gertrude Jekyll in her book Colour Schemes for the Garden *uses the word associate in terms of linking plants together for a common purpose; she writes, 'the duty we owe to our gardens is so to use plants that they form beautiful pictures'.*
Join the two interpretations together, including with the evocative quality an approach to, and insistence on, colour harmony, and there is still the matter of shape, texture, and foliage pattern. Plant relationship might be a better description.

suggest that there is a sufficient variety of plants to suit every soil, need, and purpose. The introduction of a large quantity of trees, shrubs and herbaceous plants, supplemented with bulbs and annuals, no matter how good their quality, will not guarantee a pleasant garden. That each item has been selected with care and for a particular merit of form, leaf, flower or twig colour really makes no difference, it is still only a plant collection. Interestingly enough, if the acquisition of plants is merely an alternative to accumulating stamps or fine porcelain, the satisfaction derives from ownership rather than any appreciation of what constitutes a beautiful landscape. The artistry lies in using the plants in such a way that, from association with each other, complementing or contrasting, they form fine-looking pictures.

There is no need for concern that all the associations are correct. Unlike a building or a painting, the picture can be adjusted and changed simply by moving the component parts. There is no reason why shrubs, even trees, cannot be moved three or four years after being installed, provided the transplanting is done with care and during the proper season. The time usually advised for moving shrubs or trees is loosely defined as the dormant season between October and April. So long as the weather conditions are suitable – moist and humid – shrubs with a fibrous root system will transplant without showing undue discomfort at almost any time.

That other pitfall, overplanting, is always waiting to trap the unwary. Indeed, the experienced gardener is not infrequently liable to end up in this particular pit alongside the raw beginner. Take time, therefore, not just to search out the plants which are best suited to your purpose, find out also the amount of space each will need in maturity. Your vision of a beautiful landscape, the garden intended as a place of ease and refreshment of mind, may look a trifle sparse for a year or two. Do not be over-concerned, for the gaps between the permanent framework of trees and shrubs can be filled with annuals, bulbs, and most certainly herbaceous perennials. The planting is just the first step on the way to a beautiful and harmonious garden. After-care – formative pruning and feeding, together with routine cultivation of the soil – is also important.

One piece of advice given to me as a teenager, that for once I paid heed to, was to carry a notebook and pencil always ready to hand. In the front I made notes of a practically informative nature, while in the back was recorded any plant or grouping of plants which pleased me. This has proved an invaluable aid to memory, particularly as in later years I also noted the aspect: north, south, east, or west, and the type of soil the plants were growing in. For what use the lovely compilation of pale-orange azalea underplanted with Spanish bluebells if your soil is full of lime? Possibly here it would be opportune to note that, though lime-tolerant plants such as lilac, cinquefoil, and mock orange will grow happily in an acid soil, the same forbearance is not shown by lime-hating (calcifuge) plants. Rhododendron, kalmia, and the rest of the ericaceous clan will in no way, at least not without a vast amount of effort, be persuaded to grow in soil which is alkaline.

The Elizabethans had a tolerant looseness of definition which makes us look niggling. Take lawns, for instance; any reasonable expanse of grass was a lawn to them. 'Thereon daises pied and violets blue, and lady's smocks all silver white, were equally welcome'. From A Suffolk Harvest *by Adrian Bell. There is room for artistry even in a lawn.*

Gaps in the border can be filled with bulbs. Crown Imperial, *Fritillaria imperialis* 'Rubra', combines with *Cytisus* x *praecox*, one of the most floriferous 'brooms'

OPPOSITE
Complement or contrast, they form fine looking pictures. *Narcissus* 'February Gold' with winter flowering heathers blooming in March

Gertrude Jekyll's description of 'the year's first complete picture of flower effect' is a synthesis of all the qualities embodied in a beautiful garden landscape:

The sunlight strikes brightly on the silver stems of the Birches and casts her shadows clearcut across the grassy path. The grass is barely green as yet, but has the faint winter green of herbage not yet grown and still powdered with the short remnants of mown heath grasses. The trunks of the Spanish Chestnuts are elephant grey, a notable contrast to the sudden vivid shafts of Birches. Some groups of the pale early Pyrenean Daffodil gleam level on the ground a little way forward.

Though *Penstemon hartwegii* hails from Mexico and is not considered fully hardy it survives well enough in a northern garden. The blood-red tubular flowers look lovely mingling with those of the purple-blue *Campanula latifolia*. I take cuttings of the penstemon each year in August, to winter under glass, so that all the eggs are not in one outdoor basket

At this stage should come the thought that what one considers to be a perfect piece of plant association, or a series of eye-satisfying pictures, might be to someone else no more than a jarring discord. Hopefully, the following suggestions will, even if they do not win universal approval, at least please the majority.

There is a proverb which insists that between the saying and the doing lies a long, hard road. This is truth, indeed, when applied to the making of a garden, except that most of the work is enjoyable and creative. By treating the border to be planted as a series of compartments and not as a single unit, the tricky business of achieving the right balance is made much easier. Then instead of trying to blend one plant with the next, which can be a real test of patience, there is the simpler task of joining a series of groups together, each one complete in its own right. Remember also the particular setting in which a plant association is first seen; the weather conditions and our frame of mind at the time have an important bearing on our reactions.

Each season, though it is uniquely different from the rest, yet somehow contrives to combine glimpses of the others during its three calendar months' duration. There is a misconception that winter is the doldrum time. Short the days may be, yet they offer pictures which, because they are so unexpected, are welcomed with intense appreciation. Sunlight has a softness as if filtered through sea water, which reveals subtle gradations of colour not evident at any other season. Winter colours are moss green, straw yellow, silver grey, subdued yet in no way melancholy under winter sunshine. The flowers which are in bloom then reflect this pastel-shaded quality. *Prunus subhirtella* 'Autumnalis' is typical of this fragile beauty, for the autumn cherry belies its popular name by opening a succession of semi-double white flowers from October to April. The most improbable and yet curiously attractive association that I have come across is only a short walk from here: three well grown specimens of winter cherry, two with white flowers and one with pink, growing in a chickenrun garth. On a winter day when the sunlight is filtering through flower-laden branches to glisten on the bright copper, bronze, and white of the bantam chickens scratching underneath, the grassy garth becomes a Japanese cameo.

In due season the grass is bright with violets, native daffodils and meadow cranesbill until autumn discovers the purple goblets of *Colchicum* pushing up through a scarlet and fawn carpet of fallen leaves. The autumn cherry needs always to be the centrepiece of any association, for the flowers are of such a delicate texture as to be almost an illusion. Underplant *Galanthus nivalis*, double or single, and the *Cyclamen coum*, a 3in (8cm) high native of woodland which offers flowers varying in colour from white or pink to a dark crimson throughout the winter. Include also a corm or two of *Cyclamen hederifolium* which flowers in autumn, and then spreads a carpet of marbled leaves which persist throughout winter.

Combining two shades of the same colour is often most effective. The lovely evergreen *Mahonia japonica* is handsome enough in foliage to warrant inclusion on that score alone. Dark, lustrous green leaves carried on a bush 4 or 5ft (1.2–1.5m) high form a proper backcloth to the racemes of pale primrose-yellow flowers open anytime from January onwards. An underplanting of *Eranthis hyemalis* will spread like a deeper yellow shadow under the mahonia, growing denser with each year that passes as it self-seeds to match the spreading bush. Carry interest on into summer with glaucous yellow- and green-leaved *Hosta fortunei* 'Aureo-marginata'. This is not quite so ponderous as it may seem, for the glistening purple berries of the mahonia which ripen in July are best seen with a lighter-coloured contrast. A whiff of the delicate fragrance from the mahonia flowers turns February into June, if only briefly.

Garrya elliptica's sole claim to fame over the thirty-plus years of our association, at least as far as I am concerned, is botanical rather than ornamental. When some one hundred and fifty years ago David Douglas found the 'Silk Tassel Bush' growing wild along the Columbia river and sent specimens back to England it caused quite a stir in botanical circles, for it represented a completely new genus and natural order. In fact, in my opinion, until recently that is, Archibald Menzies, who stumbled on the garrya some thirty years previously and ignored it, showed the better judgement. The dark almost matt-green leaves lack the glossy well polished charm of the camellia or even the laurel. Then in February, graceful, pendent catkins fully 8in (20cm) long are produced in such liberal profusion that a well grown bush resembles a dove-grey cascade. Close acquaintance with the catkins reveals that they are fragrant and prettily marked with pink and lime green. Unfortunately, harsh weather ensured that until three years ago I never saw the bush without scorched brown leaves, a disfigurement which made garrya unsightly to the point of ugliness until May or later. A succession of mild winters, combined with putting a male garrya, which carries the longest catkins, in the right context has given me a new appreciation of the austere, classical beauty of the garrya.

Opinions may differ as to the best association. In my own favourite grouping all the shrubs used are growing along a dry stone wall which provides an illusion of shelter. To the left-hand side facing the group is a golden privet, *Ligustrum ovalifolium* 'Aureum', one of the most cheerful of shrubs even in winter. Next comes the garrya rejoiced enormously by the bright gold of the privet. Close alongside to the right is an *Elaeagnus pungens Maculata* whose green leaves are relieved by a gold central stripe. Intermingled with the elaeagnus is a winter jasmine, *Jasminum nudiflorum*, whose cheerfully brassy yellow flowers are in evidence at the same time as the catkins of *Garrya elliptica*. The overall effect, particularly when the catkins are stirred into rippling movement by a zephyr breeze, is delightfully lovely in the flowering season, and handsome throughout all the remaining months, particularly so if the ground planting is of kaffir lilies, *Schizostylis coccinea*, whose gladiolus-like 2ft (61cm) high spikes of scarlet flowers form an embroidered hem to the shrubs during late summer and autumn.

The jasmine figures in another winter picture piece, this time

From the English Flower Garden *by W. Robinson.*

Eranthis hyemalis. A pretty early plant with yellow flowers surrounded by a whorl of shining green. When the branches of large trees are allowed to rest on the turf of the lawn, a few roots of it scattered beneath will soon form a carpet glowing in sheets of yellow in winter or spring.

For large trees, substitute modest shrubs and the winter aconite will carpet it underneath with yellow for your pleasure and delight.

An extract from A Traveller's Notes *by J. H. Veitch.*
The following is the description of a garden in Tokyo, a model of restrained aestheticism which relies entirely on shape and foliage for its effect, for there are no flowers.

The landscape garden in pure Japanese style, situated on the side of a low hill, with an exceedingly picturesque lake at the bottom. The hill, backed by Oaks, Abies firma and other large trees, is covered with many hundreds of perfectly clipped bushes of *Enkianthus japonicus*, presenting a lively green with their young shoots; amongst these are young Pines and Maples. Over the lake hang flat trained and twisted Pines.

Enkianthus japonicus *is now* Enkianthus perulatus *with white urn-shaped flowers in spring and leaves which turn brilliant scarlet in the autumn. The Tokyo garden in the fall must have been surpassingly, if fugitively, lovely.*

alongside japonica, *Chaenomeles speciosa*, with clusters of orange-scarlet flowers. The red and yellow colour combination reminds me of the rhubarb and custard of boarding-school days. Hard pruning improves both japonica and jasmine. With the japonica finger prune the young growths back to three buds during June. The jasmine should have the flower-bearing shoots cut hard back once the petals fall. The duo offered little interest for the rest of the year until a creamy-yellow, variegated ivy grew in to cover the bare wall behind them. *Hedera colchica* 'Dentata Variegata' is as handsome as its name is long.

How or why the deservedly popular *Hamamelis mollis* gained the common name of witch hazel is a mystery. One suggestion is that it derives from the fact that early American settlers used the twigs for water divining in much the same way as hazel twigs back home in England. Even the generic name 'Hama' together with 'melis', 'the apple' makes little sense except to a botanist. Such complexities apart, *Hamamelis mollis*, when the bare twigs are wreathed with large sweetly scented, spiderlike flowers in January and February, makes a picture to rejoice eye and heart. Finding the right soil is the first problem; ideally this should be a free draining yet moisture-retentive acid loam, for the roots must never dry out at any time. The second problem is finding the right companion plants. For those who boast a white-stemmed birch in the garden, or better still a grove of them, plant *Hamamelis mollis* 'Pallida' so that the yellow flowers are glimpsed between the white birch stems. Failing that, grow witch hazel planted around with that best of all winter flowering heathers, *Erica herbacea* (syn. *carnea*) 'Myreton Ruby'. The dusky, ruby red of the heather spikes do not always oblige when the witch hazel shows its yellow; when they do, sublime is the word.

Why one of the most reliable winter blooming shrubs should be so ugly for the half of the year when not in flower must mean that the Almighty, like Homer, occasionally nods. For Viburnum *x bodnantense* rejoices for long months of winter with a continuous succession of clustered, sweetly fragrant, rose-pink flowers. A 6ft (1.8m) high bush in full bloom, given a warm day, fills the eye and refreshes the nostrils, for the smell is richly all-pervading. Out of bloom, however, the shrub makes Quasimodo look like the Laughing Cavalier. A pink-flowered hybrid musk shrub rose 'Felicia' with *Iris sibirica* 'Heavenly Blue' will disguise one side. *Viburnum davidii*, male and female, so that there are turquoise berries, makes a front piece. To mask the remaining side use *Potentilla* 'Moonlight' which is continuously in colour all summer. The cinquefoil flowers, a shade of primrose yellow, open in succession from May to October.

There are plants so particular in their requirements that finding congenial companions of a similar temperament is not easy. *Iris unguicularis* is just such a one. That a native of Algeria needs to be exposed to all the meagre sunshine afforded by what passes for summer in these islands is understandable, and there are a number of plants which share this need of being cooked to a crisp. Few require a soil so arid and devoid of nutriment that it would cause anorexia in a cactus. The iris forms a grassy tuft of foliage 2ft (61cm) high; then when suited by soil and situation, during mild spells throughout winter and early spring comes a succession of flowers. There is an exquisite loveliness and delicacy to the finely veined lilac flowers, which is compounded by the season at which they choose to show themselves. They emit a fragrance of such a refined quality that it can only be fully appreciated when the flowers are cut for arranging indoors. Planted in a soil made even freer draining by a liberal admixture of oyster shell, against a south-facing wall and left undisturbed, the iris will reward patience with flowers.

After numerous experiments with sun-loving shrubs, all of them failures, *Euonymus fortunei* 'Coloratus', with glossy green leaves which are purple tinted throughout the winter, spread across and up the wall behind. A moss-covered stone figure of a rather battered cupid and a multi-coloured carpet of thyme completed the ensemble. After that, as one great plantsman put it, 'the only manure this iris needs to make it flower is patience'. As the last iris petals darken with age, so the ardent, passionate choristry of birds ushers in long awaited spring flowers.

When Iris unguicularis *was first introduced in 1845 it was considered to be a tender species needing protection in a greenhouse. Given careful cultivation and a rich soil the iris grew masses of tall leaves and gave only a few flowers in consequence. A sunny place and poor soil, as in this delightful plant's native home, will provide a brave display of flowers all through the winter whenever the weather is open.*

One of those happy accidents which somehow contrive to be lovelier than anything I plan. *Lilium* 'Coleen' with 'Ladybird' poppy

SPRING

There comes a day in March possibly, or more frequently April, when spring is for certain abroad in the land. Violets are in bloom along the copse edge or, even more encouraging, a newly prepared seed bed is steaming like a boiling kettle under a benign sun. There is a real danger with such an abundance of material available of overfilling the garden with plants which flower during the period March to June.

As politicians are to all men, so gardens need to present a fair face equally to each month of the twelve. Spring is gentle, pastel-shaded, never strident or aggressively overbearing, and the garden should reflect this. The bright colours of rhododendron are acceptable when glimpsed between the boles of trees. In the dappled shade of the branch canopy colours are muted, to be further softened by the green of young leaf. The horror of seeing a bank side covered in vivid scarlet flowers from a massed planting of *Rhododendron* 'Britannia' caused me, for the first time in my gardening life, to pray for a May frost.

Though *Daphne mezereum*, one of our rarer native shrubs, has flowers varying in shade from purple pink to dark red the colour is not intrusive. The large-blossomed form known as 'Rosea' looks particularly well underplanted with crocus 'Whitwell Purple'. Annual candytuft sown amongst the fading crocus flowers in April contributes a handsome quota to the summer scene, along with the scarlet of ripe daphne berries.

There are so many companions – shrub, herbaceous, perennial plants or annuals – which suggest themselves in the same context as *Magnolia stellata* that it is very easy to achieve a misalliance. Having seen and photographed the magnolia framed against the spring panorama of a Yorkshire Dale, the white of the flowers emphasised by the blue of a cloud-flecked April sky, it is hard to imagine them in a more perfect context. Unfortunately, portable panoramas of Dales scenery are not readily available, so attempts must be made to discover an alternative. Several 'Ostrich Feather' fern, *Matteuccia struthiopteris*, needed a temporary home and by happy chance were planted close to the magnolia. Now the pale green of the breaking fern fronds appears with the *stellata* flowers. The fern also pushes up shuttlecock growths amongst the *Meconopsis* 'Slieve Donard' whose vivid-blue flowers in summer, ably supported by the white blossom spikes of *Aconitum* 'Ivorine', make a handsome encore to the spring flowering magnolia. Both aconite and meconopsis grow to about 30in (75cm) in height, while the magnolia in ten years just tops 5ft (1.5m). To complete what is a very pleasant piece of mini gardenage the creamy-yellow *Lilium* 'Coleen', undersown with the black-spotted scarlet-flowered 'Lady-bird' poppy, an annual which grows to 18in (45cm) high – a pair in perfect accord with each other during midsummer.

Lilies planted with a well developed root system in a free draining soil are no more difficult to grow than the native daffodil. Dividing the bulbs every four years is good practice, together with

---

The variegated-leaved Daphne mezereum *was described by Philip Miller in 1759 as follows: 'Which some people are fond to have in their gardens; the plain is much more beautiful'. In the case of* Daphne mezereum *the variegation looks to me suspiciously like the discoloration caused by the cucumber mosaic virus, so, like Miller, only the plain-leaved sorts find a place in my garden.*

There is a quality about the flowers of Magnolia stellata *which I only thought to investigate after reading a description in a catalogue printed in 1902, which describes the shrub as being covered in spring with* intensely fragrant *flowers. As my bushes were then in flower, even though it was pitch dark outside, I sallied forth with a torch to investigate. The flowers, even on a dank April evening, were, indeed, delicately perfumed. In 1902 a price of 2/6d (12¹/₂p) each would have encouraged me to plant a sylvan grove of* Magnolia stellata.

Meconopsis 'Slieve Donard' *is a prime example of the late Leslie Slinger's skill as a hybridiser. The flowers are larger and carried with an expressive elegance that sets this variety apart from other forms of* Meconopsis grandis.

the annual mulch of leaf mould mixed with powdered seaweed each February.

Not all the group are of Brobdingnagian proportions, for being big in plant terms is no guarantee of beauty. A piece of limestone encrusted with silver saxifrage, *Saxifraga cochlearis* 'Minor', set in a carpet of *Potentilla verna* 'Nana', a yellow-flowered native creeping perennial, is quietly pleasant. Quite by chance I planted *Salix x boydii* nearby. This tiny willow has grown only 14in (36cm) high in as many years, yet the silver catkins, though not produced in quantity, do add their 'widow's mite'. Last year *Gentiana verna pontica*, planted, as advised, with well rotted compost within root reach, alongside the willow pulled the group into closer unity, with vibrant blue flowers shaded white in the throat. Not the easiest of the gentian clan to please, though certainly one of the most ornamental.

What are loosely defined as alpines really do provide a fascinating range of permutations for anyone who enjoys painting pictures with plants. Nor is there the same danger of upsetting the normally obliging bank manager. *Saxifraga oppositifolia* 'Wetterhorn', with intense carmine-red flowers opening in late March, matches very well with the fern-like foliage of Pasque flowers, *Pulsatilla vulgaris*. The violet, goblet-shaped, yellow-stamened Pasque flowers then carry the season on against a background of *Aubrietia* 'Red Carpet'. To balance the group there is *Artemisia schmidtiana* with foliage so finely divided it is like a filigree of silver, underplanted with *Scilla* 'Spring Beauty' for the blue-petalled bells which almost compete with gentians in their vibrant colour.

One of the more certain ways of assessing the value in garden terms of a particular amalgam or composition is the length of time it remains fixed in the memory. Those robust heralds of spring, forsythia and ribes, are forever established in my recollection as a hedging combination. Each day I passed the garden where bright yellow-flowered forsythia and deep red-blossomed *Ribes sanguineum* had been planted to form a boundary hedge. In spite of hard pruning, or maybe encouraged by the annual butchery, the bushes burgeoned into a rounded canopy of red and yellow each April. Possibly my interest was not entirely artistic for just at the point where a certain deliciously flavoured apple tree came within 'pockling' finger reach the forsythia-ribes combination was supplanted by *Berberis darwinii*. Frustration apart, the berberis with dark evergreen foliage topped by bright orange clusters of bloom gave approval to the more mundane pair. That it was clipped with similar ferocity made no difference to either health or vigour; even more to the point, it stopped small boys 'scrumping' apples.

Some plants must have agents to promote their interest over and above others possessed of greater distinction. In which case *Prunus* 'Kansan' has the services of the best publicist in the advertising business. There can hardly be a flower colour so ill suited to the pastel-tinted loveliness of spring. Yet in town and village the brazenly self-assertive, purple-pink, double flowers argue, for they could never agree, with daffodil, primrose and the native white-

There are some first encounters with plants which remain vivid in the memory no matter how many years go by. Saxifraga cochlearis 'Minor' first offered itself for my approval at a most inconvenient place on a difficult traverse across a limestone pinnacle some three miles beyond Tende in the Maritime Alps. The hundreds of little resilient points which my hand encountered (Farrer's description, not mine, of the cushion-like growth) after the hard rock face gave me a comforting illusion of security. The white flowers which are borne on red stems open in June.

The Pasque flowers, Pulsatilla vulgaris, are native to Britain and writers 200 years ago describe them as covering the Gogmagog Hills near Cambridge with a robe of purple. Legend purports it to be the Danes' flower as it grows only where Viking blood has been spilled. One old Norfolk gardener I was acquainted with over many years called Pasque flowers 'Laughing Parsley'. That flowers of all descriptions flourished in his garden may have been due in part to his resolutely refusing to give them Latin names.

Pulsatilla vulgaris seed heads are an attractive postscript to the flowers

---

John Evelyn describes the gean, our native cherry, as follows: 'Will thrive into stately trees, beautiful with blossoms of a surprising whiteness, greatly relieving the sedulous bees and attracting birds'. The gean also scores in the sunset splendour of autumn colour. The popular name of gean is derived from the French guigne. *Pliny states that the cherry was unknown in Italy till Lucullus introduced it from Asia Minor in 84 BC, and that it was taken to Britain by the Romans. Others insist that the wild cherry is indigenous to Britain.*

---

blossomed elegance of the gean, *Prunus avium*. Consider instead 'Sargent's cherry', *Prunus sargentii*, which lays a strong claim to being the most attractive of all the Prunus clan. The young foliage is bronze-tinted, while the flowers are a soft magenta pink opening during April. Then in autumn, usually early October, the foliage colours to rich crimson and orange. The ultimate height is about 30ft (9m), much the same as 'Kansan'. A drift of early flowering white trumpet daffodil 'Mount Hood' offers a proper respectful, approving undertone for both 'Kansan' and 'Sargent's cherry'. In the autumn the purple flowers of *Colchicum* – those naked ladies, herbs of the sun – look splendid pushing up through the crimson and gold of fallen leaves.

So often the first time we see a plant influences our judgement of it ever after. Certainly this is true in regard to my preference for the 'Yoshino cherry', *Prunus x yedoensis*, above all others. There are two very ancient 'Yoshino' cherries growing on a broad, grassy terrace which looks down a long wooded valley to Bolton Priory. Unfailingly each spring, early or late, the great spreading canopy 20ft (6m) high by 30ft (9m) across becomes a billowing cloud of pink flowers. To stand under those ancient trees with the sunlight pouring through the flower-packed branches and inhale the almond fragrance, the air vibrant with bee business, is to know beauty as an all-pervading presence. At the time of our first introduction, the larch planted below the terrace was just breaking into pale green leaf, while beyond the craggy buttress of Simon's Seat stood snow-dusted. The under-planting of native daffodils and the purple of aubrietia on wall and in path crevices was restrained enough not to intrude. For the autumn as the cherry leaves coloured, red-flowered, purple-foliaged 'Bishop of Llandaff' dahlia could not be improved on. As for summer? Well, there was a conveniently placed white seat and the sort of view which spans centuries and soothes the mind.

Not all of the garden lies in full sun, which is to the gardener's advantage for there are so many plants which prove themselves best suited when grown in shade. *Acer japonicum* 'Aureum' has pale-yellow leaves which can become scorched and discoloured when exposed to hot sunshine. For those on acid soil the low-growing silver-leaved *Rhododendron impeditum* is comfortably correct. Include also bulbs of 'Snake's Head' fritillary, *Fritillaria meleagris*, with cup-shaped, chequered-patterned flowers in purple and white. Forget-me-nots also, and the moisture-loving narcissus 'February Gold' suit very well and add their own petalled sunshine to the shade. For summer, the fuchsia 'Mrs Popple' with red and purple bells of flower, alongside the crisp curled, green-on-cream-edged leaves of *Hosta crispula* are neat enough not to outgrow a welcome. *Filipendula ulmaria* 'Aurea', also with gold leaves which scorch in the sun if the soil gets dry, completes the shadowed ensemble with nothing growing above 36in (0.9m) high.

There are so many vivid pictures of spring, views seen possibly only once yet which remain jewel bright in the memory; for instance, a purple-foliaged crab apple, *Malus* 'Lemoinei', which is so usefully upright in growth, rising out of a misty blue carpet of bluebells. The wine-red flowers of the crab apple could not have been paid a prettier compliment.

Summer begins to intrude yet there remains one natural garden which has for me always epitomised the truth and the mystery of the season, indeed of all the seasons. In spring primroses like carelessly scattered nosegays pattern the grass amongst white-stemmed birch along with wood violet. Then come bluebells like shadowed wood smoke drifting between the trees. Water avens and monkey musk edge the stream along with butter blobs, while colonies of early purple orchid keep a toe-hold in the open, drier hillocks. In autumn, the spun gold of dying leaf is enough to satisfy. Winter sees the elegance of silver birch naked and unadorned.

In an attempt to condense the natural landscape to fit a small garden, I planted *Betula pendula* 'Youngii', now a beautiful dome-shaped tree 15ft (4.5m) high. Primroses and all the rest are there with *Omphalodes verna* instead of eyebright which can be invasive. Cowslips seed themselves into the lawn, and only the orchid refuses the hospitality so freely offered. Pleasant, yet how can a précis compare with the unexpurgated edition?

ANTICIPATING SUMMER'S GLORY

Summer needs restraint, with so much scarlet and bright orange to tempt indiscretion. Beds are filled with multi-hued-leaved pelargoniums topped with flowers of vivid red. An edging of blue and

There is a form of Rhododendron impeditum *introduced by Joseph Rock in 1922 from the Mekong Valley region of China. A dwarf shrublet only 12in (30.5cm) high with tiny silvered leaves and darker blue flowers than other forms I have seen, it is a treasure well worth searching for. Once acquired, increasing the one to many, by means of semi-ripe cuttings available in June–July, is fairly easy.*

Amongst all the ebullience of early summer, *Campanula* 'Isobel' and *Hypericum olympicum* present a refreshing coolness

white lobelia needs only the bright yellow of calceolaria to complete a compilation that at the very least causes nausea, at worst unhinges the mind. Fortunately, attacks of this bedlamania are usually confined to traffic islands from which they cannot escape to infect nearby gardens because of the passing vehicles.

So-called 'dwarf' conifers are available in a seemingly inexhaustible array of shapes and foliage colours, and there is a temptation to use them in too many contexts. A selection of conifers offers a change in shape and foliage texture or colour. The pattern is perennial and therefore affords year-round interest. A garden overplanted with conifers degenerates into something closely akin to a Forestry Commission woodland, useful only as a rather dull nature trail. Restraint is needed, for so-called 'dwarf' conifers can in time become an outsize problem.

Picea pungens 'Globosa' with silver foliage makes a neat, dense bush possibly 4ft (1.3m) high after fifteen years. On no account let any of the associate planting intrude to spoil the shape of the conifer for ever. This warning applies in every case where a tree or shrub is selected for beauty of form. With the silver spruce I grow *Hypericum olympicum*, both the gold-flowered type and a variety with pale-yellow petals known as 'Citrinum'. Both grow 6–12in (15–30cm) high and are such short-lived though self-perpetuating perennials as to present no long-term threat to the conifer's perfection of form. *Campanula carpatica* 'Isobel' with cup-shaped blue flowers carried on 10in (25cm) high stems completes the trio. In autumn there is just *Crocus speciosus* which seeds amongst the other plants and into the bare places between. The lavender-blue, deeply veined, typically crocus flowers open to show orange stamens when persuaded by the September sunshine.

Roses are very much a part of summer's memory going back to childhood. The fragrance of a packed array of flowers mingled with the clean scent of freshly mown grass on the still air of a June evening has signalled day's end for me over many years. Roses grown en masse in a well contrived, self-contained garden fully express their own unique character, of which more later. As individuals, roses lack those qualities of perennial charm and commanding presence which are needed to form and sustain an interesting landscape. Out of flower, except for the hip-bearing species *rugosa, moyesii* et al., they are rather nondescript, lacking comeliness of form and variation in foliage. When used as focal points to a group roses need a good supporting cast. *Rosa alba* 'Celestial' makes a bush 5ft (1.5m) high with grey-green leaves, an excellent foil to the double camellia-shaped pink flowers. *Berberis candidula*, a 3ft (0.9m) high dome of small shining dark-green leaves, silver underneath, provides the positive perenniality. The flowers which open as the rose leaves unfurl are large and bright yellow in colour. 'Jacob's Ladder' *Polemonium caeruleum* suits very well in divided foliage and blue flowers with the berberis. As a foreground, there is a purple-leaved form of Venetian sumach, *Cotinus coggygria* 'Royal Purple', which is kept hard pruned each spring so that the white flowers of *Colchicum speciosum* 'Album'

When dwarf conifers are used to excess, the effect is not one of harmony, for the unnaturalness of what is after all a vegetable gnome makes me feel slightly uneasy, particularly in the deepening gloom of evening – a series of curiously hunched figures which, for so-called dwarfs, do increase in size at a quite embarrassing rate. I speak as one who has sinned and profited from the experience of a very expensive mistake when fifty per cent of the garden had to be given away. Briefly, I had many friends all with empty gardens.

The autumn crocus, of which Crocus speciosus *is a good example, need to be grown through some not too dense ground cover. The stem seems totally incapable of supporting the weight of these lovely flowers, so that they flop over to become soiled like ball gowns that have trailed over a rain-wet drive. The campanula serves very well as will thyme or dwarf forms of* Calluna *such as* 'Silver Queen'.

---

planted underneath can push through to display themselves in September. A group of *Phlox paniculata* 'Eva Cullum' which in my garden flowers pink with the shortening days of autumn, forms a cheerful supplement to the compilation. This is a group which over twenty years held a place in my select top twenty associations.

On a visit to Greece in search of the lovely, yet elusive *Paeonia clusii*, I was for a whole day diverted from my real purpose by *Euphorbia characias wulfenii*, the plant that splendid gardener E. A. Bowles of Middleton House dubbed his 'Frog Spawn Bush'. One hillside above Delphi was dotted with great clumps of this most impressive spurge. The spikes of greenish-yellow flowers, each floret with a red-brown centre, have caused many a flower-arranging devotee to shatter the commandment which forbids covetousness. Each plant, or so it seemed to my gardener's rather than botanist's eye, showed a slight difference in leaf shape or flower character from those of its next-door neighbour, and it was this that excited my interest. Growing with the spurge was a pink-flowered asphodel, possibly that referred to in the Elysian fields – home of the dead in Greek mythology – dubbed by botanists *Asphodelus fistulosus*.

A spring flowering euphorbia should really be in another chapter, except for the context in which fate, in the shape of a south country garden and a handsome bush of *Ozothamnus ledifolius*, gave me the opportunity for experiment. Both need a place in full sun with a soil so well drained that a day's sunshine means drought conditions. The Tasmanian Lacquer Bush, *Ozothamnus*, has narrow, leathery, very shiny evergreen leaves, and the coppery-red flower buds are in evidence just as the spurge flowers arrive at peak condition. The effect is better than poetry. Having established a Mediterranean corner, building on the scheme proved most interesting.

Phlomis fruticosa was too greyish-green and dusty-looking, so I passed it on to a friend. A carpet of dark-foliaged, ruby-flowered thyme tumbling over from bed to path proved a happier choice, with *lavender* 'Hidcote' giving the pennyworth of grey and blue the planting needed. Having seen the madonna lily, *Lilium candidum*, growing in conditions which even the native tortoise found intolerably hot I planted six bulbs which produced stems of incomparably lovely golden-stamened, white-petalled flowers just as the daisy flowers of the Lacquer Bush performed.

For autumn days *Nerine bowdenii* thrives on aridity and offers a quota of curious crimped pink blooms in September. Why not the asphodel, so much a part of the natural, original scheme? Attempts to introduce well grown plants all ended in failure, so I planted *Crocosmia Lucifer*. The flame-red flowers are so outrageous – they sit like out-thrust tongues on curiously geometric 3ft (0.9m) high or slightly taller stems – that the arrangement succeeds, though why it should is beyond me.

Brightly coloured annuals are an integral part of the summer scene. In the contrived garden landscape and the broader natural scenery beyond, annuals play their own distinctive part. *Lavatera*, the first annual seed I sowed as a schoolboy, still holds a place

Roses root with such enthusiasm that each autumn, whether or not new plants are needed, I take a selection of cuttings from those bushes already growing in the garden. A sheltered border outdoors, where the soil, having been used for the same purpose for many years, is very gritty and free draining, has proved ideal for the purpose. I choose young shoots of the current season's growth which are about 12in (30.5cm) long and full ripe. These are buried to at least one-third of their length and spaced 4in (10cm) apart in a trench and then firmed well in. Twelve months later a good percentage are well enough rooted for planting out in the garden.

Though an endemic of Tasmania, Ozothamnus is hardy in my garden. The highly aromatic secretion, which is so reminiscent of freshly made strawberry jam, pervades the whole garden on still warm days. In the wild it makes the bush extremely inflammable. Cuttings of young shoots made in July root quite readily in sharp sand compost.

All the Buddleia davidii *hybrids would be worth a place because they bloom in late summer and are very attractive to butterflies. To see the long racemes of fragrant flowers clustered with painted lady, red admiral and others all gorging on the nectar is worth tolerating a shrub which in flower is a joyful sight, and for the rest of the year resembles an ill-constructed clothes rack. Prunings, used as pea sticks, can be lifted at summer's end as rooted cuttings.*

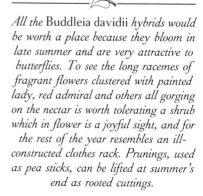

A variation on the 'Venetian Sumach' (Cotinus coggygria 'Royal Purple') with colchicum theme which I have tried this year: mauve with dark purple is almost episcopalian

Though Impatiens *form a part of summer in combination with golden-leaved berberis, there is need for a more perennial association.* Rhododendron yakushimanum *has proved that foliage complements are as richly satisfying in subtle colour shades as brightly fashioned flowers. The dark-green and soft fawn felted leaves of the rhododendron are contrasted with the bright yellow of the berberis.*

Dianthus gratianopolitanus, *the lovely Cheddar pink with its mats of blue leafage overshadowed in June by fragrant flights of fringed rose-pink flowers in number as the stars of the sky', to quote Reginald Farrer who used words in the grand manner. I would always raise new stock by means of the seed so generously offered by these same flowers.*

though in new improved varieties. Planted around the grey-leaved *Buddleia* 'Lochinch', the satin-pink flowers of the annual look very lovely. A sea holly seeded into the picture and appeared so much at home that I planted *Eryngium x oliverianum* for the steel-blue tinted stems and involucre to match the two tones of the buddleia flowers. With a bold group of day lilies, *Hemerocallis* 'Hyperion', adding a soft yellow, seasonal tone, the cottage garden effect is complete.

A garden formed only from trees, shrubs, and herbaceous perennials tends to be repetitive no matter how well contrived; with only a scarcely discernible change in height and breadth as a reward for effort, our enthusiasm is inevitably diminished. By skilful use of annuals the whole pattern and colour complex can be changed. Bulb foliage, yellowing to ripeness in midsummer, spoils the whole appearance of the garden. A sprinkling of annual seed, a different species each year, amongst narcissus, crocus, colchicum and the rest soon forms a bright blossomed screen to all the decay. Interesting variations in colour can be tried in the certain knowledge that any which go badly wrong will be safely erased by the first frost of autumn.

One of the reasons why herbaceous plants and shrubs with coloured foliage are so useful is the way they form a background to experiments with annuals. Dark-red-flowered, purple-foliaged 'Coronette' *antirrhinum* grouped with *Rosa glauca*, whose foliage is glaucous purple, is one to try. The lovely golden lace-patterned leaves of the 'Red Berried Elder', *Sambucus racemosa* 'Plumosa Aurea', tempt all sorts of outrageous experiments. Love-in-a-mist, whose blue and white flowers are in evidence most of the summer, the soft plumes of 'Squirrel Grass', *Hordeum jubatum*, like pink tinted barley, and the biennial foxglove, *Digitalis* 'Excelsior', complete a relaxed natural arrangement.

There are several more shrubs which serve as the basis for annual experiments. *Berberis thunbergii* 'Atropurpurea Nana' is a gem. There is a yellow-leaved form of the species 'Aurea' which needs to be kept in shade, so 'Busy Lizzie', *Impatiens*, varieties make a readily available associate. Working out colour schemes like this is a fascinating way of gardening on dark winter evenings – better by far than the banality of 'Trivial Pursuits'.

Though summer can never be too long, the same cannot be said of plant lists. So here is just one more summer scene using one of the absolutely indispensable hardy geraniums. Of the many, *Geranium cinerium* 'Ballerina' is creditably long blooming and only 4in (10cm) high. The typical geranium flowers are pink with dark red veins. Fragrance is important, which gains a place for the Cheddar pink, *Dianthus gratianopolitanus*, a most attractive native that forms creeping mats of glaucous grey leaves. In June deep-rose-pink flowers on 6in (15cm) high stems offer a fragrance that is fit subject for poetry. These are two shades of pink which blend very well yet need something dark foliaged to set them off. *Daphne retusa* is a neat evergreen shrublet growing slowly to 14in (36cm) high by 18in (46cm) across in ten years or so. The intensely

fragrant deep-purple flowers open in May, to be followed in due season by large berries.

Strangely enough, the *Saxifraga oppositifolia* mentioned in the shade border context has a place here. The foliage in the brighter light is silvery white. I had noticed this same curious characteristic some years previously when exploring a valley in the mountains near La Grave. Plants growing in the shade showed only pale-green foliage, those in the sun were silver encrusted. Apparently the leaf tips are equipped with a special gland which can regulate loss of water by transpiration. On dry days when the plant is losing a lot of moisture to the cooling process of evaporation the gland secretes lime which dissolves in the water. As the water evaporates on the leaf surface the lime is left to shut down the stomata and so reduce an excessive loss of moisture during drought. Once the drought ends the lime encrustation dissolves, leaving the leaf free to resume the normal transpiration process. It is strange that the procedure employed by plants of absorbing water-carrying nutrients through the roots fuels the photosynthetic process which is the basis of all life on this earth. The excess water once the minerals are removed is lost by means of the unblocked valve in the case of purple saxifrage and most other plants.

Crocosmia 'Lucifer' better placed, I now agree, against green, not nerine pink

A layer of sandy compost used as a mulch under the berry-laden branches of the daphne usually discovers at least one or two self-sown seedlings in due course.

AUTUMN

*Writing of my last garden:
'Loveliest of all cherries here is* Prunus
sargentii, *growing to 20ft (6m) high
with soft pink flowers measuring
1½ inches across. In autumn the leaves
turn brilliant scarlet, the display lasting
in a favourable season for several weeks.'
That was in 1967 and* Prunus
sargentii *has not changed a leaf tint or
petal shade in the intervening years.*

Autumn is, surely, the most complete of all the seasons. There is such an overflowing abundance of colour that there are moments when perfect is not a misapplied description: a bed of dahlias seen across a mist-hung lawn in early morning, a beech grove turned to a cathedral of golden light as the evening sunshine pays a final tribute to end a lovely day. Suddenly the twittering concourse of swallows that for so long hawked low over the lawn, or dipped to skim the still pool to a ripple of life, are gone. Instead, a lace veil of cobwebs shrouds the garden and a silence so profound that the sound of foraging rooks three fields away is loud enough to be an intrusion. Autumn is a time of joy tinged with sadness, where days do not pass but drift away through avenues of colour and fruitful abundance.

First indication that another garden year is passing, the Sargent's cherry leaves change green for scarlet and gold. Often one branch of the horsechestnut will quickly follow suit, and the stage is set for the carnival.

Not all the colour is of death or a prelude to decay. The *Cyclamen hederifolium* push up pink and white flowers round the variegated holly whose green berries are already tinged with red. A *Caryopteris x clandonensis* makes a better accommodation for the ivy-leaved

A lovely autumn alliance between *Caryopteris x clandonensis* and *Cyclamen hederifolium* 'Album'. Usually, the cyclamen flowers appear before the marbled leaves which are a feature all winter through

Fuchsia 'Tom Thumb' intermingled with *Saturea montana* – lovely, and compact enough at 15in (38cm) for the smaller garden

cyclamen, with grey leaves and powder-blue flowers. There are problems persuading *Gentiana sino-ornata* to thrive away from areas of heavy rainfall, or where the soil is alkaline. Where this attractive plant can be grown, let the group be commendably large so that when the trumpet flowers open the soil is hidden under a screen of vivid blue. *Astilbe chinensis* 'Pumila', with 12in (30cm) high spikes of dusky-pink flowers, looks fine alongside the gentian. To throw dappled shade over the bed there is 'Paper Barked Maple', *Acer griseum*, arguably the prince of the clan particularly when the leaves turn scarlet edged with gold. Fuchsia add the elegance of contrasting shape with 'Mrs Popple' providing the right shade of red and purple. The maple is lovely even after the leaves fall, when sunshine through the peeling (ex-foliating) bark provides a halo for each twig and stem in cinnamon-gold light. Though *Acer griseum* like most of the maples can be grown from seed, be prepared to sow a thousand to be certain of one germinating. Fertile *Acer griseum* seed is rarer than Australians at a temperance meeting.

For gardens where the soil is acid a combination of heather and hebe is good. Plant three or more *Calluna vulgaris* 'H. E. Beale' which gives a display of rose-pink double flowers right through late summer into autumn. The intense coloured violet blossom of Hebe 'Autumn Glory' opens on 30in (75cm) stems, thus matching in stature those of the calluna. For over twenty years this colour scheme has held its place in a very competitive autumn scenario. As a centre-piece, *Acer palmatum* 'Dissectum Flavescens' would be hard to surpass for beauty of form. The foliage turns glowing orange at the first exposure to autumn frost. Fuchsia 'Tom Thumb' with carmine and mauve flowers with the *Saturea montana* would provide a similar arrangement for those gardening on lime.

Gentiana sino-ornata *is a quite invaluable Chinese species for those who garden on lime-free soil. It has proved so readily propagated that it is really a bad nurseryman's plant. Lifted and divided in March, each plant will fall into any number of nicely rooted single thongs. Division at any other time is a very chancy affair.*

Rhus typhena 'Laciniata' and pamps grass in an autumn-colour corner

Tropaeolum speciosum, the perennial flame nasturtium, either refuses to grow or flourishes so luxuriantly that it covers the whole garden. Nevertheless, *Tropaeolum* mantling a silver variegated holly with pale-green leaf and vivid scarlet-keeled flowers is a sight to gladden the eye. Summer offers the main display, although flowering persists into autumn with the perfect embellishment of mandarin-blue berries. A low growing 8–12in (20–30cm) high *Saxifraga fortunei* 'Wada's' offers purple-red leaves and a cascade of white flowers as a hem to the holly skirt.

There is very little incentive to contrive plant associations unique to the autumn season. So many of those plants selected for spring, summer and winter announce autumn with a change of leaf colour that all contribute to this grand climax, which is better expressed by the word Fall. *Amelanchier laevis* is expressively beautiful in spring when the white scented flowers mingle with the bronze-tinted young growth. Then in autumn the leaves take on rich tints, an intermingling of red, purple and bronze. Also plant a female form of stag horn sumach *Rhus typhina* 'Laciniata', which turns orange and yellow. The silver plumes of pampas grass, *Cortaderia selloana* 'Pumila', will add an illusion of smoke to the shrub's flaming leaf colour. Tone the extravagant mixture down with a bush of 'Lads Love', *Artemesia abrotanum*, that hoary green, feathery herb more often seen in the company of rosemary and lavender.

Soon, only the russet of the leaves retained on the beech hedge long after all the rest have fallen remain as a reminder of the autumn festival.

'Where first I met the bitter scent is not lost for the key is there in the spray plucked from the doorside bush. Old Man or Lads' Love, the hoary green herb with its memories of Aconites, Meadow Cranesbill and ancient Victoria Plum trees.'

Winter is the time for drawing up plans for the year ahead. There may be a whole new garden to design, or just a border.

There is more to designing a garden than merely filling all available space with flowers for one season. Interest needs to carry on year round, which means arriving at a proper balance between flowers, form, foliage, and bark. One important consideration is the situation. To take my own plot as an example, on an exposed site 700ft (210m) above sea level, a high proportion of evergreens is essential, otherwise the site appears more naked and windswept than it actually is. The same style of planting in a suburban or inner city garden would prove depressingly dark and gloomy in winter.

There are so many variations in foliage, colour, and texture amongst conifers that the novice can easily be tempted into overplanting. A judicious mixture of conifers in combination with other multi-hued foliaged evergreens: holly, heathers, elaeagnus, for example, makes an excellent beginning of a landscape. The 'Westonbirt' dogwood with sealing-wax red shoots bright polished by winter sunshine, carpeted underneath with snowdrops and aconite, would have relieved even King Richard's discontent.

Softer colours, snowdrops close clustered around a white-stemmed birch, or winter flowering heathers powdered with snow, are unfailing persuaders to optimism. A catkin-hung branch on the twisted hazel looks even more curiously convoluted when seen against the angry orange red of a February sunset living Ikebana. Alpines are a means of bringing spring memories of mountain landscapes into the smallest garden early in January. A cold frame or unheated greenhouse provides all the protection required. There, the flowers of saxifraga, crocus, narcissus, and rhododendron will open petals unstained by weather and safe from hungry gastropods. Strange how some flowers carry with them into the garden the quality of their natural habitat.

The first snow of winter can be turned to our advantage. Great clods of clay left fresh turned and totally intractable in October will by the following April disintegrate into a fine tilth under the merest caress of a rake. Seeds of meconopsis, primula and others which are slow to germinate will be roused from dormancy if sown in pots and left outdoors to be snowed on and frozen.

Pruning is a year-round preoccupation, but with a greater emphasis on the winter months. I pay particular attention to plants trained over walls or fences. To make certain none of the ties are so tight as to restrict growth, I cut all the stems free of their supports and do any pruning which is necessary before securing them again with twine or raffia.

There are always times when the peculiar beauty of winter catches me unawares. When the leafless branches of winter flowering viburnum are decked with pink flowers whose fragrance reminds me so vividly of May while it is yet only February. When the variegated holly by the pool is laden with berries as it is this year – a green, gold and scarlet garden complete in one 10ft (3m) high bush. When the winter flowering iris opens its delicate pencilled flowers on a south-facing wall, with sprays of yellow jasmine above.

Witch hazel branches wreathed with yellow spider-like flowers add fragrance as a bonus to mere colour

5

From the Four Corners of the World

The Giant Redwoods in their native home tower up to 350ft (107m) high. Drenched by Pacific ocean mists and left undisturbed for 2,000 years, they are, compared to man, immortal.

Oh, you dyspeptic people, who despise the pleasures of others, and with peevish pens depreciate rapture into rhapsody, it is already clear that you must not come with me to Tibet. For there is loveliness and glory everywhere on those far hills.
The Rainbow Bridge, *R. Farrer*

One fact which soon dawns on the apprentice gardener when working around the borders and enquiring into the needs of the plants growing there, is how very few of them are native to these islands. Where, then, do they come from and how did they get here? Many well established favourites, familiar even to non-gardeners since early childhood obviously do grow wild somewhere. The most surprising aspect of all is that plants from so many countries with climates and soils so completely different from ours can be successfully grown here without undue effort.

To follow the route taken by Masson in South Africa or Douglas through Redwood country in California, or even Farrer amongst the Dolomites, reveals just some idea of the difficulties they must have surmounted. Modern transport shortens the perspective. We can reach in hours locations which took those early plant hunter explorers months or even years. What is certain is that considerable sums of money were gambled on sending expeditions to remote, near inaccessible, unmapped and unexplored regions in search of new, hitherto unknown plants to satisfy the demands of an ever growing market.

That some of the plants have been changed out of all recognition by selective breeding at the hands of hybridists may not be quite so obvious. Any relationship between the dahlia growing wild alongside a grass-grown track in Mexico and the enormous, garishly coloured soup-plate-sized flowers exhibited at shows all over this country in autumn would be hard to see just by merely looking. Surprisingly enough, according to report, it was only in the eighteenth century that the sexual nature of flowers was recognised and the process of plant procreation fully understood. Plant hybridisation then is not one of the ancient arts. Yet common sense in the shape of paeony, chrysanthemum, and prunus from China, or dahlia from Mexico suggests that some form of selectivity other than cross-pollination was practised by pre-eighteenth-century gardeners and botanists.

IN ANCIENT TIMES

Theophrastus, born 300 years before the birth of Christ, was a gardener in practical terms and a botanist of distinction. In his book

Inquiry into the Growth of Plants he writes of roses, white and pink, comparing flowering times and fragrance, with the added comment that the most sought after in respect of scent were imported from North Africa. Is this, then, the first recorded incident of plant hunting? Could Theophrastus have achieved sufficient influence with Alexander the Great to persuade him to send back any interesting plants discovered on his many victorious campaigns into Europe, Cilicia, Syria, Persia, even India. After all, Theophrastus and Alexander shared the same tutor in Aristotle, and though there was an age difference it would not be too fanciful to imagine that their paths did cross. Certainly there would be increased trade with the countries conquered and the talk of myrtles, gillyflowers, and iris suggests that gardeners then as now were great swappers of plants.

Interesting possibly yet hardly relevant in respect of British gardens except that what was once Greek very soon became Roman. Julius Caesar we know visited Britain in 55BC and the Romans were able to colonise, if that is the right word, or at least establish settlements in southern Britain soon afterwards. In the absence of modern antibiotics, Roman soldiers would most certainly carry with them herbal remedies for treating wounds or disease. Home cooking, that sure alleviator of home sickness, would necessitate a judicious use of those culinary herbs native to the sun-soaked Mediterranean. Trade would soon be established and once Roman gardens were laid down (the Flavian palace near Chichester was begun in the first century AD) then plants would be imported to give them authenticity. For the Romans adopted gardening as Pliny records in his *Observations on Natural History* and, as with so many things, developed it as an art form. On the subject of rose and lily he writes 'Oils and condiments of them both have a resemblance and affinity one to the other'.

One of the healing herbs, according to writers of herbals, carried by the legionaries was *Lilium album*, our *Lilium candidum* or madonna lily, a very old inhabitant of English flower gardens. Pliny is almost lyrical in the extravagance of his prose:

> Now Lilies be set and sowed after the same manner as the Roses and grow as many ways. This vantage moreover they have of the Roses, that they will come up of the very liquer that distilleth and droppeth from them, neither is there in the world an herb more fruitful, in so much as you shall have one head of a root put forth often times five hundred bulbs.

Careful observer that he was, it seems incredible that Pliny should indulge in such a fanciful suggestion, that lilies regenerated themselves from their own nectar; observer extraordinary certainly, gardener questionably. For in planting and cultivating the madonna lily, the gardener must have noticed how they spread by vegetative means, bulb from bulb.

The petals of white lilies infused in oil were once used in the treatment of painful and obstinate tumours. They are also described in *The British Flora Medica* as a favourite domestic remedy for cuts.

Physalis alkekengi franchetii from Japan is a very happy wanderer in any ordinary garden soil which is free-draining. The 3ft (1m) long flowering stems need to be cut as the Chinese lanterns show orange colour, then dried off and preserved for use in winter flower arrangements

Lilium candidum which, I suspect, was brought to Britain by the Roman legionaries

OPPOSITE
Paeonia have a quiet, reflective quality
(*Lotherton Hall, near Leeds*)

Figs are well suited to container growing, and fruit well on a south-facing patio or terrace

A fanciful theory to suggest that the white lily arrived in Britain with the Roman legions, there is no proof to support the suggestion; equally, there is no evidence to the contrary either.

The Romans did import vines, a sweet apple, fig, mulberry (black), medlar, walnut and sweet chestnut, all of them familiar garden plants to this day. The plants mentioned as Roman imports were also in the garden where I began my own professional career. Did the pungent smell of walnut leaves bring thoughts of home to legionaries from Gaul or Tuscany, for the fragrance is unmistakably evocative? Figs oozing purple juice so redolent of hot sunshine, and grapes more acrid in taste possibly than those from the Italian vineyards, were still better by far than any fruit native to Britain. There were also the herbs coriander, garlic, rue and borage, amongst others, together with several sorts of vegetables, and almost certainly *Papaver somniferum*, the opium poppy.

THE MONKISH INFLUENCE

When Christianity came to England late in the sixth century, the religious houses founded in various parts of the country doubtless provided themselves with gardens. The monks and friars practised herbal medicine for they were apothecaries on the one hand and apostles on the other. In monastery and convent gardens a wide variety of herbs were cultivated in addition to foodstuffs. There was also constant trafficking to and fro between the Continent of Europe and England which brought hemp for rope making, cherries from Turkey according to a tenth-century herbal, the peach or Persian apple and much else besides. By the tenth century 'Wort beds', our version of herb and herbaceous borders, were well stocked with the basic ingredients for making up herbal remedies.

Was it in some friar's pack, I wonder, that the paeony was carried to Steep Holm where it still grows wild? Or was it introduced by the historian Gildas when he sought refuge on the island from the Saxon invaders, as some historians suggest? The same species *Paeonia mascula*, 'The Male Paeonia', used to grow wild in the Cotswolds near Winchcombe where there was also a monastery – coincidence enough to suggest an introduced garden escape rather than a native plant. Paeonia or Glukyside is also described by the botanist Theophrastus and was held in high regard by the ancients as a herb of healing. Named after Paeon, assistant to Aesculapius, the god of medicine, it is not surprising that the plant was held with a veneration amounting to awe. It is natural to assume that *Paeonia mascula* held a proud place in monastic gardens.

Stand near the temple of Apollo at Delphi, then search for the paeonies growing wild in the mountains beyond and discover that some plants are like ley lines spanning centuries, linking yesterday, today and tomorrow. Surely, a plant so much used in medicine and growing wild in the Mediterranean region would have been, like the white lily, an essential part of a Roman camp surgeon's medical pack. Should Julius Caesar and not some itinerant friar be given the credit for its introduction into England?

Cottage gardens over the years have proved invaluable sources for plants which, though once widely grown, had then lost popularity as garden fashions changed. Many of the old hybrids of tried and tested virtue are being used in modern plant-breeding programmes.

THE CRUSADERS DID THEIR PART

The Crusaders, the Knights Hospitallers, and the Templars were closely connected with the monasteries and possibly contributed some of the plants. And not just to the monastic gardens, for what better solace to a lonely wife with her husband absent for years on end than regular consignments of plants carrying with them reassuring messages of love and devotion? Grown in the castle garden, they would add a new quality of unusual beauty and a splendid form of one-upmanship. 'Just a little something Sir Percy sent from Spain or Jerusalem' – a real conversation stopper. There is no question that gardeners then as now took 'slips', divisions or seeds for their own use and the cottage garden idiom was founded.

HERBS AND HERBALISM

The interest in plants continued to be medicinal rather than ornamental, the cult of herbalism becoming ever more irrational as the doctrine of plant signatures gained popular acceptance. Herbs with yellow sap would be suitable for treating jaundice, while those with spotted leaves, like pulmonaria, served the same purpose for lung disorders.

The precise date when love of flowers for their beauty rather than for any edible or medicinal quality first revealed itself is not accurately recorded. Poets, no doubt, would be the first to extol the beauty of flowers. Only when the need for the expression of beauty in flower-filled gardens provided the demand would the means of supplying the wherewithal to satisfy it be found. Chaucer wrote of 'Vyolet and Cullambine with Gilliflowers and Sops-in Wine', while Shakespeare had his lilies of all kinds.

GARDENS OUTSIDE THE CASTLE WALL

Gardening literature records the prevailing fashions of the times. Most of the books are concerned with the grand landscape and the plants grown in manorial gardens. For all that, they offer an interesting comparison between then and now.

Then, with the establishment of the Tudor line a more settled time arrived; law and order once firmly instituted brought peace of a sort. New houses, grand, modest, and small and without the need of fortification, offered the prospect of a garden somewhat larger than that imposed by the limitations of space inside a portcullis-shielded castle wall. The stage was set for men like William Turner, a clergyman by calling, a botanist by inclination, to draw up an accurate list of the plants growing in England. In 1548 he published *Names of Herbes*. Thomas Hill wrote what must be one of the first specifically English gardening books, *A Most Briefe and Pleasant Teaching How to Dress, Sowe, and Set a Garden*. Then came Gerard, the barber-surgeon who must obviously have found time to learn a great deal about growing plants, for in addition to his own garden he was in charge of the Lord Burleigh demesnes, one in the Strand, the other in Hertfordshire. In 1596 he issued a list of the considerable number of plants presumably growing in those same gardens. The historical significance of this, the first indication of how many imported as opposed to native plants there were under cultivation at that period, is really incalculable. There is no date given for when each was introduced; though some are described as new, others must have been growing in gardens for some time. A year later he published the now legendary *Herbal.* In it he describes damask roses and others which are non-native imports from Europe. What a remarkable adventure story and record of garden history those early imports would have provided had each generation produced a Pliny, a Hill, a Gerard, or a recorder of similar calibre. John Parkinson, who thirty-three years later published *Paradisi in Sole Paradisus Terrestris* or *A Choice Garden of all sorts of Rarest Flowers* offers another glimpse. Tantalising little snippets from other gardener-botanist recorders serve only to whet the appetite for more intimate and detailed descriptions.

For instance, who was the Mr Coy living at Stubbers in Essex where the North American yucca first flowered? A certain John Goodyear made a list of the plants growing at Stubbers which proves that Mr Coy must have had regular contact with the New World. How and why, and more important what was the contact? Were the plants merely incidental to a more lucrative trade or the prime source and reason? There must have been plant collectors since pre-Christian days in China, Mexico, the Mediterranean and elsewhere. In such places with civilisation advanced enough and with law and order established, cultured minds surely found expression in the making of gardens, particularly in China and Japan which are still a rich resource for plants.

THE FIRST ELIZABETHAN AGE AND THE TRADESCANTS

The Elizabethan age was a time of great prosperity; Britain ruled the sea routes and increased trade was the reward. One outlet for all the accumulated wealth was found in the building of grand houses and the laying out of geometrically precise pleasure gardens. The wealthy owners then vied with each other in collecting together the most interesting plants then available, with rarity a prime recommendation. No doubt new plants were brought in as a form of speculative trading by seafarers, though in a casual, random manner.

Enter then the John Tradescants, father and son, from East Anglia. The father at least hailed from Suffolk. John junior was born at Meopham in Kent in 1608. In 1609 Tradescant senior was hired by Lord Salisbury, who was then building a magnificent house at Hatfield, to work as a gardener. Possibly the dearth of interesting plants available at the time became more obviously apparent when the garden, which is proportionate to the house in size, needed stocking. Whether the wish for new, more interesting plants was the motivating force or the desire to outdo his neighbours in having the finest collection of rare and exotic plants makes no matter. Suffice it that John Tradescant was sent post-haste to Europe to find what the nurseries there had on offer.

Tradescant travelled first to France in search of 'rootes, flowers, seedes, trees and plants'. Certainly in Paris the haul included

Tradescantia virginiana, one of my favourite herbaceous perennials, is given scant praise by Parkinson: 'The soon fading Spiderwort of Virginia, or Tradescant his Spiderwort is of late knowledge, and for it the Christian world is indebted to that painful and industrious lover of all Nature's varieties John Tradescant, that brought it out of Virginia'. John Tradescant may have had the genus named in his honour, but it was known in Europe in 1590 before he was born, so must have been introduced by someone else.

Yucca flowers are now an accepted part
of the summer garden scene

glasshouse fruit such as pomegranates. From there he journeyed to Brussels and Leiden. Did he visit the garden at Leiden where Carolus Clusius grew his tulips raised from seed sent to him from Turkey by de Busbecq? No mention is made of buying tulips, only iris, portingal quince and other fruits. The accent is very much on the edible rather than the ornamental. On moving to St Augustine's Palace at Canterbury as gardener to Lord Wotton, Tradescant ventured some of his own money in an expedition to Virginia on condition that any new plants discovered there were sent to him. One of them was 'Silk Grass' or spiderwort to which the name *Tradescantia* was given.

The next trip was to Russia attached to a trade mission. This was a profitable venture in botanical terms for Tradescant noted all the plants he had seen, plus collecting a large quantity of specimens and stock for the garden including larch, a valuable timber and ornamental tree. Then to Algiers where instead of doing battle with pirates he very sensibly botanised ashore, leaving fighting corsairs to the more hot-blooded members of the party. Corne flagge, *Gladiolus byzantinus*, he described as growing abundantly. Inevitably it was the edible which had priority, 'Algiers Apricot', which quickly gained such popularity that it was featured in most noblemen's gardens. In due course, Tradescant became royal gardener to Charles I.

Fortunately, his son, also called John, had inherited his father's passion for plants and gardening plus the same adventurous spirit. In 1637 he sailed to the Americas to Virginia to gather all varieties of flowers, trees, plants which he sent back to his father in Lambeth. *Tradescantia virginiana*, the lovely blue-flowered 'Moses in the

Of all the plants introduced by Tradescant junior, it is the lovely Moses in the bulrushes, *Tradescantia virginiana* 'Isis' (*x Andersoniana*) which has given me the most pleasure and best service. Given any reasonable soil and a modest share of the sun, it is a herbaceous perennial which will flower continuously from mid-June into October. In my thin soil the height is at most 18in (45cm), with flowering undiminished in spite of the spartan conditions

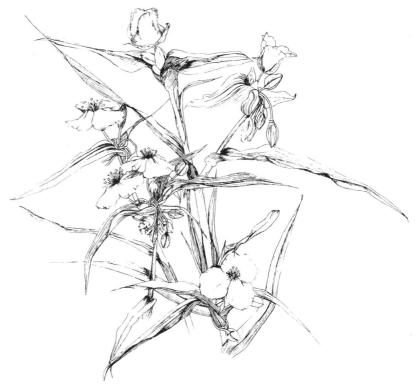

Bulrushes', false acacia, *Robinia pseudo-acacia* and the gracefully elegant *Lilium canadense* are enough to assure John Tradescant a proud place in horticulture's hall of fame. There was much more, including a plane tree, *Platanus occidentalis*, which in due course was planted alongside an already established *Platanus orientalis*. The American *Sycamore P.occidentalis* is not the easiest of trees to grow successfully, but it survived to cross-pollinate with the European plane to produce the London plane, *P.acerifolia*, the best known street tree of all time. The Tradescants can make just claim to laying a foundation stone on which to build other plant collections over the following three centuries.

Considering the difficulties which those early pioneer plant collectors had to overcome, it is surprising that any of the plants ever reached their destination. The slow journey by porter, cart, and sea, through climates totally at variance with those to which the plant was accustomed, must have killed all except the few with iron constitutions. Yet botanist explorers showing extraordinary courage and endurance continued to penetrate remote, bleak, and frequently dangerous regions to study and collect plants.

The London planes, according to Sir Herbert Maxwell, have been accused of being chief agents in inflicting influenza, bronchitis, and catarrh upon the inhabitants of the metropolis. 'It has been seriously affirmed that when the seed vessels of the plane break up in dry spring weather, the air is filled with minute spicules which act as an irritant upon human throats and noses.'
That P.x acerifolia *is now* P.x hispanica *in no way reduces the London plane tree's value for street planting, owing to its tolerance of atmospheric pollution and ability to put up with very severe pruning.*

THE TRICKLE BECOMES A FLOOD

Joseph Banks was a wealthy man who presumably enjoyed all the advantages which rank and possessions brought then as now. Botany, particularly the study of plants in the field, was his passionate interest and the driving force which sent him first to Newfoundland where he collected native plants and learned the ways and means of a field botanist. A stern initiation this must have been in so bleak, dangerous and inhospitable a region. Once embarked on his career as a committed plant hunter, the man's restless genius had him engaging himself to an expedition to the South Seas under Captain James Cook aboard the *Endeavour*. After calling at ports in South America, the expedition arrived in Matavai Bay, Tahiti. Could there have been a greater contrast than that offered by the Arctic fringe flora of Newfoundland and the tropical vegetation of a South Sea island? Banks, dedicated botanist that he was, must have thought this was Paradise after the ghastly near-death of sea sickness to which he was prone.

Next to New Zealand, then to New South Wales, *Terra Australia Incognita*. The harbour in which the ship dropped anchor was called Botany Bay in recognition of the wealth of plants growing there, all of them new, each one to be recorded, classified, collected root, branch, flower and seed, for that is the way of systematic botany. On the way back to England the ship called in at Cape Town, where Banks was given a glimpse of the astonishing variety of the native flora. This practical experience convinced him of the need to train specialist collectors who would be better equipped to cope with the difficulties encountered in the field.

Francis Masson was the first of many and he went to South Africa. To study the South African flora is a never to be forgotten experience. Vivid pictorial images follow each other in such rapid

Pelargonium violareum on the Langeberg, South Africa. The soil is sandy, dry, and sun baked

Pelargonium, *popularly known as geranium, have been grown in European gardens since the eighteenth century.* Geranium africanum, *as it was then called, gained immediate acclaim. 'This plant has every Recommendation to the Regard of those who delight in vegetables, Beauty of Flower, Fragrance and a peculiar Elegance in its whole Aspect. It is accordingly an universal Favourite',* wrote John Hill in the Compleat Body of Gardening *in 1757.*

When is a geranium not a geranium? The answer, of course, must be, when it is a pelargonium. Those plants known to most gardeners by the name geranium are, in fact, pelargoniums. Pelargoniums are native to South Africa, particularly, and form a large and complicated genus. To the gardener they are those ivy-leaved (as illustrated), zonal, regal, and hybrid geraniums which for generations have been planted in unrecordable millions in beds, borders, tubs, and hanging baskets to rejoice summer with their brightly coloured blooms. No cottage window is, even now, properly furnished without a pot of scarlet geranium (pelargonium)

succession that they merge into a blaze of colour like some giant surrealist painting. The wagon tracks are cut 14in (26cm) deep into solid rock. In Masson's day his own iron-shod waggon wheels were the first to bruise that same stone. Yet, no doubt, the mandarin-blue humming birds hung poised above pink heather blossom were just one of the splendid visions to greet Masson and his companions. Possibly he would not be so impressed at seeing *Pelargonium peltatum* covering a 10ft (3m) high thorn bush in pink butterfly flowers. After all, he had not seen it grown as the ivy-leaved geranium exclusively in hanging baskets. Violence and danger which were ever present probably heightened his appreciation of the beauty spread all around. In spite of the difficulties he encountered, Masson collected a colossal quantity and variety of plants. Fortunately, pelargoniums, one of the common plants growing in South Africa, will stand long periods of de-hydration and therefore survived the long journey back to England. Erica also grow in many colourfully varied species and were such a sensation in gardening Europe that special greenhouses were built to accommodate them. Arctotis, amaryllis belladonna, gladiolus, ixia, 'Bird of Paradise' – strelitzia, and arum lily are just a few of many hundreds of plants introduced to gardens by Francis Masson – a living, flowering memorial to a great man.

Masson collected briefly elsewhere. Canada was one country which provided him with *Trillium grandiflorum* and Kalmia amongst others. But all pale into insignificance when compared with his monumental efforts in South Africa as the first of the Kew-sponsored collectors.

There were other collectors sent out from the Royal Botanic Gardens at about the same time: Archibald Menzies, William Hooker, and Dr Abel. These then were the means and Banks the motivating force, and it was he, with memories of Australia ever fresh in mind, who dispatched Allan Cunningham to New South Wales in 1816. There he collected and sent home *Banksia*, the genus named after his guide and mentor, Sir Joseph Banks. Eucalyptus and *grevillea* were also notable introductions made by Cunningham. What is immediately obvious, when reading journals and field notes written by these early plant hunters, is the incredible courage and fortitude they displayed. Had the motivating force been the lure of gold, precious stones, or some other easily negotiable form of guaranteed access to wealth and position, the tenacity of purpose would have been explained. Instead, the 'Golden Fleece' for which these latter-day Argonauts were searching had no fixed price tag; the rewards, if any, were therefore modest. Floods, terrain so impassable that progress on foot was difficult, and finding drinkable water were constant problems. In the Lachlan river area the Aborigines provided a threatening presence to distract from the peaceful business of botanising. Repeatedly, in accounts of expeditions like those undertaken by Cunningham, the fact that collecting specimens is merely the beginning is emphasised. Time must be spent in preparing and then packing seeds and plants for dispatch on the long hazardous sea journey back to England. Then comes the problem of transport to the nearest harbour where there is a shipping company willing to take responsibility for such a perishable cargo. In spite of all the difficulties he encountered, Cunningham continued tirelessly travelling, searching out and exploring new territory and collecting the plants he so obviously loved. Apart from a brief return to England, he spent the rest of his short life collecting in Australia and New Zealand.

SUDDENLY HISTORY GAINS FLESH

There comes a stage in any historical survey when the shadowy figures described in the written page take on vivid life as of the recent past. There is no logical reason why this transition in historical terms from distant to recent past should happen for me with the advent of David Douglas, for he was born almost 200 years ago. Though I have stood in a cave which sheltered Francis Masson and followed tracks he must have used in the Cape, the bare historical bones never took on the warm flesh of reality; the man's purpose was clearly defined but his personality obscure, as with all others up to the time of David Douglas.

That the boy was father to the man is proved by his early years, for from the first Douglas found an absorbing, near all-demanding interest in the natural world surrounding his family home in Perthshire. School must have suffered because of his truancy in pursuit of this interest, for at the age of ten he was made an apprentice gardener on the Earl of Mansfield's estate. So often circumstances combine to favour and fuel a passionate yet untutored intelligence, and thus it was in the case of Douglas who showed such an enquiring interest in plants that he was allowed to use the books in the earl's library. After further training as a member of staff employed by the Royal Botanic Gardens, Glasgow, he was sent by the London Horticultural Society on a botanical expedition to North America.

Being wet, cold, half starved and lonely seems to have been the common lot of plant hunter explorers, and Douglas shared in full measure the experience of all the rest. In his journals he describes the luxury of sleeping on a bed of pine branches and the enjoyment of eating freshly caught salmon, for the few provisions durable enough to serve as basic rations had to be supplemented with anything the surrounding land offered. Food it seems was a constant problem and yet Douglas continued collecting plants with undiminished energy. Sometimes when wet, hungry, and possibly more than a little homesick, he reflects rather despairingly on his future prosperity, and yet most of the time pangs of hunger and fatigue are ignored in his unremitting pursuit of plants. The Douglas fir, *Pseudotsuga menziesi*, was discovered by Archibald Menzies, but David Douglas has the credit for its introduction to this country. So many garden-worthy plants were collected by the indefatigable Douglas, the majority of them hardy enough to be grown outdoors in most areas of the British Isles, that it is

David Douglas kept a journal in which he recorded details of his travels. The description of a view on the approach to Grand Rapids brings the whole scene vividly to life.

The high mountains in the neighbourhood which are, for the most part, covered with pines, some of which grow to enormous size, are all loaded with snow; the rainbow from the vapour of the agitated waters, which rushes with furious rapidity over shattered rocks and deep caverns producing an agreeable although at the same time a somewhat melancholy echo through the thick wooded valley; the reflections from the snow on the mountains together with the vivid green of the gigantic pines form a contrast of rural grandeur that can scarcely be surpassed.

*Garrya elliptica is easy enough to
propagate by means of semi-ripe
cuttings taken in early July, trimmed
then inserted into a compost of two parts
sharp, lime-free sand, one part
sphagnum peat.*

surprising that so few, if any, honour his name. *Acer circinatum*, so
brilliant in autumn colour, or the *Abies* he collected could surely
have been a *douglasii*.

Delphinium cardinale which I found growing on a dry hillside in
California amongst poison oaks, the branching stems like red-
flowered candelabra, was introduced by Douglas. After a five-mile
walk through alkali dust in search of the plant, I got some small
idea of the dynamic energy displayed by Douglas. *Garrya elliptica*,
whose 8–10in (20–26cm) long silver catkins gladden February days
and are much coveted by flower arrangers, is another popular
importation. The list of plants also includes several *Penstemon* of
note, the annual *Clarkia* and the lovely yellow-flowered dog tooth
violet, *Erythronium grandiflorum*.

One of the unforgettable experiences of my life was to stand
amongst Giant Redwoods at sunrise and watch what had been dark
shapes in the grey light become towering, copper-tinted green
columns – unbelievably majestic, even though I was prepared for
the experience from seeing pictures, reading accounts, and studying
the 90ft (26m) high specimens growing in Scotland. How must
Douglas have rejoiced in the cathedral yet somehow conversational
quiet of those centuries-old trees. Douglas died in tragic circumstances in Hawaii, gored to death by a wild bull when he fell into
a pit which had been dug as a trap for catching feral animals – a
terrible end to a life committed to the gentle pursuit of botanical
exploration.

THE CHINESE INFLUENCE

America may have been the New World in the idiom of human
investment, but it was to a world old in both civilisation and culture
that interest turned early in the nineteenth century. China had been,
as it to some extent still is, a land shrouded in mystery, a place
worthy of legend. Some of the apocryphal stories about the plant
and animal life which existed in China then still persist, even if the
flights of imagination are a little less inventive in the twentieth
century.

That the tales of dove trees and paeonies which grew like trees
were found to be true on investigation only served to fuel the fires
of interested avarice. For China proved to be a treasure house of
rare and beautiful plants which is still, nearly two centuries later,
unexhausted. It is a country of vast distances, inaccessible
mountains, hidden valleys, in many ways made even more
inscrutable by a culture, tradition and values totally at variance at
the time with those of this country. Indeed, little has changed except
that plants from China have had an influence on European gardens
beyond anything even the most outrageous travellers' tales or
romantic visions could have anticipated.

Robert Fortune, born in Berwickshire and trained at the Royal
Botanic Gardens in Edinburgh, was the man chosen by the London
Horticultural Society to test the quantity and quality of this
reported Chinese botanical treasure house. For this work he was

The dove tree, Davidia involucrata,
*makes a robust, medium-sized tree of a
lime-like character. In May the large
white bracts which accompany the small
inconspicuous flowers render the dove
tree briefly beautiful. The apprentice
nurseryman who, much to his manager's
chagrin, sold a* Populus x candicans
*'Aurora' to a customer as being better
value than the expensive* Davidia *had
more of the truth, I suspect. 'Aurora'
with creamy-white, variegated leaves
offers a longer season of interest, if not
so shapely a tree.*

to be paid £100 a year all found. The instructions were admirably brief and simple: one, to collect seeds and plants of an ornamental or utilitarian kind which had not been grown in this country previously; two, to find out all he could about Chinese gardening and farming. This, no doubt, included information on climate and its influence on plant growth. Fortune proved himself over the years a cool, clear-thinking, level-headed practitioner well able to adjust to most situations. Well equipped, he arrived in China during the summer of 1843 to find what he reported as a dying civilisation, and in some areas an extremely hostile indigenous population. Once away from the coastal areas, soured by their contact with European traders, he found less antipathy, although while collecting on the hills outside Canton he was attacked, beaten, and in grave danger of being murdered. One hazard he encountered must have brought vividly to mind the way in which David Douglas met his death. Wild boar traps in the region where Fortune was plant hunting were made by digging flask-shaped pits which were then partially filled with water. These were carefully disguised with branches and brushwood so that any animal which ventured to cross over the flimsy camouflage broke through and drowned. These were diversions only; for the rest there were hillsides covered in azalea smothered with flowers and paeonies in such variety that those he sent to England caused a sensation when, in due course, they produced flowers.

Part of Fortune's success as a collector lay in his ability to pass as a native Chinese, since he had acquired a working knowledge of the language and a pigtail to give it further authenticity. In addition to collecting plants in the wild, Fortune took every opportunity to visit any nurseries within the various districts through which he was passing at the time. This served to embellish the already formidable list of plants which he introduced to enrich gardens in this country. Any one of those selected here would have justified him as a collector: lovely yellow-flowered *Jasminum nudiflorum*, which has lightened February's gloom for generations of gardeners; *Mahonia bealei*, which could, with justification, lay claim to being the most handsome of evergreen shrubs, displaying primrose-yellow flowers which are sweetly fragrant in late winter; and *Viburnum tomentosum*, now a form of *plicatum*. This is the most architecturally impressive of shrubs; when the horizontally arranged branches are covered in creamy-white flowers carried in double rows along their upper sides, it looks like a superbly decorated wedding cake.

Fortune also introduced what Reginald Farrer, of whom more later, described as 'that most bleeding of all hearts, *Dicentra spectabilis*'. I spent fruitless hours trying to find out how it got one of its many popular names, 'Lady in a Bath'. He also introduced *Weigela rosea*, *Skimmia reevesiana*, and several rhododendrons including the magnificent intensely fragrant, five-lobe-petalled *fortunei*. A man, then, deserving of the highest honour by all who grow any of those plants carrying the appendix 'introduced by Robert Fortune'.

Jasminum nudiflorum is one of the most underrated winter flowering plants. That it will grow in almost any soil except one that is poorly drained, and flower well even on a north wall should earn our appreciation. The finest display of flowers I have ever seen was on a Jasminum nudiflorum *which had been trained over the iron framework of a garden seat and then pruned hard to shape. The effect was unusual and beautiful. Layering of young shoots in April is a trouble-free way of increasing stock.*

There are few more beautiful sights than that offered by a Dicentra spectabilis *in full bloom. Long arching stems hung with rosy-red Lucy Locket flowers appeal to gardeners and non-gardeners alike. Unlike some plant prima donna beauties, what Reginald Farrer describes as 'this most bleeding of all hearts' will grow well in sun or shade.*

THE GOLDEN AGE OF PLANT HUNTING

Joseph Hooker must have been bathed in a rich soup of botany and plant law almost from birth. His father, after a brief excursion to Iceland plant hunting, became Professor of Botany at Glasgow University, before, in due course, moving south to become Director of Kew, then as now the *alma mater* of horticulture. No doubt young Joseph noted the packages of plants, many of them new to cultivation, which were arriving from abroad in ever increasing numbers. Possibly this encouraged him to embark on a career as an explorer botanist, although after leaving Glasgow High School he studied medicine at Glasgow University and his first appointment was as assistant surgeon and botanist on an expedition to Antarctica via New Zealand, Australia, and the Falkland Islands. All this, in spite of the vast amount of plant material he gathered, was merely a prelude, however. Nine years later Hooker embarked on an expedition to the Himalaya, heralding what might rightly be termed 'the golden age of plant hunting'.

Few could have been so well qualified for the part they were to play, for Hooker was an intelligent, self-confident man possessed of seemingly inexhaustible energy. In addition, he had the unqualified support of his father, himself an experienced explorer botanist who wrote of his son's contribution, particularly in respect of his introduction of new rhododendron species, in the most glowing terms. The expedition overland from Calcutta complete with baggage train must have been somewhat in the nature of a royal progress. The arrival at the chosen base in Darjeeling some four months later is described in his journal: 'a little cleared spur of the mountains surrounded by dark forests overhanging a profound valley and enveloped in mist and rain'. His arrival, it seemed, had coincided with the rainy season. However, those same dark forests and profound mist-shrouded valleys were to reveal over the next two years an unbelievable richness of plants.

The rhododendrons alone are probably the most notable discoveries by a single individual in the history of the genus. *Rhododendron arboreum, cinnabarinum, falconeri, griffithianum,* and *thomsoni* represent just a few of the species discovered by Hooker. What a splendid spawning of hybrids has resulted from this one series of introductions. There were other things he collected; primula, meconopsis and lesser herbs, yet always it is the genus rhododendron that Hooker's name is linked with in gardening circles. One description of the Kinchin mountain range lit by early morning sunshine reveals a little of the rewards awaiting those who venture into the wilderness in search of plants. 'Peak after peak with cliffs, domes and tables of snow, it really conveyed the idea of a forest of mountains' – a glimpse of the poet behind the botanist.

For lime-free gardens the rhododendron has no equal either in beauty or variety. It is king to the rose's queen of the garden. A vast race of plants ranging in height from 6in (15cm) high Rh. lowndesii *to the tree size* Rh. arboreum *or* Rh. giganteum, *the genus erupts almost worldwide into a deluge of species. They are almost all determinedly lime-hating. Given a moist lime-free soil and adequate rainfall as on the west coast of Scotland, they will thrive. When planting, be careful not to bury the root ball too deeply; let it stand an inch (2.5cm) proud, then apply a peat mulch to conserve moisture.*

AGAIN THE SCOTTISH INFLUENCE

There is a curious similarity between the formative years of Douglas and another of the notable Scottish plant hunters, and arguably the greatest, George Forrest. Both were keen observers of nature, happier by far playing truant in some remote glen studying the natural world than poring over a book in a classroom. Born in Falkirk in 1873, Forrest showed a keen interest in nature study throughout his school days. On leaving school he worked first in a chemist's shop where he picked up the elementary knowledge of simple medicine which was to prove invaluable later on in his adventurous life. Work in a shop soon palled and his restless spirit, the motivating force throughout his life, sent him adventuring to the goldfields in Australia, then in South Africa, before returning to Kilmarnock.

The turning point in Forrest's career came when he was offered work in the herbarium of the Royal Botanic Gardens in Edinburgh, sorting, listing, and classifying the plants arriving from botanists all over the world. In this way, by force of circumstances rather than design, Forrest served the best possible apprenticeship for a prospective plant hunter. Then in 1903 at the age of thirty he was offered the opportunity by a wealthy Lancashire cotton broker, A. K. Bulley, to go plant hunting in the mountainous region of North West Yunnan and South East Tibet – a happy choice, for the area was richer in botanical terms than the mines of Australia were in gold. Forrest must have been a quite remarkable man for he quickly learned to speak Chinese. Then with commendable foresight he trained teams of local peasants to work as collectors of plants and seeds. Instead of working single-handed, there was now a team which enabled a blanket search to be made of each area visited.

For a plant hunter the plateau 11,000ft (3,300m) high between the valleys of the Salwen and the Mekong was a virgin Eden full of beautiful plants which are now household, or rather potting shed, names; and everywhere rhododendrons, *Rh. campylogynum, forrestii, bullatum, souliei*, and so many more that he really must have been spoiled for choice. In the moister, open woodland glades an abundance of primulas, gentians, and lilies offered distraction and a change of mood. What did he make of *Lilium giganteum* (Cardiocrinum) with stems towering 8ft (2.5m) high hung with white tubes of flowers? Or *Gentiana sino-ornata* like a vivid blue carpet flung over a grassy hillside? Then there was *Buddleia forrestii*, which was suggested by one authority as his most notable contribution. Lovely though the buddleia is when the branches are wreathed in cylindrical racemes of fragrant lilac flowers during late summer, it lacks for me the appeal of *Pieris formosa forrestii* whose brilliant red young growths and panicles of lily of the valley-scented white flowers are such a breathtakingly lovely sight in April.

Comparisons are odious, however, for so many of Forrest's introductions enrich our gardens today. In searching for plants he suffered incredible hardship and danger. Indeed, on one occasion he was the only member to escape, together with one servant, out of a company of seventeen strong; the rest were killed or captured by Tibetan lamas. In 1930 he made what was to be his last expedition into the area where so much of his life had been spent. He wrote letters home 'Of seeds in such abundance that I scarce

George Forrest wrote on North-west Yunnan. 'The country teems with new species, even in the central and southern regions. Much of the province is yet unexplored in the north, and north-west only the veriest fringe has been touched. There a great harvest awaits the first in the field, a harvest of horticultural novelties which will astonish us.' Almost a century since that was written we still are waiting.

Gentiana sino-ornata *planted in a cool, moist, peaty soil will flower so abundantly in September as to hide the bare earth under a carpet of erect azure-blue trumpets. The clusters of thong-like fleshy roots do need to be lifted and divided regularly in late March or early April, at intervals of no more than three years – preferably every two except in very favoured gardens. Good though* G.sino-ornata *is, a hybrid between it and* G.farreri *serves me more faithfully. Called* G.x macaulayi 'Wells', *it can lay strong claim to being the best of all gentians. The flowers, which are a lovely azure blue, open a month to six weeks earlier than those of its parent.*

Pieris formosa forrestii *in the form originally introduced by George Forrest is one of the world's most beautiful shrubs and requires a cool, peaty, lime-free soil and some shelter from late frost. Young, semi-ripe current season's growths taken with a thin heel of older wood, dibbled into a compost made up of two parts sharp, lime-free sand, one part peat, will root readily enough to satisfy even the greedy gardener.*

Gentiana sino-ornata, like a vivid blue carpet

Pieris formosa forestii, a lovely sight on a warm April day

know where to start': *Meconopsis, Lilium*, no doubt there would be bulbs as well: a glorious finale to a splendid career.

Bearing in mind that he had lost the whole of one season's work – plants, seeds, photographs, and field notes – at a guess Forrest thought the collection numbered 2,000 species, with seeds of eighty species. That he was reported dead on one occasion to the Foreign Office scarcely seems surprising. On 5 January 1932 just as he was about to return home to Scotland, Forrest suffered a massive heart attack and died. His body lies in a small graveyard in Tengyueh. After studying Forrest's letters, field notes, and the list of plants he introduced, one would find it hard to deny him the epitaph 'great', yet in a strange way he lacked a positive personality.

Unlike George Forrest who did not survive to write in detail of his experiences, Ernest Henry Wilson fortunately did. In his book *A Naturalist in Western China*, Wilson gives an account of eleven years spent in 'remote parts of the flowery kingdom'. During the course of that time he collected over 3,000 species of which 1,000 had never been grown previously, at least in European gardens. He was a quiet, determined man, infinitely patient, with an ability to reach an understanding with the native population which earned him the sobriquet of 'Chinese Henry'. Once again circumstances combined to put the right man in the place where his hitherto latent talent could discover full expression.

A British customs officer called Augustine Henry who was based in China became concerned with the despoliation of the natural forests in his area. Anxious that some sort of survey should be made of the area by a qualified gardener botanist before valuable plant species were lost, Henry wrote to Kew outlining the problem and asking for help in finding a solution. Unable, because of financial constraints, to raise sufficient funds, Kew arranged a partnership with the famous nursery firm Vietch & Sons. What was needed, according to the general consensus, was a man who could assess both the botanical value and the garden-worthiness of a plant. Wilson, having trained first in nursery work, then at the Botanic Garden in Birmingham where he studied at the Technical College, and finally gaining a position in Kew Gardens, was admirably qualified for the job.

Wilson arrived in China in 1899 and made his way to Yunnan. His top priority was to find and bring into cultivation seeds and plants of the Chinese dove tree, *Davidia involucrata*, about which Henry had written in glowing terms. He arrived at the site on the map reference given to him, to discover that the tree had gone. A search revealed further specimens which, in due course, supplied seed. During the five years Wilson worked for Vietch & Sons he must have repaid their investment in his expertise many times over. *Acer griseum*, the lovely paper-barked maple, elegant in form and brilliant in autumn colour, is now an established garden plant. *Clematis montana rubens* I bless him for each time the cascade of pink flowers with their curious musky odour show themselves in May.

The most notable of all Wilson's introductions, *Lilium regale*, found growing in only one location, a narrow valley in Szechuan,

That Lilium regale *should fail to grow on that first introduction is difficult to understand. Seed, which is the most reliable way of raising vigorous, virus-free stock, germinates very readily. Deep containers, or a sheltered border outdoors where the seed can be sown and the resulting seedlings left to grow on until they are ready for planting out in flowering positions, are the best method of propagation I have tried.*

Rosa moyesii *with single blood-red flowers 2½–3½in (6–9cm) across makes a large, erect, branching shrub. The long, handsome flagon-shaped scarlet fruits are also strikingly beautiful. Seed sown when full ripe, first in sand to stratify, then into a nursery frame, will germinate fairly readily.*

Lady's slipper – it does not look like a slipper, much less like 'Our Lady's' slipper, but cross over into Normandy (in a not dissimilar valley) and the peasants call it Sabot de la Verge. *Now it is not like a slipper but it is the very form of a Norman sabot, to a nicety. (John Crowther, Roman Road, Grassington on Cypripedium calceolus)*

Cypripedium calceolus (a plant Farrer must have found growing wild in Wharfedale) is one of our rarest and most attractive native flowers

failed on its first trial. That so beautiful a flower which had caused him so much agony to collect – indeed, at one stage he was close to death – should then fail to make the grade would have been galling in the extreme. Wilson describes his second visit to the valleys where the lily grew: 'by the wayside in rock crevices by the torrent's edge and high up on the mountainside this Lily in full bloom greets the weary traveller. Not in twos and threes but in hundreds and thousands, aye in tens of thousands.' What a picture they must have made, those legions of ivory-white, stained purple flowers filling the air with perfume. Anyone who has once grown this most regal of all lilies will never want to be without it. The list of Wilson's introductions reads like a plant roll of honour. *Hamamelis mollis, Magnolia delavayi, Rosa moyesii, Berberis wilsonae,* and the kiwi fruit, *Actinidia chinensis.*

THE YORKSHIRE INFLUENCE

Always, in any company, be they tinkers, tailors, soldiers, botanists or gardeners, there is one contradiction that somehow still contrives to prove the rule. Reginald Farrer I have come to know through reading his letters to his family and friends. The books he wrote reveal another facet of this quite extraordinary character. Farrer must have stimulated many hitherto uncommitted gardeners to take a deeper interest in the plants under their care with his vivid descriptions of his expeditions.

Farrer's was the privileged landed gentleman approach to a knowledge of plants and understanding of botany. There was no apprenticeship served either in garden or botanical institutions. Indeed, Farrer appeared to pick up knowledge of both subjects like a gourmet at a banquet, tasting here and there at the dictates of a curious botanical appetite. He was possessed of an immense intellect and intense love of plants. To gain some sort of understanding of the man we must look at his environment, beginning in the Yorkshire village of Clapham where he was born. Study the rock garden he built at the age of fourteen, which simulated a natural perch tarn and limestone outcrop. Follow the stream up through shaded woods to Trow Ghyll and meet the view of the hills and limestone pavement dominated by the bulk of Ingleborough. This then was the playground of Farrer's lonely childhood – an area rich in plant life, including the rare 'Lady's Slipper Orchid', *Cypripedium calceolus.*

After botanising and collecting in the European Alps, his ambitions centred on the Far East where Tibet and China meet. A chance encounter with William Purdom, already a trained, experienced plantsman, came at an opportune time. The two had little in common save a passionate love of plants, coupled with a fine regard for wilderness, and mountains in particular. In 1914 they left for Kansu via Peking. Almost immediately they encountered difficulties. On two occasions Purdom found himself facing mobs of tribesmen intent on murder. In spite of this and the world war which brought the expedition to a premature close, Farrer brought home a notable collection of plants. The lovely *Clematis tangutica* with soft yellow flowers and silken silver seed heads, or *Clematis macropetala*, the Far Eastern version of the European *Clematis alpina* with flowers of violet and paler ice blue, are enough to make any collector proud. Consider also *Viburnum farreri*, a medium-sized winter flowering shrub with white scented blooms opening in sequence through the darkest, most cheerless season.

Shortly after the war, this time in the company of Euan Cox – later to become a nurseryman of repute specialising in rhododendrons and living near Perth – Farrer departed once more to the East, this time to Upper Burma. In places the abundance of plants is described by Farrer as

> One simultaneous knot of colour laid on, not in dottings and pepperings, but in the broadest and most massive sweeps such as might satisfy the most opulent day dreams. The flowers blend by the acre, not by the dozen or even by the hundred, there are solid furlongs of tender pink Geranium, yellow Globe Flower, Crimson Polygonum, citron Primula, violet Delphinium, golden Anemone.

And so the list goes on.

The explorer has first to find and mark the plants in flower, then return several months later to collect the seed which must then be dried, packeted and packed for transport by mule to the nearest railway station – painstaking, difficult work. After several more expeditions, this time alone, for Cox had returned home to Scotland, Farrer climbed for the last time to his camp in the hills below the Moku-ji Pass. There after two fascinating months amongst the flowers he loved, fever struck him down and a fortnight later this remarkable man was dead. He is buried on a slope of the mountain above a little village between the Irrawaddy and the Nmia Hka. The plants he collected are growing now in gardens throughout Europe.

HISTORY YESTERDAY AND TODAY

Men and women who write their names large in the annals of history are rare. Their special qualities can only find full expression, given the right situation and combination of circumstances and habitat to nurture them. Frank Kingdon Ward, the son of K. M. Ward, Professor of Botany at Cambridge, enjoyed all the benefits which a privileged position could offer. Even though his family were not wealthy, he gained a scholarship to Christ's College Cambridge. On graduation he accepted a teaching post at the Shanghai Public School, and during his school holidays indulged in his passion for exploration, with plant collecting, it seems from his notes, merely the excuse for travel. In 1910 he was offered the post of collector to the nursery and seed firm of Bees as a replacement for George Forrest who had discovered more profitable employment elsewhere – the right man in a convenient place at the appropriate time. Had any one of the factors been missing, Kingdon Ward could easily have pursued a full-time career as a schoolmaster, with exploration as a mere incidental. Instead, he became a plant hunter and a legendary figure in his own lifetime,

Clematis tangutica is described in Reginald Farrer's field notes from Kansan as: 'A handsome ramping twiner, very abundant in limestone shingles of Tibetan rivers with a profusion of flowers like large nodding golden Fritillaries'. This describes what is a lovely species, easily raised from seed. I have grown it down a slope in the rock garden, over a low wall mixed up with pink-flowered 'Dorothy Perkins' roses, and across a cleft paling fence; in every respect a most excellent climbing shrub.

Again from Farrer's field notes: 'April 16th (1914) is an important date in botanical history as marking the first discovery of Viburnum fragrans (now farreri) growing as a wild plant'. One of the most easily grown shrubs, it is stiff and erect up to 13ft (4m) high. The flowers borne in terminal clusters are pink in the bud, then opening to white, sweetly scented, in evidence from November and continuing through the winter. Any soil suits this durable and popular shrub.

My tent was always pitched near some thundering torrent, which was music to me, and lying in bed I would watch the brilliant arch of the moon set over the mountains. Land of the Blue Poppy
F. Kingdon Ward

Meconopsis (Himalayan blue poppy) has the reputation of being difficult to grow yet, given a humus-rich, acid soil and a plentiful supply of moisture during the growing season, it presents no problems. Seed which should be sown directly after harvesting, or if this is not possible kept in a refrigerator, offers the best means of increase. To protect the young seedlings against damping-off disease over winter, add a fungicide when watering.

Meconopsis grandis will also grow from sections of root, 2 or 3in (5–8cm) long, taken and potted in sandy compost in late winter. It is not surprising that Kingdon Ward searched for it so avidly, for it is singularly beautiful.

Daboecia cantabrica 'Alba', whose racemes of glistening pure white flowers above darkly green foliage are utterly delightful to see. One of the loveliest shrubs for planting with a fringe of gentians in a peat-rich, acid soil. I found the 'Alba' form growing wild on a hillside in Connemara and, for once, consider that the plant in cultivation is better than it was in a natural habitat

for the plants he introduced were like the choicest selection from a botanical Aladdin's cave. During his first trip to the Yunnan–Tibetan border he first saw blue meconopsis, though not the incredible *Meconopsis grandis* or *betonicifolia* which was later to create such a sensation. Why men like Kingdon Ward overcame the most incredible dangers, risking death from accident and disease in the face of difficulties of a magnitude we can only guess at, in order to search out plants which might not even grow in Europe, would need a close psychological study to discover a logical explanation. Moreover, Kingdon Ward disliked snakes intensely and had a morbid fear of heights. That he should choose to search for plants in areas where he was in daily contact with both defies comprehension.

In 1924 he accompanied the Earl of Cawdor on what at first appeared to be a geographical exploration to the Assam Himalaya. On this expedition he found and sent back specimens of the blue poppy, and later collected seeds of *Meconopsis baileyi* (*betonicifolia*). When the flowers were exhibited at a meeting of the Royal Horticultural Society they excited the most extravagant comment. The effect on anyone seeing those bright blue flowers for the first time is the same now as it was then, for they are sensational. Kingdon Ward became an immediate celebrity, but his main concern was to return at the earliest possible moment to the mountains, their serenity, beauty and very remoteness spiced by the element of danger for those who question their inviolability.

There were no problems now in attracting sponsors, and Kingdon Ward was soon busily engaged on the 'Edge of the World' as he described the frontier between India and Burma. There in the mountains of the Irrawaddy-Brahmaputra divide he found an abundance of primula, rhododendrons and cassiope: the *Primula beesiana*, parent of so many hybrids between itself and other candelabra species, and the lovely pale-yellow *Primula florindae*, the Himalayan cowslip growing in the bog conditions it requires in the garden state. Kingdon Ward continued collecting and exploring for plants until his sixty-eighth birthday found him climbing above 11,000ft (3,300m) on Tagulum Bum in Burma. This trip secured a fine haul of seeds and plants, as did his last at the age of seventy in the Southern China hills.

In retrospect Kingdon Ward was the last of the great plant hunters, those legendary figures we honour each time we rejoice over one of the plants they brought back. There have been others since, equally tenacious. Comber, Rock, Ludlow, and Sherriff all made a valuable contribution, yet always it is those early men of the 'Golden Age' who earn our regard. There were people like Younghusband or Stewart, army men who found relaxation in off-duty hours studying plants in remote regions of Tibet, India and elsewhere, who contributed much to our gardens. Of all the post-World War II botanical explorers, the partnership between Ludlow and Sherriff proved most notable. The seven journeys of plant exploration they made included Bhutan and South East Tibet, areas previously unexplored and rich in plant life.

Many years ago I landscaped and then planted the banks of a stream which ran through the garden I had charge of for twenty years. Several of the primula used in the initial planting were from the Irrawaddy-Brahmaputra region and included P.beesiana *and* P.florindae. *From the outset they flourished in the moist, acid loam, cross hybridising and self-seeding so that each June/July the 300yd (270m) long stream side was transformed by a kaleidoscope of colour into a miniature Himalayan valley. Given the right conditions, all the* Candelabra Primula *will naturalise in this way.*

Diascia are natives of South Africa and yet grow quite contentedly in a Yorkshire garden. They have a place in full sun and a free draining soil to root into. The pink flowers grow on 12in (30cm) high stems

6

Brief
but Beautiful

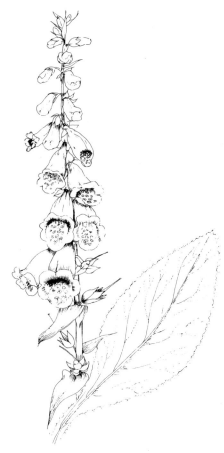

Consider for a moment the perennial garden. The slow growth of trees, shrubs, and even perennials is to some extent an unchanging process. Contradictory though this may seem, the alteration year by year is in bulk rather than feature. A change of expression is not hard to find. By planting short-lived annuals and tender perennials the whole character of the garden can be transformed for a season. Though the onset of winter restores the original familiar pattern, we come to it refreshed by the change.

An annual is defined as any plant which can be raised from seed to flower to seed during the course of a single growing season. A half-hardy annual usually needs a longer time to complete the process, so must be started early in greenhouse, frame, or on a heated window-sill. In due course, these tender beings are planted outdoors in late May. There are also biennials which spend the first year establishing a framework on which the flowers appear the following year. A plant which is monocarpic may grow one or several years before flowering and seeding; after this due process of procreation it dies. Tender perennials are those usually extremely floriferous colourful plants, which, though they can survive what passes for summer in Britain, are killed by winter's chill. These must be stored in a frost-free place. Dahlias are one of the best known examples of a tender perennial.

Bulbs, though many of them if left outdoors will survive and spread must, because of the one contribution they make, be classified as brief though beautiful.

There is no doubt that those who are considering growing annuals, biennials or tender perennials will find raising the necessary stock each year from seed or cuttings a cheaper alternative to buying in. Gardeners relying on outside suppliers will find themselves limited as to choice. The self-sufficient gardener can plunder the seed catalogues like a latter-day Captain Morgan and find interest and satisfaction in the whole process of seed sowing and pricking out. There will be expense, of course. A greenhouse, with possibly a frame for hardening the seedlings off in, is almost essential. This need not be heated, although it offers much more latitude if heat of some description is laid on. The alternative is to use the window-sills inside the house as propagation benches. Cover the sill with polythene, or better still

Foxgloves, especially the hybrids 'Excelsior' and 'Foxy', are attractive biennials for cultivation in an informal shrub border

one of the long trays used for growing-bag culture, to avoid damage to the decor. Care is needed over watering, for carpets unlike lawns do not respond to a daily damp-down except by growing mould.

There is nothing complicated or difficult about run-of-the-mill seed sowing. Specialist genera, rhododendrons, some alpines, orchids and others, need carefully contrived composts and equable growing conditions. Most of the brief but beautiful plants are amazingly tolerant in regard to composts and minor details like temperature which in a greenhouse shoots into the 70s°F when the sun shines, and falls to the mid 40s°F overnight. Most contrive to survive and grow. Such simplicity of purpose makes annuals a very effective antidote to the complex world outside the garden boundaries. The arguments over better and best composts for a particular purpose are not worth entering into. Peat-based mixtures for short-term work are lightest to carry, cleanest to handle and reliable in quality. The loam-lovers argue about the difficulties of watering plants growing in peat-based composts without just cause. There is no substitute for loam in certain cases; for the rest peat or pulverised bark serve very well.

Standard seed trays are marvellous compost wasters unless the seedlings are going to grow on in them until the roots have used up most of the feedstuffs available. The argument against leaving them in seed trays so long is that pricking them off to provide each one with light, space, and freedom from excessive competition is just about impossible. Flat trays, about 1in (2.5cm) deep give sufficient depth of root run to get most annual seedlings up to the first true leaf pricking-out stage, which halves the cost of seed-sowing compost, as any politician would assure us, 'at a stroke'. Stagger the sowings at ten-day intervals so that the seedlings come ready for handling at comfortable intervals and not all together.

Seedlings sown in shallow trays will suffer if not moved on into standard depth seed trays at the correct time. Balanced growth with any plant which matures in the space of a single season is of the utmost importance. Overcrowding, starvation of nutriment or water, indeed, any cultural condition which impedes healthy growth, leads to loss of flower. Therefore, as soon as the seedlings are large enough to handle carefully, transfer them, evenly spaced out, into a seed tray. A dinner fork is a most efficient tool for lifting annuals out of a nursery container so that they suffer minimum root damage. A fork with the two outer prongs cut off is the best tool when handling minuscule seedlings, a full-size, four-prong, standard dining article for the rest. Dibbers are rounded, evenly tapering pieces of wood cut in varying lengths and thicknesses. These are made from hardwood, hawthorn, or, for a Rolls-Royce quality, yew, and will last even full-time gardeners a lifetime. There are four in my potting shed that have served three generations and are just getting to the stage of being too short to hold comfortably.

Most seedlings are pricked off singly. Exceptions are the cluster plants: lobelia and alyssum where half a dozen seedlings are dibbled into one hole to make a decent-sized flowering clump when bedded

'Blue Eyed Susan', 'Foam of the Meadow', 'Love in the Mist' and 'Busy Lizzie', well-loved summer flowering annuals, are so beautiful that I cannot do without them; yet they flower for such a short time, occupy a good deal of space and leave an unsightly blank as the blossoming gives way to seeding. By growing annuals scattered about amongst shrubs and other perennial plants I can enjoy their brief, glorious season, then as the beauty fades the seed ripening stage is hidden by the burgeoning of growth all around. Seed allowed to shed naturally in the autumn grows up to repeat the process each succeeding spring.

Marigolds are a good example of the short-lived and beautiful annual. The crisp, sunshine-bright colouring of the petals brings a note of cheer to the dankest summer day. The single-flowered forms – 'Silvia' and the 'Marietta' varieties – are pleasantly informal. One of the easiest annuals to raise from seed, either sown under glass in March, or outdoors direct into the open ground in late April

Crocus 'Whitwell Purple', one of the great survivors

out. Annuals are not necessarily merely 'bit' players on the spring, summer garden stage. For anyone taking over a virgin, treeless, shrubless, even lawnless plot, annuals offer the lovely alternative to a barren first year. They will grow and flower well with the minimum of cultivation, seeming actually to prefer a poor soil to one that is richly fertile. This amiable characteristic is not to be exploited, except at the expense of a lot of work later. Dig the soil to clean it of weeds and other undesirables like builders' leavings or similar unsightly debris. Work in a little organic matter at the same time to improve the soil texture rather than its fertility. This makes preparing a seed bed easier or, in the case of half-hardy annuals, planting out a pleasurable rather than wrist-jarring business. A week or so before sowing or planting, work in a dressing of superphosphate at the rate of about 1oz (25g) per sq yd (sq m); this element encourages strong root action. For the old adage applies to most plants, annuals included, 'Look after the root and the top takes care of itself' – unless a slug decides otherwise, of course.

Choosing what varieties to grow is not the head scratching, heart searching business that it is when designing a shrub or herbaceous border. Annuals are like the swallows, an impermanent though welcome denizen of summer. What we do not like one year can be changed for something totally different the next, which allows for a splendid extravagance of ideas and outrageous experiment. Though time adds lustre to all things, the first garden I made as a teenager was almost entirely planted with annuals and is the one which lives colour-bright in my memory. Soil, situation and weather combined to produce a display of flowers which, as a neighbour commented, 'lifted his cap off each time he came out of the house'. In all the years since, I have never dared to try those same bold colour patterns which succeeded so well in that glorious summer.

Hardy annuals sown direct into the open ground serve several useful purposes. They can be sown to cover the dying foliage of spring flowering bulbs and colchicum, turning morbid decay into something beautiful. The soil should be loosened sufficiently with a rake to provide a tilth, possibly working in a dusting of fertiliser at the same time, for bulbs unless fed do not flower and though annuals flower better in poor soil they do need a readily available food supply in the early stages to make sturdy growth. For, in the case of annuals, the shortness of their tenure in the garden is more than compensated for by the brilliance and abundance of the flowers they produce. There are some annuals better suited for bulb cover than others. Candytuft is one, the old-fashioned hyacinth-flowered *Iberis amara* native to Europe. An interesting name derivation here, for Iberia is the old name for Spain. The fragrant white-flowered variety grows about 15in (38cm) high, while the multi-coloured 'Fairy Mixture' is a midget of 9in (23cm). Both will self-seed themselves, given the opportunity. Though *Limnanthes douglasi*, which honours the plant hunter of that name, has the happy ability of self-seeding into anything which passes for soil, it does so on

Candytuft (*Iberis umbellatus*) sown in spring to flower in summer, or during August to bloom in October is, for me, essential company

occasions with weed-like freedom. In spite of this, 'Meadow Foam', as it was called by colonial Americans, is a cheerful annual whose white saucer-shaped flowers have an egg yolk-yellow middle. As one exasperated gardener on a moist clay soil once described limnanthes' self-perpetuating ability, 'In a light soil it is persistent, in a heavy soil it is ubiquitous, in a damp soil ineradicable'. I remember this portrayal very well from having to go and check the word ubiquitous in a dictionary – everywhere pervasively present – it is an apt description of limnanthes' durability. Should there be a ground hugging *Cotoneaster dammeri* nearby, then encourage limnanthes to sow itself amongst the network of prostrate stems, for the two agree most handsomely.

There are other annuals which are so perfect a manifestation of summer that they are a never failing presence each year. For example, godetia, those 'Farewell to Spring' of California, of which there are so many hybrids available. Those with double blooms, in particular the 'Azalea'-flowered mixtures, are colourful enough, yet are so blowzily indifferent in form. Instead I grow the dwarf bedding varieties with single flowers, allowing the plants to ripen and shed seed each autumn and thinning out the naturally regenerating seedlings the following May. A carpet of salmon-pink and crimson flowers will be a sure reward.

Limnanthes douglasii will self-seed all around the garden

Where weeds are likely to present a problem, as they are in soil recently brought into cultivation, it is advisable to sow seed of hardy annuals in straight rows rather than broadcasting it. This makes weed control and seedling thinning easier without losing any of the casual informality which is a part of an annual flower's charm.

This year Eschscholzia *'Daffodil' seeded in with the limnanthes and pushed up 6in (15cm) high shuttlecocks of ferny foliage and pale-yellow flowers through the network of cotoneaster branches. So another name has been added to the lengthening list of desirable annuals.*

To ensure against mishaps and make certain all the empty spaces are filled, I sow a percentage of selected annual seed in a frame. Lavatera, Chrysanthemum coronarium *hybrids, and* Agrostemma *are most useful, tall-growing gap fillers. The seedlings must, however, be kept well watered after transplanting to their flowering positions or they never bloom well.*

So many of the most colourful annuals come to us from America, in particular California. Considering the difference between the hot sunshine there and the grey dankness which passes for summer here, it is surprising they grow at all, let alone bear such abundant crops of flowers.

The name *Eschscholzia* always makes me grateful that most plant collectors had easy-to-pronounce names like Douglas, Forrest, and Farrer. Possibly J. E. Eschscholz had virtues to offset his unpronounceable name. The Californian poppies have that silken texture of petal combined with grey-green feathery leaves which can only be described as elegant. The 6in (15cm) high, yellow-flowered *Eschscholzia* 'Sundew' makes effective bulb cover in the rock garden. Elsewhere in the garden the taller growing multi-hued 'Thai silk series', 'Monarch mixed', or 'Harlequin' bring a hint of Californian brilliance to the borders.

Gaps have a most unpleasant knack of showing themselves in the herbaceous border just at that time in spring when it is too late to order replacements. A shrub which looked the picture of health at leaf fall in autumn fails to show a sign of life in spring and has to be pulled out. This leaves an empty space which seems immediately to become a focal point and a source of irritation. Annuals do make marvellously efficient fillers of such unexpected vacant places and most effective colour schemes can be tried out at very little cost. Taller growing varieties, of clarkia, for example, will serve as a mask to disguise some early blooming herbaceous plant with their colourful flowers.

For this sort of 'gapping up', to use a forestry term for space filling, very positive plants function the best. *Lavatera* in its many varieties is always my first choice for they make such handsome bushy foliage plants. 'Silver Cup' and 'Tanagro' with trumpet-shaped, satin-pink blooms, and the glistening white-petalled 'Mont Blanc', are handsome enough to compete for space in any company.

Nicandra physalodes, with pale-blue flowers and curious papery lantern-like seed cases, at 36in (92cm) high, makes a useful gap filler in the herbaceous border

Then there is the annual delphinium, the elegant and beautiful larkspur which, like its perennial kin, offers a change of shape in slender spikes of flowers. From the 12in (30cm) front of the border dwarf Hyacinth-Flower mixed, to the 3ft (0.9m) tall Giant Imperial Special, which is so suggestive of cottage gardens, larkspur will perform well.

The best known of all annuals is the 'Pot Marigold', *Calendula*, with the name derived from the first day of the month defining the continuous flowering character of this most ingenious plant. The common name of 'Pot Marigold' is derived from the petals being used as flavourings in soups and stews. They are also useful as a colourful addition to salads and stir-fry dishes. Sowings made in September will give flowers in May, successional sowings then from April until early August should see plants continuously in bloom all the year round. They have a curiously expressive flower shape and colour which is hard to place in a garden. A little too much of the dandelion gold and not enough of the rose red.

In contrast to the ponderous and durable qualities of *Calendula* is an annual from south eastern Europe, well named 'Love in a Mist', with grey-green thread-like leaflets resembling filigree lace. At the tips of each stem, cupped in the leaflets, are carried large blue, pink, rose, or white flowers. The knowing gardener leaves the *Nigella damascena*, to give the love in a mist an authentic botanical title, to grow on and develop the large rounded, green-stained, purple fruits which are such a feature in autumn flower arrangements.

FORMAL OR INFORMAL

Hardy annuals are so expressive of the natural, casual, unconstrained style of gardening that they do not take kindly to what is popularly termed bedding schemes. Half-hardy annuals have been adapted by selective breeding to the rigid disciplined formality of massed planting. The geometrically precise arrangements of beds in front of town hall or in the local park would be nothing more than a colourful, untidy mess if sown with hardy annuals, whereas half-hardy varieties conditioned by breeding and upbringing to standardisation are ideal for this stylised, formal type of gardening. Each individual in a seed tray of half-hardy annuals will be as near identical one with the other as the hybridist can make it. When planted out, a bedding scheme is seen as a brilliant pattern of colours not as a collection of individual plants. Possibly this is why the mass-produced bedding plants, for example salvia, pelargonium, stocks, or asters look totally out of context in a cottage setting.

Hardy annuals can be grown and made to look very effective in a bed devoted solely to their cultivation. But not as a follow-up to spring flowering tulips, polyanthus, or wallflowers, for they do not vacate the ground until too late in the season. For this purpose half-hardy annuals are ideal as they are not ready for planting outdoors until late May. First then consider the rather limited purpose of annuals which can be sown direct into beds in late April or early May for flowering late July.

An old herbal dating from the fourteenth century preserved in the Royal Library, Sweden, describes how, if you look wisely on the marigold early in the morning, it will preserve you from fevers during the day. Culpeper, in his Herbal *writes 'that they are a little less effectual in the smallpox and measles than saffron'.*

Of the references to marigold that I have read so far, the most poignant of all is that penned by Charles I when he was a prisoner in Carisbrooke Castle. 'The Marigold observes the sun, More than my subjects me have done.'

Though a native of South Africa, *Phygelius aequalis* is hardy enough to survive most winters outdoors without fatal discomfort. The informality of a cottage-garden-style border and company of deep-purple or blue-flowered plants suits the orange-buff, tubular, slightly curved blooms of this 30in (76cm) high perennial very well. The 6–9in (15–23cm) panicles of blossom are in evidence from July to October. A plant worthy of a sheltered corner and a free draining soil

Eschscholzia, the lovely plant with the unpronounceable name, seeds itself in any light, dry soil

OPPOSITE
Wallflowers, colourful and fragrant biennials, growing with tulips and forget-me-nots

The sweet pea was the flower of the Edwardian period; a favourite of Queen Alexandra as a decoration for all festive occasions, it held pride of place.

To quote one enthusiast, 'The Sweet Pea has a keel that was meant to seek all shores, it has wings that were meant to fly across all continents, it has a standard which is friendly to all nations, and it has a fragrance like the universal gospel, Yea, a sweet prophecy of welcome everywhere that has been abundantly fulfilled.' More a eulogy than a speech.

The Concept and Design

In a large border the individual varieties should be used in bold groups. This is essential, as any tendency to make the sections too small results in a border which is fidgetily indefinite. Work out a scheme on paper and order the seeds required well in advance. When drawing up the plan, make the various groups irregular in outline. Let taller varieties drift through almost to the front of the bed to break up the line. Also choose enough scented varieties so that when the plants are in flower anyone walking down the length of the border is conscious of subtle yet pleasing fragrance. For this reason a bed of annuals backing onto a hedge of sweet peas is particularly effective, and for cutting and arranging in vases they offer beauty and utility in return for the small amount of space they occupy.

Compact plants up to 18in (46cm) in height are available in a wide range of colours, and though clashes never occur in nature according to legend, the wise gardener errs on the side of caution. Blends of different shades, gentle contrasts with whites and pale yellows as catalysts to bolder scarlets, vivid blues, and orange, all make for a beautiful, harmonious whole. Should courage fail, or artistry be in doubt, use mixed colours like the bee-busy anchusa 'Dawn' or alyssum 'Pastel Carpet'. As the annual border more than any other part of the garden offers such opportunity to use colour as an artist uses paint, names of varieties listed here would be

Annual *Dianthus* derived mainly from the species *chinensis* provide a link between the formal and informal. For hybrids like 'Queen's Parade' (illustrated) and 'Telstar' blend into any surroundings. They add summer colour to the rock garden, look perfectly at home growing in a tub on a patio, or compete successfully with other highly specialised bedding scheme plants. I grow them in scattered groups with pansy and candytuft in the most informal way possible

There is one plant combination that I unashamedly repeat almost every year: a grouping of dusky red-flowered fibrous-rooted begonia around a dwarf and neatly cone-shaped Picea pungens 'Moerheimii' with intensely glaucous blue leaves. Be the weather dourly damp or bright with sunshine, this combination succeeds though others fail.

superfluous when a seed catalogue supplies all the details and an order form as well.

WELL REGULATED AND MULTI-HUED

Half-hardy annuals fit so neatly into the seasonal pattern that they might have evolved precisely for the benefit of gardeners. As the petals drop from tulips and wallflowers or viola take on the tired look that earns them a place on the compost heap, the first flowers are opening on salvia, petunia, begonia, and the rest of the annuals raised from seed in boxes and pots under glass during late winter and early spring. A week before the plants are due to be installed in their flowering positions give them a dilute liquid feed just as a conditioner.

Once the spring flowers are cleared from the beds, dig the soil over with a border fork, working in some well-rotted compost and a dusting of blood, fish and bonemeal or similar slow-release fertiliser at the same time. Annuals do not need a lot of feeding or they run to leaf instead of flower. The evening prior to planting everything out, give the boxes and pots full of plants a thorough drenching to make certain the compost is absolutely saturated. Unless the soil in the bed is exceptionally dry leave any watering there until the planting is completed. There are things more tedious than planting out into a soil made sticky by watering, but there is no point in making a rod for one's own back. A better method is to saturate the bed by putting an overhead sprinkler to work after planting is completed. This settles the soil intimately in contact with the roots and gets the plants away to a flying start.

Fibrous-rooted and tuberous-rooted *Begonia*, though by no means the easiest of bedding material to raise from seed, are very reliable no matter what the weather during summer. Usually the reason for poor germination is not the quality of the seed, rather the inadequacy of the sower. Begonia seed is so tiny that it should not be covered at all. To avoid accidents mix the fine seed with dry sand before sowing the combination over the carefully levelled surface of the compost. Begonia flowers are very attractive when seen in dappled shade under light canopied trees. The dark purple-foliaged varieties around a silver-leaved pear, *Pyrus salicifolia*, look very handsome.

Impatiens, the modern 'Busy Lizzie' hybrids, are also good colourful shade brighteners. Though really a half-hardy perennial, they perform equally well when treated as annuals. The 'Busy Lizzie' are plants for all purposes: shade and sun, porch, patio, windowbox or hanging basket. Out of all the varieties there must be a colour blend to suit every taste.

Pelargonium, the so-called bedding 'Geranium', are one of the more remarkable examples of the modern plant breeder's skill. A few years ago the only way to be sure of trueness of colour and uniformity of height was to raise all bedding geraniums vege-tatively from cuttings. Now seed sown in a heated propagating frame will produce identical sized flowering plants by early summer, all with blossom of the same shade. As a variation on the eternal geranium and Calceolaria theme, the pink geranium 'Apple Blossom' grouped around a *Chamaecyparis pisifera* 'Boulevard' is pleasant. On a brighter coloured theme, F1 Scarlet Diamond series 'geranium' with *Juniperus x media* 'Old Gold' is dramatically bright. The *Calceolaria mexicana* is infinitely preferable to the bedding sorts and looks delightful when grown with purple heliotrope.

Antirrhinum have a flexibility denied to the majority of bedding-scheme plants because they refuse to be standardised into unvarying mediocrity. Though the thousands laid out in beds each year grow to the same height with identical flower colour they still express a delightful individuality which prevents them looking like so much vegetable paint. Antirrhinums then can be used for mass bedding, or as gap fillers anywhere in the garden. There is such an infinite variety of annuals to choose from that even Methuselah with all the summers he enjoyed, did not succeed in trying them all.

This Year – Next Year – Sometime Undoubtedly

Plants which take two years and more to flower and then become material fit only for the compost heap need to have exceptional qualities to overcome what, after all, is a serious garden disability. Yet some of the near legendary cottage garden plants are of a biennial persuasion.

'Canterbury bells', *Campanula medium*, is a popular biennial from southern Europe. The large, semi-double flowers which earn for it the nickname 'cup and saucer' look delightful growing in company with sweet william, teasels, foxgloves, honesty and iceland poppy in a cottage garden composition. All are well known biennials.

In our temperate climate the usual method of raising biennial plants is by means of seeds sown in early summer. During the months following germination when temperatures are high the seedlings make rapid growth. During the cooler months of autumn flower buds form to be displayed the following year. Some biennials do not follow so rigid a pattern, for when conditions are unfavourable they take two or three years to reach flowering size. Many biennials can be persuaded to flower like annuals in the same season if the seed is sown early in the year under glass.

Do Biennials Pay Ground Rent?

Thought must be given to where the seedlings will spend the first flowerless year making vegetative growth. In the kitchen garden possibly, where straight rows are normal and young plants can be properly cared for. Wallflowers, one of the most popular biennials being a member of the same family as cabbage and other *Brassica*, also attract the same pests and diseases, so care is essential to see that they fit neatly into the four-crop vegetable rotation.

Pansies and violas are best treated as biennials; good plants with a superabundance of flowers are the reward for this consideration. Most biennials are sown direct into prepared beds outdoors in early

When I first raised antirrhinum from seed sown in home-made composts based on the John Innes recipe which has loam as the main ingredient, I had few problems with germination or growing on. The introduction of peat-based mixtures forced me to pay more particular attention to sowing technique. The seeds must only just be covered or germination is too long delayed and erratic. The temperature is not so critical, though 65°F is the minimum for optimum growth. Synthetic nitrogen used as a substitute in John Innes composts, when the hoof and horn used in the original composition became scarce and very expensive, also caused problems. Newly germinated seedlings fell more easily prey to damping-off diseases, it appeared to me, when this synthetic nitrogen was introduced.

Once known as Coventry Bells, they are described in Herbals four hundred years ago, and so are deserving of a place in modern gardens for that reason alone. One author states, 'The roots of the Coventry Bells are esculent and admired by some for their pleasant taste, they are frequently boiled and eaten like Rampion which is, of course, a relation'. In the sixteenth century rampion was known as 'little turnip'. Canterbury Bells, Campanula medium, *do not have the same fleshy root and taste like boiled soil.*

*There are several reasons why seeds fail
to grow or germination is delayed. The
temperature may be too low; cold soil or
compost is a common cause of failure.
When sowing outdoors in early June,
dry soil is often to blame for the non-
germination of many biennials. Water
the soil thoroughly so that it is saturated
to field capacity and keep it moist
thereafter. Do not sow too deeply, again
a common fault with seed sown in drills
outdoors. When in doubt, hand cover
small seeds with a specially prepared
sandy compost. Some seeds,
delphiniums and nemophila, dislike high
temperatures and germinate best at
65–70°F.*

*Pansy and viola, so neatly differentiated
by gardeners, are members of the same
genus,* Viola. *Most if not all the
cultivated species are perennials and I
include them under brief but beautiful
because there is never a month in the
year when a member of the clan is not
in flower. The popular pansy,* Viola
tricolor, *is a native of Europe including
Britain. The numerous varieties
developed from this species are now listed
under* Viola x wittrockiana. *In
addition to a legion of varieties which
flower from May to September, there are
now hybrids which, given a sheltered
corner, commence blooming in autumn
and continue throughout the winter into
spring. The Universal F1 mixed are the
latest example of pansy which have this
winter flowering characteristic. They
give exceptional value also as cold
greenhouse or conservatory plants, and
are easily raised from seed.*

June when all the work of planting up summer bedding has been
done. Wallflowers will need transplanting into nursery beds and the
tops nipped out a week or two after this to encourage bushy growth
by the time they are ready for the final move to flowering positions
in late autumn.

Biennials do fill a niche in the garden. Canterbury bells and sweet
william look well in the herbaceous or mixed border. Foxgloves,
meconopsis, viper's bugloss, honesty, and aquilegia, which are also
treated as biennials, look lovely in a copse or woodland setting.
Never worry if the copse is the shrub border and the woodland only
a tree; the pattern of light and shade the shrubs or tree supply is
enough to provide the stage and set the scene. By compost or peat
mulches the gardener can then build up the woodland-type humus-
rich soil which such plants thrive in. To glimpse foxglove or
meconopsis flowers across the garden in the patterned sunlight cast
by the tree branches is reward enough to compensate for the
growth-only, barren years. Or that fragrance from the wallflowers
which is so delightful on spring evenings can be distilled only in
proper quality by massed ranks of flowers. Such profligate
disregard for expense is only possible for the average gardener
when stock is home-raised from seed.

As for viola and pansy, the two which botanists insist no garden
should ever be without, they are easily accommodated, free
flowering, beautiful plants. The multiplicity of popular names gives
some indication of how well regarded this gem of a flower has been
and still is down through generations of gardeners. The word
'pansy' is a corruption of the French pensée, for thought. 'Love in
Idleness' is another; 'Pink of my John' and 'Three Faces under a
Hood' are just a sample. The various members of the pansy family
make shift to grow and comply with any pattern. Sun or shade, the
flower my mother always called 'Tittle my Fancy' gives value for
money with ten out of ten for effort.

A Touch of Mexico

Though dahlias are perennial, forming a food store in swollen underground tubers which carries them over from one year to the next, only in favoured localities can they survive overwintering outdoors. This is the only flower to offer a proper tribute and orchestration to the grand climax of autumn. Selective breeding has transformed this lovely Mexican wayside weed into a specialist flower. Dedicated growers of all the various named forms from small Pom-pom to Giant Decorative strive after perfection of form which only the experienced grower can properly appreciate, and the end for them justifies the eight months' cultivation.

For the rest, dahlias are of the autumn landscape, seen across the glistening silver of a dew-wet lawn – a hint of mist to filter the morning sun and the brilliance of flower colour, delicate, lambent, like something not of any season but rather an illusion of all. They will flower during the first year from seed; the Coltness hybrids and Collarette are quite admirable in this respect if sown in February under glass. Then by selecting the best colour forms when the flowers appear for storing over winter, the dahlia becomes a true perennial. One root of dahlia will provide upwards of twenty cuttings which in turn will grow to flower by mid-July. The cuttings will have flowers identical with the plant they came from, so colour schemes can be planned in advance and not be haphazard as with seed-raised stock. The memory of their fugitive loveliness has gardeners reaching for seed catalogues almost as the last petal falls.

Dahlias are of the autumn, colourful as a Mexican market place during a fiesta. Like most garden plants, dahlias will flower all the more profusely in a well prepared soil. The digging in of organic matter – well rotted compost, farm manure, or whatever potentially humus-forming material is available in the autumn – will ensure that the soil is in prime planting condition the following May. Because dahlias in full bloom in September make such a pleasing brilliantly barbaric sight I also apply a base dressing of organic fertiliser two weeks before planting the seedlings, cuttings, or tubers in their flowering positions. The amount of space each is given depends on the variety; 18in (46cm) each way will be adequate for bedding types, with an average of 24in (61cm) for the rest. To encourage the production of flowering side shoots, pinch out the growing point in late June or early July, otherwise this terminal shoot forms a premature flower which inhibits the development of shoots which will carry the main display of bloom in September.

7

A Hint of Grandeur

There is also a personal interpretation of the word grandeur. Farrer expressed it in his description of the wisteria growing in the Kameido Lake garden in Japan.

| Wisteria in trail of lilac mist sweeping from the sky, and a delicate cloud wreath of Wisteria rising softly from the dark and silent water, in which the descending streams of colour vapour are mirrored. The world seems to melt in the quivering heat into a shimmering violet haze.

R. Arkell on roses:

What is a nation?
Just the same old garden
With a different name,
It may be here, it may be there
We grow the same roses everywhere.

So often a poet can express in one short passage what it would take someone less gifted a whole page to explain. Certainly gardeners at some stage in their adventure aspire to grow roses. Success and failure, minor trials and triumphs make a bond between each one, whether the scene of operations is a postage-stamp patch or a domain of many acres; the world is small because we grow the same roses after all.

There are so many ways of defining the word grandeur. Where used to describe a mature oak or cedar, the word reflects dimension indicating a respect of age and stature. The same term used to explain a flower-filled alpine meadow with the snow-capped peaks of mountains in the background acknowledges magnificence of appearance, a sublime majesty which is awe-inspiring.

Then there is grandeur as in the quality of being grand, which is incapable of exact analysis because it is a combination of many different elements. This is why a word which so effectively serves to describe a 300-year-old oak tree serves equally well when used in respect of a rose. This is not to imply that an expression which can be used in so many different contexts loses thereby any of its definitive qualities. In the plant world grandeur can be as much a degree of nobility and stature as it is of excellence.

ROSE – QUEEN OF FLOWERS

Notice how little the name 'rose' varies between different nations. In Greek – Roden, in Latin – Rosa, and in so many European languages the same word, Rose, suffices with minor variations, as if, Foulkard suggests, 'nature, having apparently in this generous distribution designed to offer these flowers to all people as the type of grace and beauty'. Yet a camellia with the same elegance of form and loveliness of flower may be portrayed as handsome or splendid, but lacks the positive qualities which warrant the all-embracing grandeur.

Anyone searching for reasons why the rose lays such a strong claim to the title 'Queen of Flowers' would discover a family history which has been well recorded. The flower is so ancient that almost every country, European and Oriental, has its own mass of rose legend and written chronicle; yet even so, much of the story, at least the early chapters, remains obscure and lost in the waste-land of pre-recorded time. For the rose as we know it today is a result of a union between East and West, with one root of the family tree in China and the other in Europe, and man, the plant hunter, botanist, hybridiser, in turn providing the means which enabled the marriage to take place. Even so the rose, ancient or modern, lacks certain qualities that in any other plant would be considered essential. Majesty of stature, elegance of contour, and perennial interest. A rosebush out of flower is a nothing, and after pruning a less than nothing landscape of cut stumps and a horse manure mulch. Yet still roses enjoy near universal acclaim as the epitome of excellence in more than garden terms.

The reason why is not hard to find, it is identifying the qualities which is impossible. To walk in a garden with roses in full bloom is to discover some part of the answer. The flowers have a velvet-textured quality that gives a depth to petal colour in which the eye becomes immersed. Fragrance distilled from the flowers when they are warmed by the sun spills out in such abundance that on still, calm evenings the garden is filled with the refreshing perfume. The qualities are the same whether the garden is in Portland (Oregon), Paris, Lyon, St Albans or Aberdeen, for roses are not of one nation or any single period in history, they are timeless. Possibly this is the secret that they have gathered for themselves through the slow passage of centuries – an extraordinary quality which makes them immortal.

Though roses flourish in most soils, it is the heavier loams and clays which suit them best. Such soils provide the nutrient-rich root run that is so essential to any rose's well-being. During the first 26 years of my professional gardening life, all spent cultivating glacial clay soils, roses throve in my care like the proverbial green bay tree. Damask or noisette, hybrid tea or floribunda so long as the routine of prune, feed, and mulch was adhered to, roses were a feature of summer which suffered no competition or substitution. A move to light loam soils destroyed any illusion that the success with roses up till then had been due to my skill. Without the constant moisture provided by the clay soil roses became the miffs and mopes of the garden, prone to every sort of ague and ill.

So the first priority must be that of ensuring a free draining, yet at the same time moisture-retentive root run. On all soils this means digging the site of the rose bed over to a depth of 15–18in (38–46cm), working in at the same time well decayed compost or manure. All improvement of the lower levels needs to be done at this stage, for once the roses are planted up, mulching over the surface each year with rotted manure, compost, peat or pulverised bark will be the sole means of maintaining the soil in a friable state. Feeding may not be quite as essential with shrub roses as it is with hybrid tea or floribunda for they do not have to produce a whole new crop of fresh young shoots each year; nevertheless, it is good garden practice. Three oz (75g) per sq yd (sq m) of specially formulated fertiliser in March will be sufficient.

Pruning of shrub roses over the first two years should be so adjusted as to produce a strong framework of branches. Before planting prune all top growth back by two-thirds to an outward-facing bud. During the growing season rub out any shoots which are weak, badly placed, or growing across the centre of the bush. The second spring prune the growth made the previous summer back by about half to an outward-facing bud. In subsequent years prune only enough to keep the bush in good shape and peak flowering condition.

'Zepherine Drouhin' is the most popular of the bourbon roses and a favourite of mine going back to childhood. The thorn-free branches and vivid pink flowers which are very sweet scented and borne from June until Christmas in most years, earn this of all roses a special place in my affection. During my late teens I had to pass along a path lined with 'Zepherine Drouhin' roses when checking that various gates were tight closed against livestock and marauding rabbits. On summer evenings the fragrance from the hundreds of flowers filled the air around my head. Sixty-three 'Zepherine Drouhin' were trained over rustic trellising which bounded three sides of the garden in my care for twenty years. The bushes in full bloom formed a pink, fragrant background to the lower growing bedding roses.
Grown as a climber over a trellis shoots extend up to 12ft (3.66m). Given unfettered freedom as a large bush the height is reduced to a manageable 6ft (1.83m) as the branches arch over at the tips.

Heavier loams and clays suit roses best, as 'Sunset Song' obviously agrees, judging by the crop of flowers

OLD OR NEW – A MATTER OF PERSONAL PREFERENCE

In garden landscape capability there is no way that the modern bedding rose can be compared with the roses which the Empress Josephine grew in her garden at Malmaison. For the rose at that stage remained almost exclusively a European development not yet influenced by the Chinese roses. The varieties commonly grown then flowered once, usually in June. While the rose garden in June offered a compilation of scent and colour, a festival which acknowledged the arrival of summer, for the rest of the year there was little the damask, bourbon, gallica and others had to offer. Yet the old roses when given the right stage on which to display their undoubted charm are as essential a part of the June scene as they were in the Malmaison garden.

Rather than segregating them, a near impossibility in the modern small garden, incorporate the old roses into a mixed border with carefully selected herbaceous plants. *Rosa gallica versicolor* of the curiously flecked dark- and light-pink flowers gains in quality from an association with the lime and grey green of 'Ladies Mantle', *Alchemilla mollis*, whose fine, silky-haired leaves hold drops of dew to glisten like quicksilver in early morning sunlight. The blue spring flowering delphiniums are a contrast in shape and a complement in colour to those of the roses growing amongst them. To obtain just the right colour shades raise quantities of delphinium plants from seed. Select the most suitable varieties from these as they flower, then take cuttings the following year. The shoots which push up from the crown (root) of the delphinium in spring,

Though *Alchemilla mollis* is so useful a source of foliage and flower for indoor arrangements, it is also an indispensable piece of the garden-design jig-saw. Growing wild in company with geum and forget-me-nots, or in gardens, this is a very companionable plant

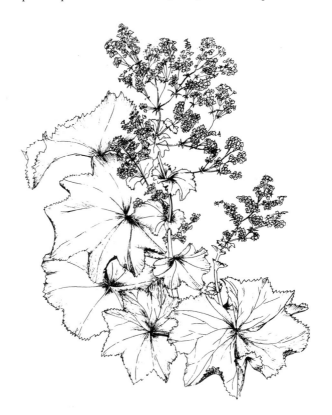

The polished mahogany-coloured bole of *Prunus serrula* with 'Peeping Tom' daffodils in spring, to be followed in summer by the majestic *Cardiocrinum*

if cut when about 4–5in (10–12cm) long, make suitable cutting material for rooting in sharp sand. Try pale-blue delphiniums with, sprawling over a rustic paling support alongside, *Rosa* 'Tour de Malakoff' whose cerise and magenta flowers turn rich violet with age, or the incomparable *Rosa* 'Madame Isaac Pereire' with voluptuous quartered flowers in deep madder, distilling a fragrance which can only be described as excellently fruity. These courtesan flowers are also lovely when cohabiting with the peasant-cultured 'Meadow Cranesbill', *Geranium* 'Johnson's Blue'.

Possibly it is in the cool shadowed twilight that some colours show to best advantage and so it is with *Rosa* 'Madame Pierre Oger', a bourbon whose creamy blush turns a rich shade of pink on sunny days. In the twilight the blooms take on a luminous

The Eryngium *seeds itself into the most improbable places when the soil is well drained and the border open to the sun. The prickly flower heads are very useful for drying to use in winter arrangements with other preserved material. Many of the best hybrids are listed under* Eryngium x zabelii.

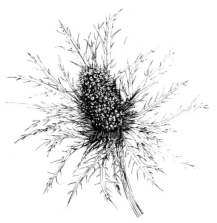

Eryngium alpinum grows 24in (61cm) high and is a beautifully executed plant – displaying deeply divided blue-green lower leaves and steel-blue flower heads

happy chance some seedlings from *Eryngium* 'Miss Willmott's Ghost' seeded around and amongst the rose branches to enhance the effect in the gloaming, while also serving to link the rose with a boskage of lavender all grey and blue – a picture to persuade an excess of time wasting. Failing all the rest, let 'Zepherine Drouhin' hold a place, trained over yet not tied to a triangle of poles, so that the branches arch over to become a pattern of deep-pink, sweetly scented flowers from June until autumn. A clematis, 'The President', trained over the supporting poles enriches the picture by opening a succession of medium-sized rich purple flowers, first in May, then again in August. Walk amongst your roses as the air cools at the close of a hot June day and share silent communion with the unrecorded thousands who down the centuries have done the same.

The modern HT and floribunda roses change identity quickly. New varieties in ever increasing numbers are introduced to supplant those just planted so that these lovely and useful garden dwellers are in danger of being treated like so much floral paint. There are those such as 'Peace', 'Silver Jubilee', 'Evelyn Fison', and 'Picasso' which survive all attempts to supplant them. Always place these roses in blocks of a single colour, never mixed, as if in simulation of a surrealist painting, the product of a formless dream. Let each colour be seen against the smooth green of lawn, not the toneless grey of flagstone or fawn of gravel, (more of this later).

A Cinderella Grandeur

The splendour may be brief for only a few short weeks while the flowers last, as with *Yucca gloriosa*. The 'Adam's Needles' of California, with erect crowded panicles of creamy-white flower bells carried on stems 6ft (1.8m) high, is an arrestingly beautiful sight. Cedar of Lebanon as a background to the yucca proves that Solomon in all his glory, at least for this flowering time, could not compete.

Who could deny to a well flowered colony of 'Golden Ray lilies', *Lilium auratum*, a share of the word grandeur? For these splendid bulbous plants with stems up to 6ft (1.8m) in height, carrying a dozen or more of the flaring trumpet-shaped ivory-white flowers with a distinctive gold bar down the centre of each petal, are superbly expressive. The fragrance which is a notable part of this lily's charm needs no close enquiry, for it reaches out in greeting across the garden. Plant the bulbs 6–8in (15–20cm) deep, even as much as 12in (30.5cm) deep in light, fertile soil amongst low growing shrubs, and the result cannot fail to please.

So many lilies have a regal quality which is only fully apparent when they are placed in the right context. *Lilium superbum* growing amongst the Redwoods in California, *Lilium candidum* framed against the living mythology of a Grecian landscape, deserve in those locations the appellation 'grand' while in the garden they become merely beautiful. Not so the 'Giant Lily' *Cardiocrinum giganteum* from western China which, even transposed from its native, tree-bedecked gorges into a garden setting, still maintains an imposing presence. They need a deep, very humus-laden rich soil to thrive. In the dappled shade cast by a light-foliaged *Acer griseum* or *Prunus serrula*, the immensely stout flowering stems rise 8–10ft (2.5–3m) high. From the top the long, trumpet-shaped blooms of lime green on white flowers splashed maroon in the throat open in late summer. The seed pods are a pleasant afterthought. Unfortunately, this paragon of a bulb dies after flowering but leaves offsets behind to continue the line.

Rhododendrons lose much individuality when grown as a massed planting into a great amorphous boskage devoid of shape and character. There are species which, when given a sheltered situation, will grow into specimen plants with a grandeur which commands admiration. *Rh. arboreum* from the Khasia Hills is one. To see the globular heads of blood-red flowers covering a bush 20–30ft (6–9m) high framed against snow-covered mountains is to discover a new interpretation of the word beautiful.

Possibly the splendid *Rhododendron falconeri* introduced from Sikkim by Hooker in 1850 impressed me because I saw it first with the blue and white of the Irish Sea as a backcloth. The large, deeply veined leaves, rust red underneath, combined with the huge dome-shaped trusses of bell-like, waxy-textured, creamy-yellow flowers each splashed with purple in the throat, filled the eye. A tree 25ft (8m) in full bloom deserves and needs at least an hour of quiet appreciation. Both *Rh. arboreum* and *falconeri* require shelter and a moist humid climate to thrive, so a woodland setting suits them.

To choose one other which is tougher, more robust, while still retaining the essential qualification, there is *Rh. decorum*, introduced by Fortune from Szechwan. The flowers are large, flared-funnel shape, either white or shell pink, and open in May. With the scent from thousands of fully open blooms filling the air with their ripe melon fragrance and the panoply of spring all round, *Rh. decorum* improves on excellence.

On investigation the plants which qualify for the description grand grow numerous in the memory. Magnolia, of course, have an immense presence and several are positively grand. *Magnolia mollicomata*, with flowers like pink water lilies arrayed along the naked branches, is one of the many glorious plants which came to gardens from Tibet. Perhaps the magnificent evergreen foliage, glossy green above and rust red beneath, of *Magnolia grandiflora* makes it supreme champion. The intensely fragrant, creamy-white flowers open over several months. One garden in America is forever held in my memory for the magnolias filled it nose deep with their delicate perfume. *Magnolia grandiflora* is what in human terms would be called a slow developer. Fortunately, there are two forms of the species, 'Exmouth' and 'Goliath', which flower at an earlier age than the parent. Planted in a rich, moist loam in a sheltered position, their beauty can be enjoyed to the full.

Cherry trees lack some essential quality which, lovely though the blossom-mounded branches appear against the blue April sky, just fails to earn them the final tribute of grandeur. There is one

Yucca gloriosa has clumps of narrow rigid, spine-tipped leaves on a stout trunk-like stem. Top this with an 8ft (2.5m) high spike carrying a crowded conicle of creamy-white flowers, each petal shaded purple on the outside.

The much lower growing Yucca filamentosa *and* Y. flaccida *are also reliably hardy. For an enclosed courtyard or patio garden there is* Yucca recurvifolia *with spikes of creamy-white flowers carried in dense, erect panicles on 3ft (0.9m) high stems. Given sunshine and a dry, free draining soil, the yucca will flourish.*

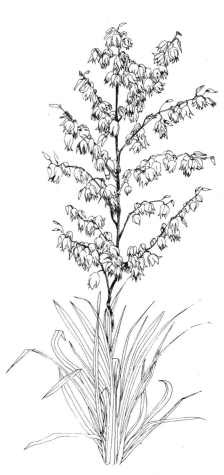

Yucca recurvifolia is the most widely cultivated of the clan, while *Yucca filamentosa* (illustrated) takes less time to reach flowering size – usually two or three years after planting

All rhododendrons may be propagated by layering. Branches which are suitably placed so that they can be easily pulled down and buried in the soil are the most convenient. Make a cut on the underside of the branch, the younger wood roots most readily, half way through, then 2 or 3in (5–8cm) long. A match stalk or piece of sphagnum moss inserted into the wood will hold the two cut surfaces apart so that they do not just heal up instead of growing roots. Dust the wound with rooting powder, then peg the branch down firmly so it is buried 2–3in (5–8cm) deep in a compost of peat, sand, and lime-free soil. A heavy stone placed on top will hold all firm, and in dry weather keep well watered. In eighteen months a layer will have sufficient root to be cut free from the parent bush.

The large flower trusses of *Rhododendron loderi*, most floriferous of the decorum offspring, dispense a most refreshing fragrance

exception other than that mentioned in regard to *Prunus x yedoensis* (Chapter 4), when the location, the mood, and a perfect spring day made the difference between merely beautiful and grand. For the Mount Fuji cherry, *Prunus* 'Shirotae', in full bloom under late April sunshine looks like drifted snow, so dazzling white is its blossom. Standing under the flower-laden branches inhaling the bruised almond scent on a warm day, I could appreciate the reason why the Japanese name for this lovely tree is 'Snow White'. Below me the pine-covered hillside dipped down into a grass-green valley, and spring in all its splendour was abroad in the land.

MAJESTIC BROAD LANDSCAPE GRANDEUR

Catalpa are such lovely late summer flowering trees, that even with the immense weight of competition there is at that time of the year as the borders spill over with colour, they hold a place. Most of the species grow into medium-sized, wide spreading trees with attractive foliage. Some shelter is an absolute necessity for the leaves are easily bruised and shredded by wind. The wood also is brittle and liable to be broken under heavy snow or by strong wind. As a courtyard tree catalpa is quite superb as the panicles of foxglove-like flowers open in July. In *C.bignonioides* these are white with yellow and purple markings, while in *C.fargesii* the petals are soft pink-spotted dusky red, stained at the base with yellow. To sit under a catalpa on a hot summer day, cooled by the sun-filtering lime-green foliage while enjoying in the most intimate detail the quality of these lovely flowers, is a privilege reserved for those who trouble to grow and know this interesting tree. There is a form of *C.bignonioides* with yellow leaves, soft hued and velvet textured, which only reaches full and perfect form in the sun-warmed most sheltered of corners. Only once, in Italy, have I seen a mature specimen of *C.bignonioides* 'Aurea' growing full and perfect of leaf. In the clear bright sunshine it was a tree of shimmering gold.

Centuries have passed since the Romans introduced the sweet, or Spanish, chestnut to Britain, which probably explains why *Castanea sativa* is now naturalised and accepted as native, particularly in the eastern counties. In July when the yellowish-green male and female catkins are abundantly displayed the trees are a handsome sight. Though, as children will testify, it is when those deliciously chestnut-red nuts are falling that the tree achieves full beauty. Gathering basketfuls of ripe nuts from a carpet of yellow leaves with the pungent aroma of autumn, the essence of the season all around should be in everyone's experience. Perhaps it is in Studley Royal Park leading to Fountains Abbey where *Castanea sativa* achieves true expression; towering majestically, the crown of branches lifting from those curiously convoluted stems, with herds of fallow deer grazing amongst them – sublime grandeur indeed.

Beech are not the most comfortable trees with which to share garden room, yet where space allows they are so elegant that even the oak must take second place. Had the beech, *Fagus sylvatica*, developed a root like the oak, *Quercus*, which delved deep into the

A pergola covered in 'Golden Rain' *Laburnum x vossii* with ceanothus and ferns adding their quota to the distinctive grandeur (*Newby Hall Gardens, near Ripon*)

LEFT
Catalpa bignonioides, with soft-textured leaves and orchid-like flowers is my favourite of an exceptionally well endowed clan. The specimen in my last garden encouraged many hours of sun-blessed contemplation

soil so making it possible to grow other shrubs, herbaceous perennials and the like in association with it, then finding a place for this most beautiful of all trees would have been less of a problem. Unfortunately beech is surface rooting and even moss has difficulty in surviving root competition and overhead shade. Were it possible to become sufficient of an aesthete with a superior appreciation of what is beautiful, then a single well grown beech tree might serve as a complete garden with a lawn to provide a vista across which to contemplate the object of our admiration. Then in winter there would be the silvered grey and lime green of the bole holding aloft for appreciation the broadly fashioned yet delicately outlined canopy of branches. Spring would spread a haze of pale green to deepen into darker shaded summer, while autumn discovers copper and gold above and below in the feet-nestling carpet of fallen leaves. There are many forms of *Fagus sylvatica* with leaves purple, golden, even pink edged, though few improve on the quality of the parent.

Though there are only four species included in the genus, cedars are one of the most popular trees for specimen planting. *Cedrus atlantica glauca*, the 'Blue Cedar', judged on year-round performance is one of the most spectacularly beautiful trees. The leaves are silvery blue and this coupled with the sheer overpowering bulk of the branch canopy in maturity gives it a grandeur that, because of the leaf colour, is never gloomy. This sets it apart from the other species and varieties of cedar which have a suggestion of the funereal about them: a churchyard connotation which on grey days can be depressing. Given a broad landscape around them and blue sky above, then 'Cedar of Lebanon', *Cedrus libani*, with its picturesque tiered arrangement of branches which gives the mature tree a characteristic flat-topped look, and the pendent character of *Cedrus deodara* are undeniably grand.

For the same reason that they grow to an outrageous size, only someone who has no intention of living with the garden more than twenty years ever plants a horsechestnut. *Aesculus hippocastanum*, native of the border region between Greece and Albania, is really not a good garden tree. This in spite of the beautiful picture it presents when the whole canopy becomes a giant candelabra as the stout erect 'candles' of white flowers light up at the tips of every branch during May. Unfortunately, no other plant can survive within the sphere of influence of the common horsechestnut, so even though it is amongst the most beautiful of flowering trees, only in avenues or open space parkland can it really be tolerated.

Davidia, the legendary dove tree, was a celebrity long before it was introduced into cultivation by E. H. Wilson nearly a century ago. The distinctive beauty of *Davidia* is in the large, conspicuous, snow-white bracts which subtend the tiny clustered flower heads. At first these are lime green, they become pure white as the flowers mature. The petals and bracts are hung on long slender stalks and when stirred by even the slightest breeze they are like white flickering Buddhist prayer flags. The bracts are most noticeable at dawn or twilight when the slanting rays of sun pick them out.

One of the most curious espaliers I have ever seen is in a friend's garden where a Cedrus atlantica glauca *has been trained to cover a garden wall. The tiered arrangement of branches are like tinselled silver ropes pulled taut across the stonework. Careful pruning over thirty and more years has produced a remarkable wallscape.*

Cedars, especially those from Lebanon, span the centuries from the temple built by Solomon to the present day. They have an enduring quality which defies time

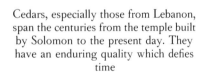

Davidia makes a medium-sized tree thriving in most soils so long as they are moist yet well drained.

Taking grandeur in the magnificence of appearance interpretation, there is no question that the 'Chilean Fire Bush', *Embothrium coccineum lanceolatum*, collected by Comber in the Norquinco Valley qualifies for inclusion here. The lustrous dark green of the leaves are of a shade which perfectly complements the scarlet of the flowers that open in late May. A free draining lime-free soil which is, in contradiction, not prone to drying out completely in summer is that preferred by this most lovely small tree. A specimen grown from seed will reach about 24ft (7m) in eighteen years. In a woodland setting where the sun can strike through to light up the flowers, this is a tree of quite incredible beauty when in bloom.

There are some trees which impress more by elegance of outline than ever they could in quality of flower. The most widely grown of all weeping trees, often planted in the most ill advised situations, is quite probably *Salix x chrysocoma*. Certainly it is the tree which suggests all that is gentle and beautiful in a pastoral idyll. The arching branches extend into slender golden-yellow shoots which hang in a gracefully pendulous curtain to sweep the grass or water below. It is in the context of grassy mead and slow moving river or still lake that *Salix x chrysocoma* shows all those qualities of elegance and grace which focus attention and admiration. All too often it is planted in a garden so small that, being fast growing like all willows, only by recourse to annual butchery can it be kept within manageable bounds. Ultimately, only removing what after years of hard pruning has become a grotesque travesty of a tree affords the final solution. Undoubtedly a tree to be admired in its entirety across a broad expansive landscape.

To stand under the might, branching canipy of a mature oak is to sense in small measure something of the strength and fortitude this most enduring tree projects. There is a quality of beauty in the rugged strength and a vibrance of life in the wide flung branches which is somehow symbolic. Stand long enough and it would not be difficult to believe each and every oak inhabited by a sylvan semi-deity.

Oaks of all kinds grow best in deep, rich soils. They are deep rooted so it is practical to garden all around beneath the branch canopy. A mature specimen will take up all the space which a modest sized garden affords and still, like Oliver Twist, demand more. There are both deciduous and evergreen species contained within the genus *Quercus*; most grow to noble proportions and live to a great age. To achieve immortality one could do worse than plant a sapling English oak, *Quercus robur*. Over the decades of the youngster's slow progress to maturity succeeding generations might pause to reflect on things other than the mere business of living, and call down blessings on the head of the gardener who wielded the spade.

Embothrium will grow in slightly alkaline soils if well mulched with peat or forest bark. A soil which is moist, shelter from cold drying winds and a place in the full sun are modest enough demands for the brilliant display of flowers which are the reward of our diligence. Seed is not set every year, and I wonder if, like so many of the scarlet-flowered Chilean plants with honeysuckle-shaped blossom, it is adapted for fertilisation by humming birds or specialist insects.

So much a part of the English legend, the oak is the best loved of all our trees

Spring is a word capable of so many interpretations, for of all the seasons this is the most difficult to predict. There are false dawns which encourage hope each year. Days, even in February, so benign that bees forage busily over crocus flowers and bird song is loud on every side. These pleasant interludes – 'weather breeders' as the dalesmen call them – are usually a prelude to a prolonged spell of frost and snow. Often in May, just when the apple trees are in full bloom, there comes a sharp frost to blight the crop. St Dunstand is usually blamed for this sort of mischief. In a late blossoming season, a clear night which threatens frost is known as a John Frankum night. Apparently a certain John Frankum made a sacrifice in his orchard with the object of getting a specially fine crop of fruit. The punishment for this piece of perversion was a ruinous frost.

Epimedium versicolor 'Sulphureum' makes a patterned ground cover for shady places where the soil is never subject to drought, and is moderately fertile. The flowers open on 12in (30cm) steams in early spring

Farrer's describes *Erythronium revolutum* as having 'invaluable grace for cool choice corners of the rock work. Perhaps the best yielding delicate Turks-caps in the loveliest soft shades'. I plant the tubers 4–5in (10–12cm) deep in the autumn and am rewarded by the yellow flowers borne aloft on 8in (20cm) high stems in April
(right) Purple flowers of *Rhododendron russatum*, and white cherry blossom – an enduring spring memory.

Then there comes a day when the wind veers from east to west. The soil steams like a boiling kettle, and all the pent-up energy is released in a great upsurge of growth and frenetic activity. In company with most gardeners I would enjoy the season more if the sudden change of weather did not always catch me with so much work demanding immediate attention – seed sowing, lawn mowing, pruning and planting all to be completed in a day only twenty-four hours long.

It is impossible not to pause and take full measure of all the season's quality. No matter what the weather there is always an underlying, somehow youthful gentleness, combined with a pastel-shaded loveliness which defies analysis: It is not just one sight or sound, more an amalgam of so many things: a patina of multi-toned green spreading over field and hedgerow; curlew's call mingled with all the other bird song into a grand choristry, cherry blossom and daffodil, the scent of wallflowers and slowly lengthening days mean that more time is spent outdoors than in.

Establishing a routine is the only way I can make certain essential work is completed at the correct time. Otherwise I start seed sowing, am

distracted by a rose left unpruned, or some herbaceous plant which should have been lifted and divided a month ago. Now, if sowing vegetable seed is the order of the day, though the world shakes, I adhere strictly to that. I might pause en route to the tool shed and admire a bird's eye primrose, or the scent from 'Mezereon' flowers.

There is work in the greenhouse which fully occupies all those days when rain or, whisper the word, snow makes outdoor tasks impracticable, tomatoes and cucumbers to plant up, half hardy annuals to prick off, and peach blossom to fertilise.

In the diary I mark what my family call the 'deadline' days. 24 April is noted as the earliest day on which hardy annuals can be safely sown outdoors. In my callow youth I tempted fate by preparing the soil for sowing on the first day warm enough to work outdoors in shirt sleeves, often during March. After several years of seeds not germinating, a watershed of 24 April was arrived at.

So much of gardening is concerned with the present, and yet in reality is an anticipation of the future. Even as the tulips planted last October open to rejoice May, so thoughts turn to planting gladiolus and other bulbs: *acidanthera, Galtonia candicans, Ixia* and the rest. Of

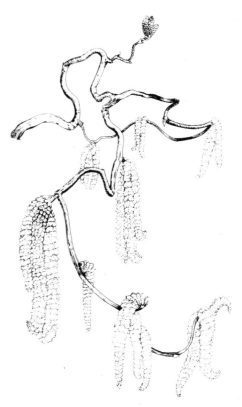

The curiously convoluted stems of twisted hazel *Corylus avellana* 'Contorta' festooned with yellow lambs-tail catkins heralding the spring

course, the bed for dahlias – so essential a part of the autumn scene – was made ready six months ago, though never do I plant this native Mexican outdoors before 21 May, no matter how kindly the spring. I can blame St Dunstan for frosting the fruit blossom, only myself if the tender shoots of the dahlias are nipped. A thought occurs to me that it was a mistake to honour a Swedish botanist by naming this lovely flower after him – the Mexican name cocoxochitl is much better. What a splendid title The British Cocoxochitl Society would have been.

Gardeners are fortunate in being outdoors during the season which sees life everywhere resurgent. I am sure that we all embark on each round of seed sowing and planting convinced that this year really will reveal our own personal Eden, perfect and unblemished, free from scourge and serpent.

Nigella damascena can be sown direct where it is to flower. Love-in-a-mist is a beautifully descriptive name for this 18in (46cm) tall hardy annual

8

A Hint of Subtlety

To achieve a dramatic effect by using brilliantly coloured flowers in a massed display is not difficult, though it could be compared with using a bludgeon to command admiration. Huge blocks of orange marigolds alongside regiments of vivid scarlet pelargoniums will make a dazzling show and bring gasps of astonishment from all who see it. Such an arrangement lacks the essential degree of harmony which makes it liveable with. For to be assaulted by colour at every turn destroys all the sense of tranquil quiet which is one of the prime benefits to be derived from growing plants.

The design needs to improve the quality of the environment in which we live, while providing at the same time a means of expression for personal skill and creative artistry. There are as many ways of achieving this most desirable end as there are gardens and gardeners tending them.

Spring is the season which best illustrates the subtle use of what is really differing shades of one primary colour. A hint here, merely a suggestion there, just variations of green tints build up a picture which is compellingly beautiful while still defying analysis. Try to separate the component parts and we find that individually they are insignificant, only as a united whole do the shades of green, embellished here and there with points of colour from the flowers, gain full expression. All these subtle degrees of colour can be combined to good effect in the choice of plants used to furnish the garden. The perfection of art in garden design is to conceal art.

Though the individual units of the design may lack the splendour portrayed by a cherry mounded down with pink blossom, they have a softening influence on the more violent colours while still maintaining a quiet beauty which is perennial. The value of coloured stems was brought vividly home to me when following a road bordered by thickets of *Cornus alba*. The day was one of showers and sunshine and the rain-wet stems of the dogwood glowed an even brighter red when lit by the sunlight. Two varieties of the species 'Westonbirt' dogwood, *Cornus alba* 'Sibirica' with brilliant crimson shoots, and 'Spaethii' which has strikingly variegated golden and green leaves, are also pleasing to the eye. Possibly in the smaller garden the 'Westonbirt' dogwood which is less robustly vigorous would be the best value. Hard pruning each year in spring will result in a fresh crop of young shoots which have the brightest of scarlet bark.

The chestnut blossom is raining steadily and noiselessly down upon a path whose naked pebbles receive mosaic of emerald light from the interlacing boughs. At intervals, once or twice an hour, the wings of a lonely swallow pass that way when alone the shower stirs from its perpendicular fall. Cool and moist, the perfumed air flows without lifting the most nervous leaf or letting fall a suspended bead of the night's rain from a honeysuckle bud.

A quiet composed picture drawn in words by Edward Thomas, which is totally harmonious and simply subtle.

There is no doubt that flower scent, subtle yet evocative, improves the quality of the environment. A group of the annual *Nicotiana* 'Sensation' will fill the air with fragrance from brilliantly coloured flowers. Height in bloom 24in (61cm)

A well designed herb garden where the eyes are soothed by quiet colour tones, and the nose by a combination of herbal fragrances

OPPOSITE
The beech tree is at all seasons beautiful. In autumn, as the leaves turn colour, it is majestic

---

From a diary I kept in 1973

Nearly every day of the year my work takes me at least once amongst groves Of indigenous birch and always, at all seasons, they are lovely. Some have thrown up four or five stems as a result of being damaged in youth instead of just one, and these are the most picturesque. Now when I plant seedlings I head them back to near ground level then thin the shoots to three or five as they break and have a miniature grove.

Less conspicuous than the cornus though with curiously convoluted shoots as an added attraction, a form of the 'Pekin Willow' *Salix matsudana* 'Tortuosa' makes a most effective winter silhouette. The branches and twigs which are twisted like corkscrews are distinctively pale yellow. They look especially beautiful as the young leaves break in spring.

The various species of birch are possessed of such graceful elegance that this combined with the marbled white of the stem makes them noteworthy trees, for they hold our interest all the year round. Most need the sort of space any small tree requires to do itself justice. *Betula pendula*, the 'Common Birch', has a white stem which in those forms that really are pendent has a classical grace. In winter the delicate twig tracery, which gradually turns plum purple at the approach of spring, is revealed in all its artistry. A group of snowdrops clustered about the white bole of the tree serves as a compliment to, rather than an embellishment of, the 'Lady of the Woods'. Other species of birch share the white-stemmed character; *Betula costata* and *jacquemontii* are particularly well endowed in this respect but they lack the balanced, well proportioned elegance of *Betula pendula*. All show the same obliging acceptance of most soils and situations. Only when the leaves fall from the deciduous trees in the autumn is it possible to make a proper evaluation of their overall shape. The silhouette makes such an important contribution to the character of the garden in winter that it is a wise gardener who seeks to know well all the virtues before buying.

Regular pruning out of the dead and older stems of Rubus cockburnianus *is essential to ensure a full complement of young shoots. The rose can be pruned at the same time, for as with the bramble the young shoots are the most ornamental. The thought occurred to me after the spring pruning was completed this year that a ground cover of 'Soft Shield Fern' would complete what is an already pleasant combination of shapes and pastel colours.*

The various forms of maple are in many cases so stiffly geometric that they lose all character and influence once the leaves fall. *Acer griseum*, the delightful 'Paper Bark Maple', with flaking cinnamon-coloured underbark is an exception. The 'Snake Bark Maples', *Acer davidii, pensylvanicum* and in particular *grosseri* with young stems which are mid green, beautifully striped with white and lime green, are attractive at all seasons.

Though several of the cherries have ornamental features other than ephemeral flowers, only the Manchurian *Prunus maackii* with shining gold-tinted flaking bark and the Tibetan *Prunus serrula* with stems of a rich mahogany colour are year-round contributors. Grown in combination with the oriental hellebores, whose flowers when the plants are grown from seed can be any shade from dark purple through pink and cream to lime green, the burnished stems of both cherries gain extra quality and importance.

Roses are not usually accused of subtle modesty, but *Rosa omeiensis pteracantha*, the 'Mount Omei Rose' from western China, though unassertive in flower really is possessed of the most formidable array of translucent scarlet thorns. When lit from behind by rays of winter sunshine they give the appearance of having been dipped in the blood of some unfortunate sacrificial gardening delinquent. *Rubus cockburnianus*, the well named 'Whitewash Bramble', whose gracefully arching stems are covered in a white bloom makes a good intermix with the rose – a white-robed penitent at the sacrifice of the miscreant.

LEAVES – LONGER LASTING THAN FLOWERS

Coloured foliage which includes any variation on the predominantly green is of such importance that there is a great temptation to overuse it when drawing up the overall plan of the garden. Too much variegation reduces the planting to a pale imitation of Joseph's multi-coloured coat which earned that unfortunate a temporary burial followed by exile.

The common holly, native to Europe and Africa through to China, has been cultivated for centuries. Judging by the number of varieties on offer, holly seems to have produced a variegation for each decade of its existence as an anniversary present. Certainly, there is no more beautiful or durable evergeen shrub or tree for the garden than *Ilex aquifolium* in green and variegated forms. There are those which are striped, edged, or marbled with tones of silver or gold in so many permutations that the only way to make a selection is to go round a nursery and see them growing, then pick the one which pleases best. Because hollies are so tolerant of pruning there is no problem keeping them within bounds. They do form a near perfect focal point around which to paint all sorts of extravagant pictures. A skirt of *Cyclamen hederifolium* to grace the autumn, lovely peach-flowered *Tulipa batalinii*, or the early blooming white- and cream-petalled *T.tarda* – none more than 6in (15cm) high – will bloom to welcome back the swallows. Choose a female holly for the scarlet of the berry against the leaf colour.

Cyclamen hederifolium flowers in autumn before the leaves appear. The blooms in varying shades of pink to white with a spot of dark crimson at the base of each segment have an elfin loveliness which is very appealing. The leaves are like those of the common ivy in shape, attractively marbled white on dark green and waved at the edge. In soils which suit them they thrive and self-seed all about to form well flowered colonies.

There is such a bewildering range of crab apples with purple foliage that selecting just one or two from the many is not easy. Of those on offer *Malus* 'Lemoinei' is neatly upright in growth with flowers that are commendably large and of a deep wine red. *Malus* 'Profusion' blooms a little later than 'Lemoinei' and has more interesting coppery-red leaves. All the red- or purple-foliaged plants show to better effect when associated with blue flowers.

Berberis are amongst those under the near indispensable label. Discounting their value as flowering and berrying shrubs, they earn bonus points for foliage also. *Berberis thunbergii* 'Aurea' is a neat shrub with bright golden leaves which preserve their pristine character all season when grown in a north-facing border. Another shrub which fits neatly into the same context is *Rhododendron yakushimanum* whose young growths are the colour and texture of silver-grey suede. Possibly the cherry-pink buds of the rhododendron flowers are too shocking a shade to be called subtle; fortunately, they turn to creamy white as they open. The various forms of *Berberis thunbergii* with purple foliage are best represented for garden purposes by 'Atropurpurea Nana'. This is a dwarf variety forming a neatly rounded bush some 24in (61cm) high in ten years with handsome red-purple foliage. Golden-leaved *Thuja orientalis* 'Aurea' and blue and white spring flowering *Anemone blanda* serve only to make a good plant even better.

What a cause for regret that the various forms of *Acer palmatum*, the incomparable 'Japanese Maple', are so very capriciously unpredictable. There are no rules which can be applied in regard to the cultivation of this plant. On acid clay their behaviour was impeccable, on light sand growth and all-round quality of leaf left nothing to be desired, whereas in good quality loam they have sulked and moped like any over-indulged debutante. From the bronzed crimson-leaved *Acer palmatum* 'Atropurpureum' to the soft yellow-green lace-patterned *Acer palmatum* 'Dissectum Flavescens', the Japanese maples are worth every indulgence the gardeners' patience will allow. Grow the 'Atropurpureum' with gold- and green-leaved hosta and the lovely pale-yellow flowered *Meconopsis regia*, for they agree very well. Of the 'Dissectum' forms with finely divided leaves there are in addition to 'Flavescens', purple-leaved and bronze-tinted varieties also. There are few more beautiful sights that the garden affords than a dome-shaped *Acer palmatum* 'Dissectum Flavescens' rising out of a carpet formed by vivid blue-flowered *Omphalodes verna*, the 'Blue Eyed Mary' of cottage gardens. All the Japanese maples are best suited when planted in a moist yet well drained acid soil. Shelter from the east wind which blasts the tender young growth is another prime essential.

There is no question that there are some shrubs with variegated or coloured foliage which because of their ability to thrive in most soils and situations are more useful for general planting than others. *Weigela florida* 'Variegata' is in the 'all things and any garden' class. Each leaf is edged with creamy white, and though it looks just a little bit 'chocolate boxy' when the rose-pink flowers open, the fall from grace is only brief. So why not compound the felony by

Evelyn employed all his rich command of descriptive vocabulary to express his opinion of holly.

Above all the natural greens which enrich our home-born store, there is none certainly to be compared to the Holly, insomuch as I have often wonder'd at our curiosity after foreign plants and expensive difficulties to the neglect of the culture of this vulgar but incomparable tree. Is there under Heaven a more glorious and refreshing object of the kind of glittering with its armed and varnished leaves then blushing with their natural coral? It mocks the rudest assaults of weather, beasts or hedge breakers.

An *Ilex aquifolium* 'Aurea Marginata', whose dark-green leaves edged with gold are rendered even more strikingly handsome by a complement of red berries.

Sunlight-patterned acer leaves

The well named 'Whitewash bramble'
Rubus cockburnianus

planting bright-blue-flowered delphiniums or pale-lavender-petalled *Iris sibirica* alongside?

Cornus mas has only one brief season of beauty when the naked branches are covered during February with an abundance of the small pompons of yellow flowers. There is a form of the Cornelian cherry, the name *Cornus mas* is popularly known by, identified as 'Variegata' which displays white-margined leaves, an encore as the flowers fade. A shrub of considerable merit which in twenty years grew to about 10ft (3m) high in a fairly exposed situation.

Though there is some truth in the accusation that *Robinia pseudoacacia* 'Frisia' is in danger of being overplanted, the reply can only be 'there can never be too much of a good thing'. Making a small tree with pinnate leaves which are rich golden yellow from May to autumn, 'Frisia' is like permanent sunshine in the garden. There is need of no more than blue sky as a background and a carpet of white-flowered *Vinca minor* 'Gertrude Jekyll' underneath, or in less pastel-shaded theme a border of lavender 'Munstead' forms a fragrant delicate contrast.

Daphne odora 'Aureo-marginata' contradicts the accepted order of things by being of a tougher constitution than the type species. Often variegations of any sort result in some weakening of the plant's constitution, but it is certainly not true in this case. Given a soil which is moist, free draining and reasonably fertile such as all daphne relish, 'Aureo-marginata' forms a neat evergreen dome of green leaves margined with creamy yellow. The intensely fragrant pink flowers open in early spring.

Evergreens which provide more than just a brief floral interest are especially useful. For years the magnificent *Pieris formosa* 'Wakehurst' with vivid red shuttlecocks of young leaves and sprays of white flowers offered a quality of beauty denied to those gardening on lime soils. For pieris are, like rhododendrons, committed limehaters. With the advent of *Photinia x fraseri* 'Red Robin', the balance was to some extent redressed because this species is lime-tolerant. The young growths are bright red in contrast to the glossy dark green of the mature foliage. Grow 'Red Robin' alongside a *Viburnum plicatum* 'Mariesii' which carries umbels of white blossom on delightfully tiered branches amongst a colony of white and blue Spanish bluebells, *Hyacinthoides hispanica*.

Amongst the lower growing shrubs with coloured foliage those plants loosely grouped under the name of heathers have no equal in the variety of choice offered. There is one drawback to their general usefulness in the garden; so many of them just will not grow in alkaline soils. Some, like the *Erica erigena*, *E.terminalis* and the hybrids of *E.darleyensis* will succeed in lime soils when well mulched with peat. Most of them, except *Erica terminalis* which hails from Corsica and blossoms in late summer, are winter and spring flowering which doubles their value in the garden. For the remaining Erica species and the romantically nostalgic *Calluna vulgaris*, the ling which spreads a purple shadow over upland moors in August, an acid lime-free soil is essential. Planted in association with dwarf conifers which offer as many variations on the gold, silver, glaucous blue and green theme as the heathers, the two combine to produce the vegetational version of grandmother's patchwork quilt. Such a combination of widely varying colours, using plants completely different in character yet not sufficiently contrasting in form, needs skilful handling in small gardens.

Growing heathers all together in a solid block leaves no room for artistry, whereas using groups of heathers round and about in the garden as points of emphasis takes full advantage of all the variations of colour in leaf and flower which this versatile group of plants offers. Just two examples: *Erica arborea* 'Gold Tips' makes a well proportioned shrub 50in (127cm) high. The bright gold of early spring contrasts splendidly with the orange-red flowers of *Berberis x stenophylla* 'Coccinea'. A dozen or two blue-flowered annual candytuft give colour as the heather's foliage pales to lime green in summer, or on a brighter note, dark red patches of *Antirrhinum* 'Coronette'. Where the soil contains lime *Erica herbacea* 'Foxhollow' with bright yellow summer foliage is beautiful in company with the prostrate blue-green-leaved, mauve-petalled *Hebe* 'Wingleteye'. Keep the erica in order or the hebe could be easily swamped.

In a climate where the sky offers more variations on a grey theme than bright blue, the golden, bronze-tinted shoots of the *Spiraea japonica* 'Gold Flame' brighten what would otherwise be a gloomy prospect. Two others from the same parent, 'Golden Princess' and 'Golden Mound', are of a similar colour and character, growing about 30in (75cm) high. As a cool foliage contrast the *Ruta*

Vinca minor 'Gertrude Jekyll', one of the attractive periwinkles which have glossy, dark-green leaves and flowers in a wide range of colours from purple, through blue, to white – distinctive low growing shrubs

―――――――――

Heathers in general need to be renewed at regular intervals, with the exception of the tree heathers such as Erica arborea *which can be treated just like any other garden shrub. Even with annual trimming* Calluna vulgaris *varieties do grow woody and untidy looking. Fortunately, cuttings made of young shoots of the current season's growth, made just as they begin to harden at the base, when dibbled into a peat and sand compost will root in four to six weeks.*

―――――――――

Acanthus spinosus has established itself so firmly in my affection as to have become one of what my family call the 'pet plants'. The dried flower spikes have featured in innumerable church festivals, courtesy of the plants growing in the garden here

Acanthus grow from root cuttings so readily that just chopping down the side of an established plant produces a crop of rooted shoots – or should that be shooted roots? When mature plants are moved the fragments of root left behind give a dozen or more youngsters to fill the vacant space

graveolens 'Jackman's Blue' or the glaucous-grey-leaved Hosta 'Halcyon' are well suited for the purpose.

THOUGHTS ON HERBACEOUS PERENNIALS

While shrubs provide the permanent framework to the garden, herbaceous plants afford the seasonal interest. Most herbaceous perennials are easy to grow and offer a choice of plants to suit all conditions from weeping bog to dry shade. Many combine good foliage with subtle artistry of flowers. *Acanthus spinosus* is a plant of such commanding presence that it really needs to be grown as a specimen in isolation. At the corner of a border or as a central feature in an island bed the deeply divided leaves and spikes of mauve-purple flowers demand admiration. A well grown specimen with flower spikes around 50in (127cm) high is an impressive sight. *Echinops ritro*, most handsome of the globe thistles with bright-blue knob-kerrie flowers, is in height and shape a proper humorous exclamation mark to the ponderous arrogance of the acanthus.

In terms of elfin comeliness *Dierama pulcherrimum*, the 'Wand Flower', is of a grace which adds a new meaning to the term refined. The thin elegantly arching stems branch at the tip into a shower of long, drooping pink bells, carried on stalks so fine they seem to dangle supported only by the summer air. A plant so easily raised from seed should be less than temperamental and, given a place in full sun and a well drained soil which does not dry out, so *Dierama* proves to be. The wiry stems arching over a ground cover of low growing heather, or blue-grey-foliaged *Hebe pinguifolia* make all else around seem gross by comparison.

There is a plant, discovered in western China by the redoubtable monk Abbé Delavay, which compares with *Dierama* in elegance of form and that is *Thalictrum dipterocarpum* (delavayi) 'Album'.

RIGHT
The type species *Thalictrum dipterocarpum* has all the delicate grace of the white variety, except the flowers are blue

Growing a metre high with the flowers held like a fluffy cloud over finely divided aquilegia-like leaves, this plant makes a refined addition to the garden. It is lovely when grown amongst dark-flowered shrub roses or the apricot-petalled *Lilium x testaceum*.

For a long time the popular name 'Tickseed' as applied to *Coreopsis* seemed to have no basis in fact. Then I discovered that 'Coreopsis' means like a bug and refers to the shape and colour of the seeds which, until that time of enlightenment, I had not taken the trouble to look at. In America *Coreopsis verticillata* was used to dye cloth red, which presented another puzzling factor for the flowers are a lovely soft yellow. A form of *Coreopsis verticillata* called 'Moonbeam', which as the name suggests has primrose-yellow-petalled blooms, is most attractive when grown with a dark-leaved form of *Heuchera americana* called 'Palace Purple'. The fern-like foliage of the coreopsis needs a positive contrast to emphasise its own delicate quality. Both plants grow to about 24in (61cm) high.

There seems to be no other obvious explanation why some plants are regarded with such intimate affection while others receive only half-hearted acclaim. Roses are an obvious example, lavender is another and, of course, honeysuckle. All are flowers which are referred to in the fondest of terms by gardeners and non-gardeners alike. The carnations and gillyflowers have figured so largely in garden literature, always being described in the most glowing, emotional phrases, that they too must be included in the list of best loved plants. One writer even recommends a conserve made from gillyflowers as the life and delight of the human race, while Gilbert praises them as 'a cordial, extremely comforting for the noblest part of man, the heart'. There is no doubt that the fragrance of dianthus flowers, be they clove carnations, garden pinks, or the popular sweet william, has a wonderfully soothing and yet refreshing quality that eases away stress. There are so many different varieties to choose from ranging in height from 6 to 24in (15–61cm) that the best advice is to sniff each one before buying. Two well known varieties of garden pink guaranteed to pass the nose test are 'Mrs Sinkins' and 'White Ladies', both with white-petalled blooms and both well able to hold a place in any company. Grey foliage makes the ideal complement to all dianthus, though the plants selected need to be low growing. *Artemesia alba* 'Canescens' with a mass of curling deeply divided silver leaves at around 20in (50cm) high is neat enough, while *Artemesia schmidtiana* 'Nana' with bright silver filigree foliage at only 4–5in (10–13cm) high fits in very well with the smaller-bloomed garden pinks.

For the same reason, perfume more than other qualities, I include 'Burning Bush', *Dictamnus albus* with white flowers, and the mauve-petalled 'Purpureus', for they have leaves as aromatic as their florets. The scent suggests lemon groves full of ripening fruit and is crisply refreshing. Both grow to about 3ft (0.9m) high with a quality of bud and leaf which is rigidly precise. Plant dictamnus with the lovely *Iris pallida* 'Variegata' which has yellow-striped leaves and pale blue flowers, and include also the feathery grey foliage of Lad's Love, *Artemesia abrotanum*. The French call lad's

Echinops ritro, the globe thistle, is also rewarding in late summer/early autumn, when a second crop of knob-kerrie blooms appears

A garden devoid of scented flowers is merely a painter's colour palette, for a whiff of fragrance stimulates memory quicker than sound or sight. 'Lads Love', gillyflowers, sweet peas, and the whiff of smoke from burning birch logs are a part of my childhood. The clove scent of dianthus brings back memories of the old man, a retired butler, who encouraged my interest in gardening. When he offered me cuttings from one of his choice border carnations I queried as to whether it was the correct time for taking them. With all the ponderous dignity and authority acquired over years of office, he rebuked me with 'When anything offered comes at no cost, then any time is the right time'.

Dierama pulcherrimum will grow readily from seed sown into a sandy compost in early spring. The end product is a sufficient reward, for the flowers are true 'wind hovers'

love 'Atronelle' for the leaves give off a pungent lemony smell when rubbed between the fingers. This is no extravagant riot of colour, just a delicate, restful blend of green and pastel shades.

Either deep or lightly shadowed corners are of considerable advantage·to the garden, for they provide moist coolness even during the heat of midsummer. The interplay of light and shade brings out such a variety of unsuspected colour tones in leaf and flower that it is worth taking care with the planting to exploit them. *Trillium grandiflorum*, the delightful, single-petalled, pure white 'Wake Robin', revels in shade conditions. The flowers open on 10in (25cm) stems during April. Make this only a beginning, a frontal piece, with the blue Himalayan poppy, *Meconopsis betonicifolia*, or the even larger, more electric-blue-petalled *Meconopsis* 'Sleive Donard' behind, to bloom in late June.

Lighten the deeper shaded areas with a dwarf form of 'Goats Beard' *Aruncus dioicus Kneiffii*, which carries ivory-white feathery flower plumes over dark-green fern-like foliage. Though the ever reliable hosta always suggest themselves as colonisers of shade situations, *Veratrum album* or the darker-flowered *nigrum*, both with large deeply ribbed leaves, serve the purpose even better. The leaves of *Veratrum* are less likely to be turned into lace curtains by the omnivorous slug than those of the hosta.

A deep leaf mould or similarly humus-rich, moist soil is all Meconopsis *and* Trillium *ask. I would happily excavate 3ft (0.9m) deep to provide it and be rewarded by these exquisite flowers.*

Iris have such an elegance of form that they enhance any context

Iris pallida 'Variegata' (below left) can be used to provide a change of foliage pattern in shrub or herbaceous border and *I. sibirica* (right) planted alongside *Weigela florida* 'Variegata' is an interesting combination

Cool shade and a moist, humus-rich soil suit some bulbs, particularly the North American lilies which are amongst the loveliest of all that noble clan. There is *Lilium grayi* with deep-crimson, slightly drooping flowers which hails from the Alleghany mountain glades, or *Lilium canadense*, the Canada lily, which is really misnamed for it grows wild in the Appalachian Highlands and southward to Virginia as well. The large nodding yellow bell-shaped blooms open with those of *grayi* from late June into July. Even the 'Leopard Lily', *Lilium pardalinum*, from the Giant Redwood country in California grows vigorously in the same soil and situation. They have flowers with bright orange petals deepening to crimson at the tips. All these most handsome species blossom on stems 1½–2yd (1.4–1.8m) high.

Once a nucleus is established the colony can be extended at will. *Tricyrtis formosana*, the curiously marked 'Toad Lily' with mauve flowers on stiffly erect stems, is a most interesting 10in (25cm) perennial which blooms in September.

Some of the most delicately formed of tiny daffodils will not thrive in light soil which dries out in summer, and a place at the front of a moisture-retentive shade border suits them admirably. To see the *Narcissus asturiensis* growing mixed together with mauve-flowered dog tooth violet, *Erythronium dens-canis*, as they do in northern Spain brings a warm glow of satisfaction.

Even a small patch of shade can be fashioned into a mini-wetland if the soil is given a generous dressing of peat, leaf mould, or compost to hold the moisture in dry weather. A piece of tuffa or porous sandstone will provide a toehold for the tiny creeping *Arenaria balearica* from the Balearic Islands. Slowly this lover of cool moist shade will spread a carpet of diminutive bright green foliage over the stone, so like moss, until myriads of white flowers open on ¾in (1.9cm) stems to flirt and dance with even the merest whisper of a breeze. Grow the *Saxifraga* 'Cloth of Gold' like a mossy argent cushion and *S.* 'Pixie' also neatly hummock forming with red flowers as company for the *Arenaria*.

Ferns are an indispensable part of any cool shade community for they have a character and charm which is uniquely their own. *Asplenium adiantum-nigrum*, with fronds of heavy textured greenness, or the tiny maidenhair spleenwort, *Asplenium trichomanes* with opposite pairs of leaves arranged on black stems, are both worthy of closer acquaintance. There are plants so modestly self-effacing that unless they are given sympathetic company it is easy to overlook them. *Uvularia grandiflora* is just such a one, yet given close association with ferns the arching 18in (46cm) high stems, hung in May with pendent yellow bell flowers, are utterly charming. *Gentiana asclepiadea* 'Alba' is of similar character to the modest North American *Uvularia*. The curving stems carrying sprays of white flowers gain in expression against a background of ferns. Blooming is delayed in shade until September so plant also a *Fuchsia magellanica* 'Aurea' with yellow leaves and red flowers to hold court with the gentian.

One of the many rewards for planting a garden is to be found in the quantity and quality of the wildlife it attracts. Peacock butterflies clustered on the flowers of Buddleia *'Lochinch' or, for me, swallowtails newly hatched from imported eggs flying off to land on* Coreopsis *flowers: a moment of fine-textured loveliness. brighter for being often recalled.*

Festuca glauca, growing only 6–9in (15–23cm) high, forms thick tufts of grey-green leaves. The delicate, graceful, purple-tinted flower heads are a feature during June and July

Summer

tude, with so many sunlit tomorrows if all is not completed today. Scarcely has twilight deepened to darkness than a thrush from a perch high up in the ash tree announces another day, or a garrulous working party of rooks goes reaving down to the corn lands in the valley.

Most of my working days have been spent in gardens, so my memories of summers are a mixture of laborious toil relieved by interludes of such beauty and satisfaction that all the effort is made worthwhile. On many occasions, greenhouse duty had me out of bed at sunrise to pull down shades on melon frames and open ventilators on the peach and vine houses. In the evenings, returning to shut them down found me walking around in twilight. After long practice I honestly believe it would have been possible to do this with my eyes shut. For the scent from the various greenhouses would have been sufficient guide: pungent aroma of tomato, delicate fragrance of peach, and the mouthwatering bouquet of melon, then the walk back along the rows of sweet peas, and the annual border where mignonette and night-scented stock grew to steer me along the broad grass walk into the rose garden. Even now I cannot decide which is the best time to be abroad in the garden: dawn or dusk.

Astrantia maxima, choicest of the 'masterworts', provides a refreshingly cool contrast to the brighter summer flowers. All 'masterworts', with their curiously formed, paper-textured flowers are good for drying. Any soil which does not dry out in summer suits this Elizabethan-ruffed, herbaceous perennial

Summer is the lodestar on which all our gardening hopes and joyful anticipation are fixed. Recollection of July days spent in the garden provides the best incentive for all the work of preparation which needs to be done during the winter. In spring we put into practice the plans made during winter with summer in mind. The quality of crops we harvest during autumn depends to a large extent on the weather during this, the second and warmest season of the year.

Often when wearied with the sometimes laborious work of preparation I have paused to lean on spade or rake and seen the bare earth carrying a crop of vegetables, or a riot of flowers. Though there is a lot of work to be done in summer the days are long enough to allow a leisurely approach, a mañana-of-Mexico atti-

The name bladder senna so perfectly describes the inflated seed pods of *Colutea arborescens* that the botanical name seems superfluous. A useful 43in (3m) high yellow, pea-flowered shrub, sometimes found growing wild on railway embankments.

Late June, with all the planting completed, leaves only routine work, weeding, mowing, and rotational harvesting of vegetables. There is a comfortable sense after the frenetic rush of spring that I am in control. Usually at this stage the lawn mower breaks down, rabbits eat the choicest bedding plants, or moles turn the smooth-mown lawn into a ploughed field.

These are minor inconveniences which serve only to qualify the placidity of sunlit days. Always in retrospect past summers shared this quality. The reality of now is vastly different. Rain prevents me cutting the grass until it has grown so long only the hover mower will cope. Then all the debris has to be hand-raked, which takes up time which I had set aside for dead-heading roses. Just as strawberries are ripening, the weather often turns humid and damp, reducing succulent red berries to something even the blackbirds refuse to eat.

Always in the garden there is the joy of anticipation. The bed planted up with the newest HT and floribunda roses more than justifies in the colour and quality of bloom what

A border devoted entirely to the cultivation of herbaceous perennials luxuriates in the hot June sunshine

seemed at the time of planting an expensive extravagance. A note is then made to invite the less-than-enthusiastic bank manager round to share the profit from our joint investment.

Annuals offer the cheapest and least permanent way of changing the whole character of a garden, but I grow more than merely annual plants from seed. At this moment there is a seedling labelled 'Oriental Lily' now properly identified as *Lilium speciosum* in bloom. I kept the bulb growing on in a pot and now the deep-red reflexing petals of the lovely flower are filling the house with their perfume. What matter that three years have passed since the seeds were sown. In the greenhouse there is a seedling *Magnolia sieboldii* due to carry blossom next year in June. Four oak trees raised from acorns gathered under the patriarchal oak growing in the grounds of a stately home will cast a grateful shade on some labouring gardener a century from now.

9

Gardens within Gardens

The Planning of Gardens. *John Parkinson Bland writing almost a hundred years ago from the midst, as he termed it, of a horticulturual revolution:*

Nothing in gardening is so difficult as the planning of a garden; and it is peculiarly difficult now because we are still in the midst of a revolution, a return to nature, which has upset all the old ideas and conventions of garden design both good and bad. This return to nature has done much good. It has taught us to love plants for their natural beauty and to grow them so that their natural beauty may be shown to the best advantage. But it has not taught us, nor can it teach us, the art of garden design. For a garden is, and always must be, something quite different from a wild paradise of flowers, and no art can turn it into one.

From this it would seem the concept of wilderness and wild life gardening is not new, merely a resurrection of an old idea.

On thoroughness according to Reginald Farrer:

Never scant initial trouble, never despise it. Half the world's horticultural tragedies arise because gardeners, for one reason or another, fail to make their preparations complete, fail to be thorough with the long, tiresome and sometimes expensive preparatory measures.

How very true that is.

All painters, so logic insists, ought to paint what they themselves most love. For the same reason gardeners should grow those plants which they find most attractive, otherwise the whole business becomes a toil not a pleasure.

Design the garden then to suit your own personal sense of what is beautiful. Never mind if no one else finds the arrangement pleasing; so long as you the gardener are content, that is enough. A selfish attitude certainly, yet such singlemindedness of purpose is the only way of realising and finding expression for creativity and artistry. Even a small garden is like a series of segments, each one featuring or presenting a different gardening form: roses, mixed border, bedding scheme, rock garden, pool or any other specialist item which fancy dictates finds a place, though with the dimension of each scaled down in proportion to the space available.

All these individual segments must be linked together, for only in the very large garden can each unit be given enough expression to be self-sufficient. A smooth, well-kept area of grass is the most effective way of bringing the various features together. A closely mown sweep of lawn is restful to the eye, a bringer of order out of a chaos of mixed flower colours and a creator of space by lending perspective to what might otherwise appear cramped and congested. Indeed, in all things the soft green of grass is the catalyst supreme.

Grass is just another crop which like the rose or delphinium grows best in well cultivated, weed-free soil. Good drainage is as important a factor when laying down a lawn as it is elsewhere in the garden, as anyone who has struggled to cut grass during a wet summer will appreciate. Digging the soil over and removing all perennial weeds will improve surface drainage and aeration at the same time. Any rough levelling done at this stage will save backbreaking work with a hand rake during seed-bed preparation. When the soil is in poor condition the physical texture can be improved by working in well made compost, rotted manure, or any other humus-forming organic matter.

Lawns From Seed

Choose a grass seed mixture which will suit the soil and also the purpose for which the lawn will be used. Where a hard wearing sward is of paramount importance, then the mixture should include a proportion of rye grass. Modern strains of rye grass have been developed specifically for use in lawns and are very serviceable without any of the drawbacks once associated with them. Areas of lawn which are in shade for long periods need treating separately, and such pieces should be sown with a mixture which includes shade-tolerant species. For lawns to be used for sitting on, or as a means of access and ornament, then any of the general purpose seed mixtures will be suitable.

The Way and Means

Firm the soil well with·the feet and rake it down to a fine level seed bed, working in a light dressing of superphosphate fertiliser at the same time. Sowing may be carried out whenever weather conditions permit from April through to mid-October. I must admit to preferring late summer as being the ideal time during which to sow grass seed. Usually within a month to six weeks the grass has grown tall enough to need cutting with the mower blades set high, so as to just tip the leaves back to 1in (2.5cm) long. Three or four days later trim it again. During the whole life of a lawn there should never be any need to cut the grass closer than within ¾in (1.9cm) from the base.

Turfing is more expensive than seeding though it, of course, produces a lawn which can be walked on much sooner. Buy only good quality turf; just as much labour goes in laying bad turf as good, and no amount of time, effort, or expenditure will turn inferior meadow grass into a quality lawn. Apart from the obvious differences soil preparation and subsequent cultivations are the same for seeding or turfing to make a lawn. Start feeding the lawn in April and cut the grass at least once a week except during excessively dry weather or the dormant season. This, combined with regular brushing and raking to remove the dead grass which accumulates at soil level, will produce the sort of beautiful lawn which is a feature and focal point for the whole garden. Gravel, paving stones, concrete, astro turf or any other inert substance can never bring that quality of excellence to the garden which a lawn provides. For grass offers such an interplay of colour tones as the light changes when cloud shadows chase across the smooth vivid green. The scent of new mown grass is as much a part of summer as strawberries and cream, both incidentally worth any effort to attain.

The Rock Garden – for Mountain Flowers

A jumble of stones heaped in the middle of a lawn, even when decently hidden behind a curtain of aubrietia and phlox is rarely anything more than incongruous. A slavish attempt to reproduce a scaled-down version of the Eiger as seen from Lauterbrunnen, no matter how well contrived, can never be described as compatible with its surroundings. Nor is there any necessity to spend

A lawn is, in fact, any area of turf which is kept closely mown. Though a lawn is usually formed of grass, I have used other herbage including chamomile, thyme, and moss. The moss lawn was assiduously weeded to keep it free of ash and sycamore saplings, grass and other intruders to form a green velvet carpet under mature trees. Clover which I tried on one occasion was not a success as it bruises and blackens when walked on regularly.

The rules according to Reginald Farrer that govern the ideal rock garden:

Briefly, there is but one. Have an idea, and stick to it. Let your rock garden set out to be something definite, not a mere agglomeration of stones. Let it be a mountain gorge, if you like, or the stony slope of a hill, or a rocky crest, or a peak. But, whatever it be, it must have definiteness of scheme.

A closely mown sweep of lawn is restful to the eye and provides a means of linking individual features

enormous sums of money on importing blocks of limestone, millstone grit, or sandstone when all most alpines require is a well drained soil which is moisture-retentive enough not to dry out completely in summer.

Large quantities of suitable stone for rock garden construction are virtually unobtainable and when they are the cost would make even the most case-hardened bank manager blanch. The supply of top quality water-worn limestone, tuffa rock and weather-sculptured sandstone is only gained at the expense of an already sorely depleted and rapidly diminishing natural wilderness countryside. So abhor the 'almond puddings' which are heaps of soil with stones stuck in at random, with no consideration given to strata or anything else that is natural. Be disdainful of 'dog's graves', those long low mounds of soil with boulders set like a kerb edging all round, which make even less of a proper setting for mountain flowers than a concrete-covered kitchen sink. Be least of all tempted to form a 'devil's lapful' by tipping a heap of builders' leavings, composed of concrete, brick, and stone barely made habitable for plants with driblets of soil half filling the crevices. This last is the worst of all abominations for the space left between the stones which in nature would fill with soil becomes a happy breeding ground for crocus-devouring mice and omnivorous slugs.

SCREE GARDEN

Having constructed numerous rock gardens, large and small, and then had the routine maintenance of them afterwards, I would never build another. No matter how much care is taken to ensure that all the crevices are filled, that drainage is perfect, and that no pockets are left to gather water or even just stagnant air, the majority of rock gardens end up, after a year or two, covered only in the strongest, most durable plants. Maintenance – weeding, pruning, replanting – is laborious, while refurbishing of the soil is impossible without completely dismantling the stonework.

Alpines being then the jewel in the crown of my experience, the ultimate goal of the maturation process and, therefore, an essential part of any garden in my care, there came the problem of how to ensure the best possible growing conditions which could still be constructed to blend in with the overall landscape. The solution occurred to me while descending a scree slope after a day's climbing in the Alps. All around me were rock faces harsh and arid except for the occasional *Phyteuma, Androsace,* or *Eritrichium nanum* growing in a soil-filled crevice. At my feet was a scree formed of broken rock fragments mixed with soil and naturally composting vegetable matter supporting a thriving population of the most rudely healthy alpine plants. Not the commoner, coarser growing alpine meadow sorts, the *Veratrum nigrum, Campanula barbata,* or a lusty *Geranium pratense.* Instead there were *Linaria alpina, Geum reptans,* and in one completely stable, grassed-over scree the delectable *Cyprepedium calceolus* with mountain avens, *Dryas octopetala,* for close company. From that moment I became a student first of scree formation and colonisation, then an enquirer as to how best to turn them into a garden feature.

Screes are formed by the slow weathering process breaking down the rock face – frost and thaw, wind and rain, even sunshine constantly wearing down the most durable of stone. The broken pieces tumble down the steep slope to form loosely packed, unstable scree. Plants scatter seeds amongst the loose stones, at first the annual species, *Linaria alpina, Papaver alpinum,* and *Erinus* which die after a brief, glorious season, then rot to form humus. This rich compost enables the perennials, both herbaceous and shrub, to gain root hold and bind the loose formation of stone firmly together. Fed by nutrient-rich water from the melting snow above, a scree becomes the plant equivalent of a breakfast-in-bed, four-star hotel. For a brief time I revelled in this, for me, completely innovative discovery, only to be made aware that others had been that way before, even to the extent of writing books on how to construct screes and moraines in the garden.

How best then to condense centuries of weathering process into scree formation in a garden over not centuries or years but rather mere weeks of time? Choose, to begin with, the most open site which the garden offers. Keep well out of range of root competition from trees whose branches also drip remorselessly onto any plant growing under them after every shower. Select that place which is

In and out of all the great mountain chains lives *Eritrichium nanum* but high, high up, far above the highest of the *Androsace,* so high that, except with luck, the mere walker can rarely hope to meet with it. Into chinks of the great granite precipices it makes its little cobweb cushions of down that in their time are hidden by the dense mass of its dazzling sky blue blossoms.

I read the above passage from Reginald Farrer's My Rock Garden *before seeing* Eritrichium nanum *growing in the mountains. Even so, I was totally unprepared for that first encounter. The flowers are of that quality of blue which is so electric that they are quite overpoweringly lovely.*

Aubrietia 'Red Carpet' makes abundant growth to hide an ill-constructed rock outcrop

That first view of *Saxifraga retusa* forming a dense, matted mass of shoots along the shores of a mountain tarn remains one of my most vivid memories. Snow-topped mountains, mirror imaged in the crystal-clear water, and the all pervading quiet added to my sense of splendid isolation.

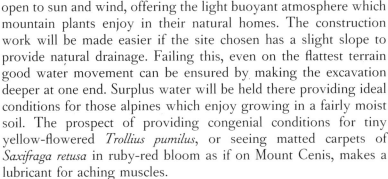

From Alpine Flowers *by* W. *Graveson*

The two phases of alpine and water gardening can be blended into an harmonious whole. The pool and scree becomes a much haunted spot. There the mind is full of pleasant and fruitful reflections.

open to sun and wind, offering the light buoyant atmosphere which mountain plants enjoy in their natural homes. The construction work will be made easier if the site chosen has a slight slope to provide natural drainage. Failing this, even on the flattest terrain good water movement can be ensured by making the excavation deeper at one end. Surplus water will be held there providing ideal conditions for those alpines which enjoy growing in a fairly moist soil. The prospect of providing congenial conditions for tiny yellow-flowered *Trollius pumilus*, or seeing matted carpets of *Saxifraga retusa* in ruby-red bloom as if on Mount Cenis, makes a lubricant for aching muscles.

Excavate the soil to a depth of 20–24in (50–61cm) sloping at the furthest point, if the site is level, to 26–30in (66–75cm). Put the fertile top soil to one side, making sure that all perennial weeds are cleaned out at the same time. As for the inferior subsoil, if it is sandy spread it on the vegetable plot during winter digging. Intractable clay is best loaded onto a skip or truck and taken away. The next stage is to lay a 12in (30.5cm) bed of broken stone in the hole to form the free draining base of the scree.

To make sure the fine topping mixture is not washed down amongst the stones cover them with newspaper, leaves, reversed turf, or coarse peat. The topping-out planting mixture is made up of three or four parts of weed-clean excavated soil, three parts peat, one part finely crushed bark, and five parts of ¾in (1.9cm) crushed stone or gravel. Any plant needing a less spartan diet can be given a handful or two of potting compost around the root at planting time. A further refinement would be to include an underground watering system to enable watering and feeding to be carried out in a completely natural way. There is an even better way of making provision against drought killing the precious scree plants and giving yet another attractive feature to the garden at the same time; simply construct a pool at the highest point. When the water level in the pool drops, top it up so full that the surplus seeps down into the scree. This is so natural a combined feature that it brings into the garden something of the same aura of what is wild and beautiful as the plants do themselves.

THE MOUNTAIN TARN, OR POOLS FORMAL AND INFORMAL

Blending a pool into the surroundings is not particularly difficult. Even a small water feature when introduced into a garden becomes a focus of attention, while at the same time projecting of itself a reflective quality which is pleasantly soothing to the senses. To see house martins dipping low to ripple the pool's surface as they drink, or glimpse mirrored in the stillness the flowers of the iris, astilbe, or primula planted about in the margin, is just a part of the magic quality water brings to any landscape, great or small.

When the pool is joined with scree the surroundings will be clear of light-impeding obstructions. For a pool, like the rock garden, needs to be well away from trees. Roots tend always to grow towards moisture, and deciduous trees shed leaves which foul the water and cause an imbalance in the carefully contrived pool community.

The setting and location of the pool really decides its shape. In a courtyard or formal garden this will need to be precisely geometrical, a square, rectangle, circle or whatever best suits the overall design. When the style of gardening suggests informality the shape of the pool should reflect this and, fortunately, modern waterproof liners make things much easier. Give time, thought, and consultation to deciding the precise shape of the finished article. Use a hosepipe or thick rope to resemble the outline, then lay sheets of newspaper down to simulate water. Remember that, once installed, unlike a greenhouse or garden shed, a pool becomes a fixed asset.

No longer does the would-be pool owner have to mix and lay huge quantities of concrete. The pre-formed pools and rubber type or PVC liners have so simplified the work that a crash course in engineering is not a prerequisite to making a pool. The new Absat liners are reported to outperform the conventional PVC and rubber type previously recommended, with a guaranteed lifetime of twenty years plus. As with most construction work in the garden, installing a pool involves moving large quantities of soil, for the filled level of the water after completion should be at least 24in (61cm) at one point. This safeguard is essential if fish are to be free from any risk of injury during prolonged periods of frosty weather. The base can taper off towards the edges leaving a level platform 14–16in (35–40cm) wide all round the perimeter to be covered with 6–12in (15–30cm) of water. Variations in depth will enable a much wider range of plants to be grown, for some aquatics need a greater covering of water than others.

Once the soil is removed to the required depth: 30in (75cm) for a final water depth of 24in (61cm), check to make certain there are no sharp-edged stones, pointed fragments of root, or pieces of glass to punch holes in the liner as it settles into position under what, after all, will be quite a considerable weight of water. To make assurance double sure, lay a 4in (10cm) layer of soft pebble-free sand over the whole area to be covered by the liner. Make a final check with straight edge and spirit level to make sure the edges are flat, so that the water fills in rim level all the way round. To have a pool brim-full on one side, while showing 6in (15cm) of liner on the other is a mind-unhinging experience, especially when it is impossible, short of dismantling the whole installation, to do anything to rectify the mistake. Stretch the liner evenly over the excavation and place stones, planks, or various members of the family around the edge to hold it taut. Run the water into the stretched liner gradually moving the restraining weights as it settles into position on the sand, with no pleats or wrinkles. This makes a splendidly leisurely way of completing the construction work. Trim away the surplus liner and disguise the edge with gravel or stone chippings, paving flags, or grass, depending on whether the pool is part of a formal or informal design.

Reginald Farrer on building a rock pool. Beyond general hints and recommendations I can preach no definite gospel. There is no royal road to gardening. I myself have bought with much failure the joy of some success.

OPPOSITE
A streamside planting with candelabra primulas (*Harlow Car Gardens, Harrogate*)

BELOW RIGHT
Dodecatheon media grows wild in North American open woodland, meadows, and moist prairie lands. I grow numerous plants from seed the shade border or near the pool. 'Shooting stars' describes the flowers perfectly.

BELOW
A shadow-patterned pool, with *Caltha palustris* 'Plena' in early spring (*York Gate, Leeds*)

The Better Part is Choosing the Plants

Alpines can be planted at any time during the period March to September, but water plants are generally best put into position early in their growing season during spring or early summer. Though the main glory of the pool will be found in the extraordinarily beautiful blooms of water lilies, there are other plants which, though less colourful, are almost of the same importance in terms of providing a healthy habitat. In the pool as elsewhere in the garden all planting must be done with a purpose. There are those plants defined as oxygenators which utilise waste products that would otherwise quickly turn the water into a foul-smelling bilge, while at the same time releasing oxygen. They perform, in fact, precisely the same service under water that the majority of green-leaved plants provide on dry land. So a complete water garden feature should include water lilies, floating plants, marginals, deep marginals, and oxygenators. Add to the abundant

flora an equally essential fauna in the shape of the Ramshorn snail, *Planorbus corneus*, and ornamental fish of various sorts and a pool becomes such a thriving, populous source of interest that leaning on a hoe quietly watching all the activity is a part of the daily routine. A well planted pool is a completely autonomous, nearly self-maintaining world, once the individual units are correctly balanced. The plants and snails utilise the abundance of mineral salts and algae that result from the waste products of the fish, while in return giving shade and protection with their foliage to the fauna which share the habitat with them. The foliage of all the various plants should not be allowed to cover more than 60 per cent of the water surface. Having introduced water as a feature, there seems little point in hiding it under a uniform green, though seasonally flower-decorated, camouflage.

Planting can be done either into beds made up on the pool bottom or, very much to be preferred for maintenance purposes, into baskets specifically designed for the purpose. Fill the pool a week before the plants are to go in so that the water is properly aired and at the correct temperature. Use a good quality heavy loam made from decayed turf or good garden soil to fill the baskets and put a special sachet of slow-release fertiliser, tailor made for aquatics, at root level. Fresh manure should never be included for that encourages the growth of algae, but a little well rotted compost

or manure is acceptable. Remove all dead or damaged tissue before planting up and firm the roots in well, even to the extent of pegging or tying them securely to the container. Cover the soil surface with gravel to prevent it floating off when lowered into the pool. Most important, thoroughly soak each basket after it is filled so that no air is left in the soil to bubble up and disturb the gravel topping.

Oxygenating plants have no root system, so they need a pebble or similar non-toxic weight fastening to the stem just as an anchor to hold them to the bottom of the pond. *Hottonia palustris*, with handsome submerged leaves and spikes of palest lilac-coloured flowers in June, is a useful oxygenator of water.

Fish, snails, and any other fauna are best held in reserve for at least three weeks to allow time for the pond to produce a habitat which will suit them.

For the linking of pool to garden choose plants which will happily accommodate to shallow water or just very moist soil. *Caltha palustris* 'Kingcups' which grow wild in wet northern pastures are ideal for the purpose, especially the double-flowered, exceedingly attractive, and more neatly compact *Caltha palustris* 'Plena'. Lady's smock grows wild in close association with the caltha, and a pleasant native community can be built up using garden-worthy natives. Again plant the double form *Cardamine pratensis* 'Flore Pleno', for the single spreads by seeds and fallen leaves to become in a very short time a pretty lilac-flowered pest. The ultimate height of the kingcup and lady's smock is about 12in (30cm).

Plants with grass-like foliage are useful, offering a change in shape and pattern. The form of *Carex elata* known as 'Bowles Golden' is very decorative when grown as a marginal. Sometimes listed as *Carex elata* 'Aurea', the rich golden leaves grow to between 15 and 30in (38–80cm) high.

Fortunately, the water forget-me-not, *Myosotis scorpioides*, is easily controlled, for even the very desirable cultivar 'Mermaid' can spread fairly quickly. The flowers persuade forgiveness of an over-robust enthusiasm, being clear blue with a yellow eye, opening on stems about 9in (23cm) long.

The 'Monkey Musks' – various species and forms of *Mimulus* – are all natives of America which comes as something of a surprise considering how well some have naturalised along the banks and in the beds of fast-flowing moorland streams. Avoid only one, *Mimulus guttatus* which is such an invasive weed that it even competes with couch grass. For the rest, try any which attract your interest, for the dwarf forms like 'Whitecroft Scarlet' are brilliant additions to the waterside ensemble.

Acorus gramineus 'Variegatus' with tufts of dark green iris-like foliage, striped and marbled with yellow, is best planted in shallow water where it will afford year-round colour and grow 6–8in (15–20cm) high. *Calla palustris* with white arum-like flowers in late summer is of similar quality, albeit dwarfer in stature at 4–5in (10–13cm).

Of all the iris which have proved hardy outdoors in a temperate climate, *Iris laevigata* 'Variegata', with cream and green-striped

The globe flowers represented by Trollius europaeus *are easily grown, moisture-loving plants which like the kingcups fit easily into the wetland pool complex.*

Mimulus 'Queen's Pride' is compact growing and very floriferous. Good for planting in shady corners

leaves forming a refined contrast to the lavender-blue flowers, is as beautiful as any, and grows quite happily in moist soil or water up to 6in (15cm) deep to a height of 18in (46cm). Try also *Iris ensata spontanea* (kaempferi) in any moist soil which is free of lime. The velvet-textured quality of the large, delicately veined flowers is so richly fashioned that it is no wonder that in Japan the *Iris ensata* is given the same pre-eminence as the chrysanthemum, paeonia, or cherry. Both like a rich soil, particularly the *Iris ensata spontanea*, and need to be kept in what a friend of mine described as 'the dry side of wet' during the winter months, then flooded with water in the summer. Names like Koki-no-Iro, and Gei-sho-Ui make Latin titles almost acceptable by comparison. Most cultivars grow to about 24in (61cm).

As the habitat becomes positively aquatic with the water deepening to 12in (30cm), so the plants become more specialist though no less attractive. Bog bean, *Menyanthes trifoliata*, as the popular name implies, has leaves very like the broad bean. White flowers with a curiously coquettish fringe push up out of the water in late spring.

Blue, summer flowering, aquatics are not so common, so *Pontederia cordata*, with the distinctive name of pickerel weed, in spite of growing rather large, is most welcome. It is tall, 24in (61cm), yet the light blue flowers spotted with green are numerous enough and sufficiently appealing for the regular division required to keep it in bounds to be a small price to pay.

Plants which have scented flowers are always deserving of a special commendation so water hawthorn, *Aponogeton*, figures high on any list of deeper-water inhabitants. Waxy-white flowers with conspicuous black stamens rest lightly on the water amongst strap-shaped foliage and are a feature in spring, then again in late summer. The fragrance reminds me of vanilla-flavoured ice cream. This one will grow happily and seed itself in water up to 24in (61cm) deep.

As a supplement to the floating oxygenator, *Hottonia*, mentioned earlier, a useful submerged aerating plant with pleasing feathery foliage will be found in hornwort, *Ceratophyllum demersum*.

So then to the water lilies, those aptly named *Nymphaea* of the botanist which offer such sculptured beauty of flower and leaf in return for our hospitality. They form a focus of interest when in bloom, and the foliage provides shade and a place for damsel flies to sunbathe and, on occasion, stepping stones for insect-hunting wagtails. *Nymphaea Froebelii* with deep crimson flowers is one of the very best and will grow in shallow water or deep – anything from 9 to 24in (23–61cm), a most amenable, free flowering, tidy foliaged variety. There needs to be compatibility between leaf and flower colour which is very evident with a variety called 'James Brydon', whose large rose-pink flowers sit like tinted goblets on round, dark-green leaves. 'Sunrise' is of that quality of yellow which marries with the pink and cream petal colour of the ever reliable 'Masaniello' while 'Rose Arey' with cerise-pink petals has a pleasing and very noticeable fragrance.

Primula rosea, first of the clan to flower, usually during March

Saxifraga oppositifolia growing along the banks of a stream above Lauteret, near La Grave, France

PLANTING THE SCREE

There are so many choice and interesting plants to grow in the moist soil at the lower end of the scree that it is hard to choose. Primula are an essential part beginning with the earliest to flower – *Primula rosea* with magenta-red flowers that will brighten March days – together with the tiny *Narcissus cyclamineus*. There are other primula taller than rosea's modest 12in (30cm) to carry the pageant through summer to autumn. Species of candelabra habit such as *P.beesiana*, *P.bulleyana*, *P.japonica*, and *P.pulverulenta* will cross-hybridise with a carefree promiscuity to produce a race of hybrids with flowers all shades of the rainbow. Add then astilbes with feathery plumes of flowers and the solidly respectable hosta to give foliage contrast and the picture builds into a landscape altogether delightful and different.

There are other superb moisture-loving plants. Purple loose-strife, *Lythrum salicaria* 'The Rocket', is one to grow with *Iris versicolor* and other drought-hating members of the clan. Try also *Kirengeshoma palmata*, a plant of exceeding beauty whose flowers of cool yellow open on the arching 3ft (0.9m) stems in late August. They look well in company with willow gentian, *G.asclepiadea*, which has the same habit of growth and flowers of a rich, pure blue shade. The white and blue *Aconitum napellus bicolor* completes an arrangement of great quality.

To bring the planting height gradually down to the drier conditions midway between bog and pool, *Hakonechloa macra* 'Alboaurea', a lovely, dainty, variegated 8in (20cm) high grass, is one of the choicest. Grow this alongside the lungwort *Pulmonaria saccharata* 'Highdown' with blue flowers.

There are three bulbs which need moist yet free draining soil to grow well. Two of these are the spring and summer 'Snowflakes', *Leucojum vernum* with white pendent bells of flowers edged green opening on 12in (30cm) high stems, February into March, and *Leucojum aestivum* 'Gravetye', taller at about 18in (46cm) and blooming later by several weeks with the same delicately pencilled green on white bells.

Snake's head fritillary, *Fritillaria meleagris*, is so lovely in a curiously Romanesque way that it is worth trying in any moist corner. The chequer-board-patterned flowers range in colour from mauve to white.

Geranium phaeum, the dusky cranesbill which grows wild along wood edges and damp hedgerows, may not suit all moods, yet the purplish-black nodding blooms are appealing. Put them in company with *Geum chiloense* hybrids whose deep-pink flowers add a certain lustre to the more sombre cranesbill. The *Hemerocallis* 'Stella de Oro', a neatly compact day lily at around 22in (55cm) high, will keep up a succession of canary-yellow, bell-shaped flowers over grass-green foliage.

The change over from wetland to the drier scree can be made by including the *Saxifraga oppositifolia* with red flowers in spring,

All primula seed needs to be sown immediately after harvesting to ensure that most, if not all, will germinate. I gather the capsules as they turn brown and split, then sow the seed 'in the green' to use a professional term which is a quite accurate description; for the seed is frequently not the brown colour which indicates full ripeness. If, for any reason, immediate sowing is not possible I store the seed in a refrigerator. All bought-in seed of doubtful age is given three weeks in the deep freezer which helps break even the most stubborn dormancy.

Geum 'Bell Bank' growing out of an encrustation of ferns makes a cool, shadowed picture. I planted the geum – the ferns came in with some leaf mould

and *Arenaria montana* which is slightly taller with white blooms. Just one or two weather-fissured stones will add a change in level to the flatness. Failing stones, dwarf conifers will give variations in height all the year round. Before buying be sure that any conifer or shrub is not going to outgrow the space allocated and ruin the whole effect.

Chamaecyparis lawsoniana 'Minima Aurea' will maintain the bright yellow leaf colour all year round. More important it will take twelve years or more to grow large enough to match that incredible name. *Chamaecyparis pisifera* 'Nana' is also very slow growing, making a molehill of dark green. *Juniperus squamata* 'Blue Star', as the name suggests, is neatly compact with leaves that are steel blue. *Picea mariana* 'Nana' is also very slow growing with blue-green foliage and will never outgrow a welcome. Amongst the *Thuja* the form of orientalis called 'Aurea Nana' is decidedly the most suitable, making a compactly oval bush of golden green.

Selecting appropriate dwarf shrubs is made much easier by just thinking genuinely alpine. *Daphne retusa* is reasonably easy to grow from seed and I make no excuse for mentioning it a second time for it is an invaluable shrub. Under scree conditions growth is tighter and more neatly evergreen, without inhibiting flowering. Those deep-rose-purple blooms and their fragrance are abundantly evident in early summer, to be followed by orange-scarlet berries. *Dryas octopetala*, the mountain avens, is lovely in season if it decides to bloom. The white flowers are replaced as they fade by feathery seed heads. The hybrid *Dryas x suendermannii* also makes a tightly prostrate evergreen mat, but the white flowers do not always open to full extent.

Evergreen shrubs from Africa which are reliably hardy in a temperate climate are almost rarer than hairs on a frog. *Euryops acraeus* is a dwarf shrub which forms mounds of silvery-grey leaves

My Californian fuchsia (*Zauschneria californica*) was continuously in flower from 19 July to mid October this year (1989)

smothered in June with large yellow, daisy-like flowers. Possibly the fact that the Drakensburg Mountains are its native home explains this delightful shrub's ability to survive in less hospitable climates.

Amongst the hebe only a few can be found which will remain compact enough to be admitted to the select company of the scree. *Hebe buchananii* is a very dwarf shrub with leaves like green leather. The white blossom offers only a fleeting glance of their quality in midsummer. *Hebe loganioides* is worth noticing simply because it is so un-hebe like: a dwarf 6in (15cm) high shrublet whose white flowers are borne in short terminal racemes during midsummer.

There are not a vast number of shrublets which can startle the unwary with the brilliant colour of their flowers. *Zauschneria* 'Glasnevin' carries spikes of vivid scarlet blooms from late summer into autumn and is quite splendidly self-advertising. Scree conditions are eminently suitable for this 16in (41cm) high shrub for good drainage is essential for its well-being.

High up in the mountains the plants are covered in snow for six or seven months of the year, so all the business of growing, flowering, and seed setting must be completed in the brief summer period. Flowers are abundantly plentiful and brightly coloured as they need to be for most of them are pollinated by insects, and have of necessity to be self-advertising. The danger with this telescoping of the seasons when alpines are cultivated in the unnatural environment of the garden is to have one brief period brimming over with colour followed by seven lean months of mediocrity. Though spring and early summer are the prime flowering seasons, by including annuals and dwarf perennials other than genuine alpine species the interesting sequence of blossom is continuous from February until October. Begin with the *Saxifraga jenkinsiae* which forms tight mounds of glaucous grey leaf rosettes covered in February with almost stemless blush-pink flowers. There is a tiny *Narcissus bulbocodum* from North Africa called *romieuxii* with thread-like green leaves and yellow hooped-petticoat flowers which open with those of the Saxifraga. There are other saxifraga listed in the Kabschia which are of equal worth; *S.apiculata* is one with yellow flowers, while all forms of the Eastern alpine *S.burseriana* are well worth closer acquaintance. A select list will extend the flowering season into April.

Aubrietia, if trimmed hard back after flowering, is amongst the 'must haves' without any doubt. The variety 'Red Carpet' is an excellent plant and looks particularly attractive when grown with *Arabis ferdinandii coburgii* 'Variegata' with patterned foliage and white flowers in contrast to the red-petalled aubrieta.

Campanula are another of the indispensables. After seeing *Campanula cenisia* wandering about in lime-free scree high up in the Alps I have been a compulsive cultivator of all campanula except, of course, that same slate-blue-flowered *cenisia* which so far has refused, indeed resolutely spurned, all my advances. Instead of the petulant prima donna-like *cenisia*, I grow tiny *Campanula cochlearifolia* with harebell flowers on 3in (7.5cm) stems, ranging in colour

Campanula pulla really shows a quite intense dislike of lime, which is the only fault, if fault it is, which can be found against this sovereign of the Alpine bell flowers. I grow a little colony in cool, sandy peat soil where it wanders at will pushing up tufts of bright green leaves, and then, late in the season, single pendulous bells of flowers coloured imperial purple on thin threads of stems.

In a refined lilliputian way, *Campanula cochlearifolia* is a romper spreading by underground stems. It is never a nuisance, though, for it forms little colonies of tiny, shining green leaves with 3in (8cm) high stems carrying white, fairy-thimble flowers. The drawing shows a plant growing in a hollow wall; this specimen is stronger stemmed than those planted in the rock garden

A vigorous, floriferous, suckering dwarf shrub *Zauschneria* is well suited to scree conditions

Helichrysum milfordiae in company with thyme, another lover of well drained soils and hot sunshine. A hollow wall or terrace bed suits it well

from blue to softest lavender and white. *Campanula pulla* will also colonise a corner with tufts of small glossy leaves. The pendulous bells of bright purple are borne on 4in (10cm) high stems in sufficient quantities to satisfy the most demanding gardener. These are lovely especially when sited alongside the grey-green-leaved, red on white daisy-flowered *Anacyclus pyrethrum var. depressus* from the Atlas Mountains.

Dianthus are not usually grown in scree conditions although all of the species need a well drained soil; indeed, some demand the sort of spartan diet which would give even a stonecrop malnutrition, so the free draining grit soil of the scree suits their needs very well. *Dianthus alpinus* is one of the very choice species growing wild in the European Alps. There and in the garden it grows into a close, ground-hugging mat of narrow green leaves. Large, rounded, deep-rose flowers push up on 2in (5cm) high stems during June. *Dianthus erinaceus*, like a vegetable hedgehog of glaucous green leaves topped by pairs of rose-pink flowers, will only survive outdoors in a hot, dry position. Where there is space the lovely native Cheddar pink, *Dianthus gratianopolitanus*, offers flowers of deep rose pink with a fragrance reminiscent of Malmaison carnations, which were noted for their perfume. In limited space the neater, more compact Dianthus 'La Bourboule' will perform a similar service. Grow the equally diminutive *Allium cyaneum*, or *A.beesianum* with heads of bright cobalt-blue flowers on 6in (15cm) stems as a savoury complement to the dianthus, for these attractive little Chinese

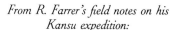

members of the onion family are worth cultivating as plants of real character.

Most geraniums look their best when allowed space to achieve full expression in the mixed shrub and herbaceous border. There are a few so small that their charm would be completely overlooked in the rough and tumble of the open garden. For though all the species and varieties of geranium have a remarkable ability to harmonise with their surroundings which makes them invaluable, they share a certain sympathy with some plants more than others. *Geranium argenteum* 'Roseum' with finely divided, silken-haired leaves and deep-pink flowers is a 4in (10cm) gem. The company which 'Roseum' finds most congenial is that of a *Helichrysum milfordiae* from South Africa which forms a carpet of silver-leaved rosettes covered in summer with crimson-backed buds that open into white, paper-textured, everlasting flowers. Grouped around a 'Noah's Ark' pine, *Juniperus communis* 'Compressa', they express a perfect example of refined elegance. Grown under scree conditions that most attractive of hybrids from *Geranium cinereum* called 'Ballerina' is less robustly vigorous, growing to a compact 3–4in (8–10cm) without any reduction in the number or quality of the

From R. Farrer's field notes on his Kansu expedition:

Geranium nepuligerum (now farreri) number F201 species nova. 'A lovely plant akin to *Geranium argenteum* in style and beauty ramifying in the topmost shale or limestone scree of the Thibetian Alps at 13,000 feet. Only two good seeds could be procured, but it is hoped rhizomes may follow'.

Geranium 'Ballerina' planted in fairly rich scree grows more neatly compact at only 3 or 4in (7 or 10cm) high

lilac-pink, red-purple-veined flowers. The mat-forming *Sedum spathulifolium* 'Purpureum' acts both as a foil and a complement with purple leaves and golden flowers which overlap with those of the geranium to extend the interest into late summer. Though most geraniums are native to Europe there is one species, *G.farreri*, which grows on red shale or limestone screes at 13,000ft in the Tibetan Alps. As Farrer himself insists, 'No other in the race compares with this Tibetan treasure as it turns the gaunt shingle to a crowded dance of its faintly flushing blossom'. In less poetic terms *G.farreri*, or as some insist it should be called *G.Nepuligerum*, forms tufts of grey-green foliage. Then in June–July the large cup-shaped blossoms with the soft apple-blossom pink shading of the petals enhanced by jet-black anthers open on 3in (8cm) tall stems.

In a fit of exasperation I moved a *Silene acaulis* from another part of the garden where it had formed not a single flower into the scree. It responded in the first and second year by covering the congested mat of small bright green leaves in stemless pink flowers. Fortunately, these for the most part have faded before those of the geranium open, for the colour is what could be described as extravagant.

In the hottest, driest, most arid parts of the scree *Sempervivum* may be planted to form a web of fleshy rosettes, especially those with marblings of brown, red, or bronze mixed with the base green colour. There are also species of house leek sempervivum, where the tightly packed rosettes are netted over with a lacework of fine white hairs. The best known of these 'Cobweb House Leeks' are *S.arachnoideum* and *S.ciliosum*. The commonest species without a hairy covering is *S.tectorum* which has the largest, most curiously coloured leaves. This, the oldest of all, was known to the ancient Greeks and illustrated in manuscripts dating back to the first century AD and the time of Dioscurides. In this country house leeks are often seen growing on stone roofed houses where they are supposed to give some protection from lightning, which explains the popular name.

Encrusted saxifraga revel in the same conditions as the house leeks, particularly if they are grouted in limestone chips which serve to increase the white encrustation over the grey-green leaves. The species most often grown are *Saxifraga cotyledon, paniculata callosa, cocklearis minor*, and *lingulata*. Unlike the flowers of sempervivum, those of the saxifraga are carried in graceful pyramids of white and pink.

Annuals, here as elsewhere in the garden, can be sown to fill in the empty spaces as they do quite naturally high on the mountain slopes. *Linaria alpina* is a short-lived perennial with blue-grey leaves and violet, orange-lipped toad flax flowers. *Erinus alpinus* grows only 2in (5cm) high with lavender-pink to carmine-red corymbs of flowers. To complete the trio, there is *Papaver alpinum*, the dainty alpine poppy with an elfin charm which is emphasised by the grandeur of the terrain in which it chooses to grow. Tufts of deeply segmented leaves support wiry stems topped by silken-petalled flowers in shades of pink, white, or yellow. Just mix the seed in a sandy compost and sow it around and about the scree.

Alpine poppies are what my daughter once described as 'fairy flowers'. Papaver alpinum *makes a poor perennial when grown in rich soil and low corners of the rock work. In scree or thin gravelly loam it forms neat tufts of foliage and flowers profusely. It makes a long tap root and dislikes being transplanted.*

When the busy world threatens a little too closely, go and share the company of the mountain flowers growing in the scree for they bring with them to the garden some of the care-eroding serenity which permeates the slopes and craggy ravines of the mountainous regions of the world.

THE ORCHARD AS A GARDEN WITHIN A GARDEN

'Hold beauty fast, she is the most certain solace for so many human sorrows.' Can there be a more perfect symbol of spring than an orchard as the trees are transformed by the annual festival of blossom? For an orchard, whether the trees are smooth stemmed or gnarled and fissured with age, communicates a gentle yet sometimes sharply poignant beauty that is always expressive of youth and all the freshness of early morning. Yet the apple also denotes autumn; even the old crab apple hung with scarlet globe fruits glinting amongst the dark-green leaves is a shrine to the goddess Pomona and a tribute to her season. There is a richness, a special quality of flavour, about an apple picked with the cool dew of night still moist on the skin which makes the eating of it a solemn rite. The smell of damp earth, of decaying leaves, all mixed up with the aroma of ripe fruit is an incense of autumn.

The names of old apples date back to the thirteenth century, Pearmains and Costards which gave the name 'Costermonger' to the people who sold the pies made from the fruit. There were the Queenings, Codlings, and Pomewater of Elizabethan times, and the Apple John of Falstaff. Then in the centuries when the country manor house reached the point of highest development there was a great surge of interest and experiment with both old and new varieties of fruit, particularly apples – Quarrendons, Nonpareils, Russets, and Cockagees. The Ribston Pippin growing in the orchard my father maintained was first grown at Ribston Hall in Yorkshire in the early 1700s. Most of the twenty or more varieties in the same orchard were the result of all the pip sowing, crossing, and hybridising which continued through the nineteenth century. Cox's Orange Pippin, still with no equal for flavour, was first planted in 1830. Bramley's Seedling, the best known cooker, was introduced over a century ago in 1876. The hybridising done by the Laxton family produced 'Laxton's Superb', 'Lord Lambourne', and the distinctively aromatic 'Epicure'.

H. V. Taylor's *Apples of England* points out that apples vary in flavour from sweet, sharp, to acid. Some have little aroma while others are delicate or strong. There are cookers like 'Lord Derby' which froth when cooked, while others like 'Annie Elizabeth' or 'Warners King' are ideal for making dumplings as cooks know well.

The old orchards took up a lot of space, for the rootstocks the trees were grown on made very vigorous growth. Now by using a dwarfing rootstock the gardener can be sure of getting a tree of manageable size which comes into crop within three years, unlike those worked on seedling crab stocks which took sometimes eight years to bear fruit. Laying down even a small orchard can be a

Yet it is the apple which is linked with Pomona, goddess of all the earth's fruits. Married as she was to a husband Vortumnus who throughout their tumultuous courtship kept changing his character and habit of employment, the unfortunate lady needed to find consolation in a quality fruit like the apple. To have a suitor appearing sometimes as a reaper, a fruit grower, a ploughman or a gardener must have been confusing in the extreme. I have a suspicion that Pomona invented cider as a solace and means of overcoming her frustration.

There is a curious legend which concerns St Dunstan and apple trees. Apparently the saint bought in a large quantity of barley to make beer, and in order to ensure a good sale for the brew, came to an arrangement with the devil. The devil would blight the apple trees so that there should be no cider if the saint would sell himself to him. St Dunstan agreed but stipulated that the trees should be blighted in three days, 17, 18 and 19 May. In almanacs the 19th is marked as St Dunstan's Day – just about the time apple trees are in full bloom. A sharp frost then and the blame is laid on poor St Dunstan.

To discover some of the mystical qualities of fruit growing there is need only to stand in an orchard as twilight changes to harvest-moon brightness. The fruit is almost ready for picking and there is all around the organic smell of moist earth, ripe fruit, and that pot-pourri of odours which combined are the tangy smell of autumn – ley lines of gardening reaching back over centuries of time to that fabled garden of the Hesperides.

rewarding and interesting hobby. By careful selection of varieties the flowering season may be extended over several weeks which increases the ornamental value. The same care must be taken to be sure the process of ripening is spread out over several months, beginning in August and continuing through into the year.

Prepare the soil well in advance of planting by turning it over with a spade or plough to get rid of all perennial weeds. Work in some rotted manure, compost, or similar organic matter at the same time. The amount of space given to each tree depends on the vigour of the rootstock chosen. Bush trees, apples and pears, need a 10ft (3m) spacing, while plums and cherries require around 15ft (4.5m) between each one to develop a full head of branches. If the orchard is intended as an ornamental feature as well as to provide a crop of fruit the spacing should be irregular rather than geometrically precise as it is on commercial holdings. Stake each tree firmly so that there is no risk of wind rock breaking the roots as they grow out to take hold in the soil.

There are quite literally scores of different apple varieties to choose from. Those listed below will give a useful return on the investment in labour and money. 'Discovery' is a new scarlet-flushed apple of good flavour if eaten straight from the tree in September. 'Irish Peach' is a smaller, sweet tasting variety which will not keep after picking for more than a few days: a great favourite this one with children who can eat large quantities with no ill effects as my brother and I proved on numerous occasions during so many Augusts when we were children. 'James Grieve' is the good all-rounder; the flowers are carmine and white and the fruit is suitable for both cooking and eating. That old favourite 'Worcester Pearmain' has fruit which if allowed to ripen on the tree are crisp and very juicy, with an aroma of ripe raspberries.

There are several good varieties ripening in October. 'Sunset' raised from a Cox's Orange Pippin is an excellent eating apple, orange and russet coloured. 'Lord Lambourne', the result of a cross between 'James Grieve' and 'Worcester Pearmain', is a variety at its juicy, sweet, rather soft-fleshed best for eating in November. Where it will grow well, no other variety of apple, home grown or imported, can remotely compare with a well ripened Cox's Orange Pippin for it has a piquancy that lingers on the tongue, sharp and most deliciously aromatic. 'Ribston Pippin' offers the nearest competition to a 'Cox', reaching greatest perfection in December. There would be little difficulty in picking out 'Ribston Pippin' in a darkened fruit store by smell alone; it has the strongest, most mouth-watering bouquet of any apples I have grown. Legend has it that this variety was grown from a pip which was taken out of an apple brought over from Normandy in the first decade of the eighteenth century. How many people have marvelled at the burgeoning of blossom against the glaucous green of young growth in spring, or relished with delight the dry, crisply sweet taste and smell over the nearly three hundred years since that first seedling bore fruit.

Apples which will keep until March and April while still retaining

their flavour are somewhat rare. 'Brownlees Russet' qualifies in the first place for the ornamental orchard by having the brightest deep-pink flowers and the fruit which keeps until April has a sharply acid taste. What memories of my grandmother's fruit loft the name 'D'Arcy Spice' conjures up. Even during April this old yellow russet apple from Tolleshunt D'Arcy in Essex carried the rich, mouth-watering crispness of autumn. It is linked always with thin bars of April sunlight through gaps in the orange pantiles throwing patterns on the straw-bedded remnants of the fruit harvest and the crunching of teeth. It is fortunate that such a useful apple should look so very unappetising to adult eyes or none would have been left for us children on those Easter visits to grandmother.

There is not the same long list of cooking apple varieties to choose from. 'Arthur Turner' is worth including for the quality of fruit, and the fact that it also acts as a cross pollinator for 'Bramley's Seedling' is a further recommendation. 'Peasegood Nonesuch' is the most dearly remembered of all, with enormous fruit golden as October sunshine, prettily striped red. Eaten as a dessert apple the flesh is crisp, tender, and sweet. When cooked it needs no added sugar. I have special regard for this variety because on one never to be forgotten day one of the enormous fruit flattened a very aggressive Rhode Island Red cockerel who up till then had attacked me on every opportunity. Being only six or seven years old and wearing shorts left me very vulnerable to beak and slashing spurs. After the Isaac Newton falling apple episode, I only had to walk past and the bird beat a dignified retreat.

Pears, even hardy varieties such as 'Gorham', are best grown on a south-facing wall in northern gardens

Selecting a fruit for eating is a leisurely experience; the sunlight suffusion of red or gold shading, the mouth watering aroma and certainty of enjoyment an essential part of the process. Straining sinews to pick an apple three inches beyond my reach reinforces a long held opinion that the choicest of the crop is always carried on the topmost twigs.

As a late keeping cooker the ever popular 'Bramley's Seedling' is supreme and must be included in any orchard.

There is more to the utility cum ornamental orchard garden than apples. Though pears require a warm, Mediterranean climate to attain full perfection they will succeed when given shelter and a fertile soil. Most flower a fortnight to three weeks ahead of apples, so they have decorative value also. Pear blossom, pure white against a vivid blue sky, with the fresh green growth burgeoning all around, is a majestic sight to be enjoyed just by planting one or two trees. 'Jargonelle' or 'Hessle', though not to be compared with the French varieties in quality of fruit, will grow well. 'Hessle' pears, like 'Irish Peach' apples, are great favourites with children and it forms a pretty rather elegant tree also. 'Gorham', a variety with much larger fruit, is hardy and very fastigiate in growth. I also include in the list that best known of all pears 'Conference' to ripen late in October, for it crops well most years. To carry the season to a conclusion 'Winter Nellis' with small heavily russeted yellow fruit will do well. For most purposes the trees should be grafted on 'Quince A' rootstock.

Plums are the most prolific of all top-fruit. In a favourable season it is often necessary to thin out the crop to stop the branches breaking under the weight as the plums swell to ripeness. 'Czar' is one which is early ripening and good for cooking. 'Victoria', the well known oval, red-fruited plum, is a regular and reliable bearer and certainly first choice in most circumstances. As a late ripening culinary plum, 'Marjorie's Seedling' is excellent. It makes a most acceptable dessert variety if the fruit are left on the trees until fully ripe. With 'Merryweather' for damson jam or home-made wine as a heavy cropping, self-fertile, thoroughly reliable backstop, an orchard could be described as well plummed.

Cherries are the most ornamental of all orchard trees when snowed over with white blossom in late April, early May. There were seven 'Morello' cherries growing in my father's garden along a north-facing wall which each year covered the honey-coloured stonework with a curtain of white. In due course the flowers swelled with a promise of ripe fruit which barely had time to flush pink, let alone turn the black colour of full ripeness, before blackbirds guzzled the lot. Sweet cherries are worth planting even though only the most incurable optimist would expect to taste the ripe fruit. Suitable varieties would be 'Early Rivers' or 'Merton Heart' which, like the 'Morello', shared garden space with me over many years. For smaller orchards and gardens choose cherries grafted on the new Colt rootstock which reduces tree size to approximately two-thirds the dimension of those grown on Malling F12 stocks, and come into crop earlier. Particularly so with the recently introduced, self-compatible sweet cherry called 'Stella' – now first choice for the garden with limited space.

Instead of just grassing the orchard down once the trees are well established the whole area can be made into a garden equivalent of an old-fashioned hay meadow. Some of the old meadows which still survive provide a fascinating example of just how many plants

Orchard plums are the most prolific of all top-fruit, and 'Marjorie's Seedling' is no exception to the rule

will flourish in grassland which is mown only once a year, usually in July or August.

Daffodils and what are popularly known as narcissus are an obvious choice. There is one old orchard which is left undisturbed apart from a minimum of pruning, where the drifts of daffodils planted, according to the owner, in 1938 have spread out into an incredibly lovely shimmering gold and white carpet. The white is that of *Narcissus poeticus* 'Pheasant's Eye', and the tall creamy-white and intensely fragrant 'Cheerfulness' which are so well named for they are in bloom with the earliest fruit blossom.

Orchards are usually bird-haunted places so that when they are transmuted into a tapestry of pink and white, green and gold, there is a swelling choristry of birdsong from the blossom-laden branches. This annual miracle of springtime never stales and, fortunately, whoever planted the original bulbs kept the colours in separate blocks. It begins with drifts of snowdrops, *Galanthus*, near the gate, leading on with narcissus in a dozen different sorts, with snake's head fritillary, *Fritillaria meleagris*, and in one corner below the hedge a small colony of yellow tulip, *Tulipa sylvestris*, holds a place. In due season cowslips, *Primula veris*, show points of yellow to tempt posy-picking children's busy fingers. Foaming heads of the umbelliferous *Anthriscus sylvestris*, 'Queen Anne's Lace', mix with burnet, *Sanguisorba officinales*, and meadow cranesbill, *Geranium pratense*. There are cuckoo flowers, *Cardamine pratensis*, devil's bit scabious, *Succisa pratensis*, so-called because the devil is said to have cut off the root in anger against Jesus, and, of course, yellow rattle, *Rhinanthes minor*, amongst others a part of the company which flourishes in undisturbed grassland. A rust-coloured tint spreads under the trees as sheep's sorrel, *Rumex acetosa*, blooms around the grey and yellow spires of great mullein, *Verbascum thapsus*.

An orchard community can be established by mixing wild flower and grass seed together for the initial sowing. Afterwards it is quite simple to extend the range of interesting wild flowers by plug planting into the sward. The cowslips, cuckoo pint, devil's bit scabious, great mullein and others are best grown in pots or in nursery beds, then transferred to the orchard meadow as seedlings. A standard bulb planter makes the ideal tool as it removes a divot of turf exactly the size of a 3in (8cm) pot. In due process of time a rose 'Wedding Day' may be planted under the strongest growing apple tree and will grow up to hang a curtain of fragrant white flowers through the grey lichen-covered branches.

Clematis montana is another very capable apple tree scrambler, as are honeysuckle and the legendary mistletoe. There are so many ways in which an orchard can be made beautiful and useful so long as the sole purpose is not fruit production. To get the maximum return in fruit, the routine of pruning and spraying has to be adhered to. The grass has to be kept close mown with a clear area of bare earth round the bole of each tree so that there is less competition for the regular application of fertiliser so essential to swell the crop of fruit. There will be no wild flowers and little bird song in such an orchard, only prodigious quantities of fruit.

Meadow cranesbill grows wild along the lanes, and 'cultivated' under the apple trees, in the Dales village of my childhood

Sanguisorba obtusa grows vigorously in competition with the grass

THE MODERN ROSE

In the chapter headed 'A Hint of Grandeur' the hybrid tea and floribunda roses were dismissed in one brief paragraph. Let me try then to explain why a flower which, after all, earns roses the popularity which they enjoy today should be categorised as a segment. There is no doubt that in quality, quantity, and length of their flowering season the hybrid tea and floribunda roses of the twentieth century are far superior both for garden decoration and as cut flowers to those cultivated by gardeners during the eighteenth and nineteenth centuries. Yet in the search for new, more extravagant colours and perfection of form in the flower some quality of refinement has been lost which is still retained by those 'old' roses. That property of fragrance combined with a flower of beauty such as Amytis, favourite wife of King Nebuchadnezzar, enjoyed as she walked under rose-draped arbours in the Hanging Gardens of Babylon in 600BC. Yet those ancient roses of Babylon, and more recently Malmaison, offered only one short season of bloom each year, then the petals fell to leave only thorns.

Once the first hybrid tea rose, believed to be 'La France', was introduced into cultivation a whole new chapter in rose history began. The queen, if not dead, suffered enforced retirement, so long live the new queen. Unfortunately, there is no slow passage of years to ripen acquaintance into friendship as with the old roses. The fashions change and new varieties of HT and floribunda are released onto the market in such rapid succession that the ink on

I sometimes think that never blows so red
The rose as where some buried Caesar bled
That every Hyacinth the garden wears
Dropt in its lap from some once lovely head.

(The Rubaiyat by Omar Khayam)

the name plate is hardly dry before it is time to erase it and write another. So then to a consideration of those beautiful and useful modern bedding roses which should not be grown in too close a proximity to the old shrub roses. There is a good reason, apart from that of hygiene, for one disagrees with the other in much the same discordant way as a modern style of architecture is at variance with a building of the Georgian period.

As mentioned in Chapter 7 roses grow best on heavy rather than light soils. Where drainage is suspect raise the level of the bed the roses are to be planted on above that of the surrounding garden, for there is a world of difference between moisture retention and waterlogging. The soil preparation is as for shrub roses. Unless the soil is naturally alkaline apply a dressing of hydrated lime at the rate of 8oz (200g) per sq yd (sq m). This really is a wise precaution with bedding roses for the soil will be treated with several dressings of compound fertiliser, plus a heavy mulch of some form of organic matter each year – a routine this, guaranteed to reduce the availability of free lime in all except a calcium-based soil. An ideal to aim for is a pH 6.5, which is just on the acid side of neutral. Pruning is an essential part of the annual routine cultivation of hybrid tea and floribunda, much more so than would be the case with shrub roses, whose deterioration when left unpruned is not so rapid and dramatic.

Any pruning which needs doing in the first year is best carried out before planting. This is, after all, the one time such work can be performed from a decently upright position. All weak, damaged, or dead shoots are pruned right out clean to the base, while those that remain are cut back to within three buds of the base. Tip the roots back lightly for this encourages the growth of fine white feeding rootlets which quickly establish a firm hold in their new quarters. After planting is completed the crown, junction between root and branches, should be buried to a depth of 1–2in (2½–5cm). This level will be maintained by annual mulching which needs to be generous enough to compensate for any shrinkage which, if allowed to continue, leaves the top part of the root sticking out above soil level.

In the average garden there is little choice of where the rose bed or beds will be situated. Choose the place most open to the sun and where the air can circulate freely through and around the bushes. Close, sheltered conditions create all sorts of problems, particularly with that bane of all rosarians, mildew, spreading a grey powder over the stems, leaves, and flower buds. This is one reason why the sunken garden proved such a disastrous failure, for only when the breeze can blow through, and sunlight gain access to coax every atom of fragrance from the unfolding petals, can roses achieve full expression free from malaise. Make sure when planting that each individual bush has enough space to develop without becoming too crowded, as much for the benefit of the gardener as the rose. To work comfortably and easily when applying fertiliser, weeding, and dead heading without suffering painful scratches is, surely, a prerequisite for all would-be rosarians.

The Very Rev. W. D. Hole, author of what is still considered to be one of the best books on rose growing wrote:

He who would have beautiful roses in his garden must have beautiful roses in his heart. He must love them well and always, with no ephemeral caprice. The cavalier of the rose has 'semper fidelis' written upon his crest and shield.

All I would add to this is the all-important 'she', for then as now, the female cares for the garden, and roses, on slightly more than equal terms with the male.

Roses come in all shapes, sizes, and flower colours, and it is easy to concentrate our attention on the HT and floribunda varieties to the exclusion of all the rest. The shrub roses have a special old world charm and would be worth a place in the garden for their fragrance alone.

PRUNING – A DETAILED ACCOUNT

Though pruning was mentioned in general terms in Chapter 7, there is need for a more detailed description when dealing specifically with bedding roses. Let those who will argue over what time, and at what phase of the moon, pruning is best carried out. In most years March offers a day so beguilingly warm that being outdoors in a garden bright with flowers and loud with bird song becomes a pleasure.

Established hybrid tea are treated differently from floribunda varieties. Strong growing shoots should be pruned only lightly back to 5 or 7 buds from the base. Those less vigorous are cut with varying degrees of severity, the weakest being shortened to leave only two buds. Before beginning any pruning proper, remove all dead, diseased, or weak wood so that the remaining shoots to be dealt with can be seen in proper relationship and perspective.

Floribunda are, of course, pruned hard prior to planting just like HT. In the second year cut the first season's growth to approximately half their length. This is to establish a strong framework which in theory at least should make the work in subsequent years much easier. In the third year cut half of the old shoots hard back to within three or four buds of the base. This should cause strong growth from near soil level. The shoots remaining should have the previous year's growth reduced by half. The following year these lightly pruned stems are cut hard back, while the rest are treated more leniently. In this way the whole bush is completely rejuvenated every two years. Unfortunately, the same restorative process cannot be similarly applied to gardeners.

Apply the spring feed at the rate of 2oz (50g) per sq yd (sq m) immediately after pruning, working it into the top 2in (5cm) during the general tidying up with a fork or hand cultivator. Never dig amongst established roses, it brings all sorts of trouble on those who are misguided enough to do so. Once the clearing up is finished put on a thick mulch of rotted manure, compost, or similar organic material to cover all the bare earth. A mulch compensates for any shrinkage, conserves moisture, and smothers weeds. In addition, such a mulch gives endless entertainment for blackbirds who in their search for food scatter debris far and wide across the lawn.

As the first flush of flower fades cut the spent bloom clean away back to the first strong bud. Just breaking them off between finger and thumb leaves a dead portion of stem to give access to some noxious disease, and slows down growth of shoots which carry the second crop of blossom. Another feed at 2oz (50g) per sq yd (sq m) applied to the soil and well watered in at this stage will ensure roses in bloom throughout the summer and into autumn.

Much has been written on the subject of pests and diseases which can attack roses. Good husbandry will reduce the risk, so do not be tempted into routine spraying for that is making a rod for your own back. Let nature, in that respect, take its course and only spray when a specific pest or disease becomes intolerable. One thing is

From The Rose and its Culture *by D. T. Fish published over a century ago.* Pruning, from being almost wholly a mere mechanical operation, has been exalted to the dignity of a science, and the old canon – cut deep or hard to find health or bloom – is absolutely reversed by the modern dictum – the less pruning the better, growth is now directed into more profitable channels than the production of fagots for the oven, or the making of charred refuse or burnt earth for the roots of roses.

Some thirty years ago I planted hedges of Prunus 'Trail Blazer', 'Green Glow', and 'Crimson Dwarf' as an experiment in a very exposed garden. The bushes came with instructions to hard prune them all the second year after planting. To make sure I fully understood the nurseryman who sent the various plants for trial arrived, complete with a most vicious looking, heavy duty pair of pruners to demonstrate. All top growth was duly cut back to within 6in (15cm) of soil level; hard pruning I would not have had the courage to carry out, yet it laid the basis of a hedge which thirty years on is still strong, thick, and beautiful.

certain, roses will survive most vicissitudes from frost, snow, drought, bug or blight to gladden summer days with colourful fragrant flowers.

There should be as much time, thought, and artistry applied to the planting of a rose garden as would be given to the compilation of shrub or herbaceous perennial border. To mix a dozen varieties of hybrid tea and floribunda roses together without regard to colour or height contributes nothing to artistry, and does even less for aesthetic appreciation. By using strong colours in bold groups and then complementing or contrasting these with lighter pastel shades, the one will gain in quality from the other. To take full advantage of the individual merits of floribunda and HT roses they should not be grown all in the same bed. The most pleasing effects are achieved with single blocks of colour. Of course, this is only practical when roses are used as a harmonious part of the overall design, and not as a collection of individual varieties, as would be the case when they are the main source of interest.

Two long borders filled with pink-flowered varieties such as 'Blessings', 'Pink Favourite', and 'Silver Lining', edging a paved walk with a lawn as a background, make a superb feature. The subtle variations on a pink theme are like the play of light over a silk shawl, always shifting yet still part of a complete whole.

One of the less pleasant experiences is to be confronted with a mixture of red and yellow. 'National Trust', 'Ingrid Bergman' and 'Velvet Fragrance' are HT roses with flowers in that shade of red which is described by poets as velvet textured. Unfortunately, this is the very shade which when combined, as quite frequently happens, with yellow produces the floral version of a very bad bilious attack. Red is the colour which immediately springs to mind when the word rose is mentioned and, in addition to those already listed, there are others with petals of that particularly inviting shade which if combined with fragrance forms the classic rose of literature and tradition. 'Alec's Red' with dark-green foliage and well formed flowers has the damask scent which should be the generous bounty of all roses. That the blooms when cut will last well in water is also worth noting. 'Royal William' is another deep-red-petalled variety with a most pleasing, fruity fragrance.

White is a very useful shade because it makes such a good catalyst to other colours. There are no pure white roses, most of those described as such are tinged with pink or cream. 'Elizabeth Harkness' with well formed creamy, scented petals makes a useful dual-purpose variety for garden display and flower arranging. 'Peaudouce' has beautifully textured petals and a very pleasant fragrance. Always when asked to select between a shapely rose without scent and another less well formed yet with perfume, the nose takes precedence over the eye every time.

Amongst the yellow-flowered roses 'Freedom' is of that rich golden colour which seems to catch and hold sunlight. A neat, compact habit and useful as a cut flower, this is a prime variety. 'Pot of Gold' is superior because, in addition to being a good garden display and cut flower rose, it has delightful fragrance.

To hold the affectionate interest of the diverse gardening public so firmly, the rose must be and indeed, is a veritable paragon of a plant. Possessed of an outstandingly lovely flower in a wide range of colours, it is capable of adapting to almost any soil or climate. For cutting as indoor decoration and for mass display in the open garden the rose is in all things good.

White and yellow roses are essential to my enjoyment of the garden in the dusky twilight of summer evenings. As the darker colours are absorbed in the fading light, so the white and pale-yellow-petalled flowers gain the ascendancy. For those who have not yet discovered the beauty of early mornings and late evenings in the garden I would suggest the year ahead would be a good time to begin on the exploration.

A rose walk leading to a formal pool is a happy arrangement (*Royal National Rose Society Gardens, St Albans*)

There are roses which combine two or more shades of colour in their flowers. These make useful bridges when used to separate two contrasting colours, so try to choose a variety which contains the two shades between which it is helping to form a link. 'Just Joey' with coppery-orange, frilly edged petals is a good garden rose and subtle enough to match a yellow to a pink. 'Lover's Meeting' is a burned Indian orange shade, lovely with dusky red 'Paul Shirville', the colour of a ripe 'Peregrine' peach with hints of pink, orange, yellow and tangerine in the petals.

To be of really top quality a rose has to be free flowering, weather resistant, and with lustrous foliage. 'Silver Jubilee' is all of these and beautiful, combining shades of pink, apricot, and peach in its flower. By happy chance my first encounter with 'Silver

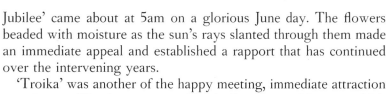

Jubilee' came about at 5am on a glorious June day. The flowers beaded with moisture as the sun's rays slanted through them made an immediate appeal and established a rapport that has continued over the intervening years.

'Troika' was another of the happy meeting, immediate attraction experiences. The flowers are a blend of orange and bronze which needs a carefully chosen background to accommodate the various colour tones. A 'Willow Leaved' pear, *Pyrus salicifolia* 'Pendula', with greyish-green leaves makes a most effective, undemanding background while remaining an attractive and graceful small weeping tree.

There are roses which continue to hold a place though other varieties come and go in seemingly endless succession. Over thirty years have passed since a bundle of bare root roses arrived on my doorstep. Amongst the half dozen varieties for trial was one called 'Piccadilly', and still the red and gold flowers maintain a place. Planted in front of a tapestry hedge made up of *Prunus* 'Trail Blazer' and 'Green Glow', 'Piccadilly' became and remains a favourite.

FLORIBUNDA – ABOUNDING WITH FLOWERS

Whereas the hybrid tea rose offers flowers so beautifully formed and perfect in shape that they invite individual appreciation, the floribunda rose presents blooms in trusses and bouquets and in such profusion as to make it a most colourful, reliable, and long-lasting bedding plant. Properly cared for, it will be in flower from June until late autumn year after year until sheer repetitive boredom demands a change.

The colour from the packed heads of flowers is so vigorously assertive that a single block of a variety such as 'Trumpeter' with orange-scarlet flowers can be too dominant a feature. By catching

'Blessings' is now an old variety in modern rose terms. I first grew it twenty-three years ago, and each June when the first buds open the friendship is reinforced

Nepeta x faassenii really is loved by cats who roll in it, chew it and in general display their affection for this grey-foliaged, lavender-blue-flowered plant in a most destructive way. A few prickly shoots from a thorny shrub such as Berberis gagnepainii *soon diverts the felines' affectionate interest elsewhere. The normal flowering time is in early summer. I prune all growth back by half as the blossom fades and enjoy a second display of colour later in the summer.*

Hebe are so very easily propagated from self-layers and cuttings of semi-ripened shoots taken in early July that I treat them on occasion as semi-permanent fillers. Many of them, including Hebe pinguifolia *'Pagei' make useful weed-suppressing ground cover.*

A different arrangement presented itself in a garden I visited recently. Hebe 'Autumn Glory', a small shrub which opens violet-purple flowers in late summer, looked right royal, or should it be episcopalian against the yellow Robinia *foliage with all bathed in gentle sunlight.*

and holding the eye vivid colours do make a modest-sized garden appear even smaller. Such considerations apart, 'Trumpeter' is a neatly compact and very floriferous bedding variety. The petal colour requires the softening influence of smooth mown grass. 'Disco Dancer' is an even brighter shade of orange scarlet which in sunlight vibrates like a fluorescent light: a difficult colour to place, yet beautiful when hedged around with catmint, *Nepeta x faassenii*. Sprays of lavender-blue flowers lifted above the greyish-green foliage serve as a restraining influence to the self-advertising rose.

Magnolia sieboldii formed a centrepiece to an interesting association of the rose 'Sexy Rexy', a paved path, a bird bath, and a lavender hedge. The use of very positive-charactered roses as units in a mixed design breaks with one of the traditional rules of garden apartheid which insists that roses are only grown with roses. *Magnolia sieboldii* is one of those obliging members of the genus which can be easily grown from seed, making experimental plantings less expensive. The foliage is of a bluish-green shade, while the fragrant white flowers with their central boss of orange-red stamens open intermittently from May to August. The small beds in the paving surrounding the bird bath were planted with grey-leaved, blue-flowered lavender. The rose 'Sexy Rexy' which has flowers of a clear-pink shade formed a crescent in the lawn to complete a lovely piece of design.

Floribunda are compatible with many shrubs or herbaceous perennials, provided these are planted so as not to interfere with the routine pruning and feeding. The so-called hand-painted roses with petals streaked or feathered with red, pink, and white make useful open garden plants. A bush of the pink-and-white-petalled patio rose 'Regensberg' with the blue-grey evergreen-foliaged white-flowered *Hebe pinguifolia* 'Pagei' has the same expressive cool quality as raspberry ripple ice cream. 'Sue Lawley' is a taller version on the same hand-painted theme.

'Iceberg' is one white floribunda which at forty years old has suffered no decline in popularity. A mixture of this and the dark-red 'Robusta' makes a notably long flowering hedge when only lightly pruned. Yellow roses afford such a cheerful tone, even on a dull day, that it is fortunate that there are several first-class varieties available. 'Baby Bio' is a pleasing, compact growing bush with large golden-yellow blooms, freely produced all summer. 'Korresia' is of a similar shade and the large trusses of flowers are scented. The various yellow shades make a pretty compliment to the plain-green or silver-foliaged conifers.

There are so many unexpected moments of rare beauty associated with roses. Even when the flowers are hidden in fading light their perfume is held on the air: an all-pervading reminder of the loveliness that will be there for us to enjoy through long, sunlit days. Though time may erode all things, yet the rose continues to build truth on legend until the position this flower holds in public esteem is assured for as long as there are gardens and gardeners to care for it.

10

The Flower Arranger's Garden

Quite often an interest in the art of flower arranging comes as the natural extension of an enthusiasm for gardening. For some, the beginning of what eventually becomes an absorbing hobby may be almost accidental. A gale force wind often catches the delphiniums in peak flowering, and rescuing the best of the shattered spikes to use as indoor decoration becomes the logical thing to do. Each spring frost threatens early flowering rhododendrons or camellia with black ruin overnight. What then could be more natural than to cut several of the most perfect blooms so that they can be enjoyed unscarred by the weather.

In the larger gardens a special border might be set aside specifically for growing flowers and foliage for cutting. There were two enormous borders in the first garden I worked in 60yd (55m) long by 6yd (5.5m) wide designed as 'cutting borders'. There, the head gardener, with me as basket bearer, selected and cut fresh flowers every day for the house. What surprised me, even though my interests at the time lay more in the direction of things edible rather than ornamental, was the way a room lit up and came alive as the vases were brought in. Great bowls filled with golden daffodils matching the April sunshine streaming in through the long windows. Or the vivid blue of delphiniums arranged in copper water jugs standing in a window recess at the turn of the staircase. The setting sun shining through onto the stems of flowers gave expression to the description vivid blue. Then in October the oak-panelled hall was filled with chrysanthemums, red, gold, bronze, and yellow in such riotous confusion that all the reckless, colourful profligacy of the season seemed to have been compressed into that one room. Even now the pungent scent of chrysanthemums conjures up a picture of an enormous urn full of the single-flowered variety 'Desert Song' which represented my first attempt at arranging flowers. For years the coppery-yellow 'Desert Song' was my favourite variety of this autumn flower.

In the average modern garden there is not sufficient space available to allow the luxury of a cutting border. A row or two of useful flowers, gladiolus, pyrethrum, pinks and chrysanthemums might be squeezed into a corner of the vegetable plot. As for the rest, they must be included as a part of the flower garden proper, serving a dual purpose of being functional and beautiful. What I

A flower arrangement, like a garden, can be too tidy; lacking something of that careless profusion and happy untidiness which allows each individual bloom or leaf a proper expression. Just as a lawn pied with daisies and the casual informality of cat mint, border pinks, or bell flowers tumbling out of a border onto a paved path provides a refreshing change from neat rows of plants and smoothly trim lawn edges.

So the romantic quality of an arrangement where delphiniums grow up together with day lilies through a framework of lady's mantle in seeming disarray is as much an expression of art as the carefully contrived, neatly symmetrical presentation in which each component has a place and purpose.

Flowers in a guest room express a welcome even more than a casual peck on the cheek. A small arrangement of flowers on the dressing table or in the window recess will encourage visitors to feel really welcome.

soon discovered is just how many plants serve a two-fold function, particularly in the case of those called upon to provide background foliage. Indeed, golden privet, laurel, *Pittosporum tenuifolium* and even camellia actually seem to benefit from a little regular, albeit judicious pruning back of over-long shoots. That a garden designed to provide material for cutting should as a result be less attractive than one laid out merely as an expression of artistic taste is just not true. So many of the shrubs, herbaceous perennials, bulbs and annuals which are prized in the garden are also much sought after for cutting. There is the usual problem encountered when deciding which plants to grow, for there are so many to choose from. The selection is made easier by concentrating attention on those plants which provide a steady supply of interesting twigs, foliage and flowers of a sort which would not be readily available elsewhere. For example, the curiously twisted branches of the 'Pekin Willow', *Salix matsudana* 'Tortuosa', are useful in winter arrangements, for they make a few very expensive flowers go a long way. In spring just as the leaf buds unfurl along the straw-yellow shoots they are a perfect associate for the daffodil. When summer brings a glut of

You can put one colour with another in a garden or flower arrangement without any real fear of producing the sort of clash which sets the teeth on edge. What would be a total disaster in a dress fabric becomes perfectly harmonious in an arrangement of flowers.

OPPOSITE
Camellia foliage makes excellent background material for arrangements – the flowers are a bonus

LEFT
Rudbeckia are such reliable cut-and-come-again flowers that they merit inclusion for that reason only. 'Rustic Dwarf', 'Marmalade', and 'Goldilocks' are a joy to see in the borders as are the perennial varieties

Remember that though a predominantly blue-flowered composition can be very lovely, the colour absorbs light to such a degree that it needs to be positioned so that light from a window falls directly on and through the arrangement. In a dark room use yellow, golden and orange-coloured flowers: marigolds, daffodils, rudbeckia and others which carry in their petals the brightness of sunshine.

Alstroemeria 'Ligtu Hybrids' are excellent dual-purpose plants. The glorious trumpet-shaped flowers offer a remarkable range of colours; orange, pink, yellow and salmon shades predominating. Sow the seed in deep pots filled with a free draining seed compost during early spring. I space sow the seeds so the resulting seedlings can be left to grow on for a year without disturbance. The youngsters can then be transferred to their permanent place in the garden. A light, free draining soil in the sun makes alstroemeria a long-term resident

flowers, then the twisted stems introduce a Japanese theme as a restrained alternative to bowls crammed to overflowing with masses of blooms.

Before starting on the work of designing, make a list of those plants which would be your first choice no matter for what purpose the garden was intended. Let the list when completed be the foundation on which the whole garden design is based. There will be afterthoughts as the work of selecting and planting proceeds, and yet it is worth noting how some of the plants on the first list remain firm favourites over many years.

Another interesting point is that plants, whether flower or foliage, that blend harmoniously together when arranged in a vase usually show a similar affinity when grown as neighbours in a border. By looking on the garden as a flower arrangement on a grand scale, working out the design becomes entertaining and educational. Trees and shrubs with interesting shapes, colourful foliage or attractive bark will be the perennial framework. They break up the flatness of the landscape and give a pleasing pattern of light and shade areas which are ever changing.

The leaves of *Alchemilla mollis* and *Bergenia* 'Glockenturn' look so beautiful with early morning sunlight slanting across them that it is worth being out of bed at 6am to see them. Now I adjust the planting so that the sunlight reaches the ground at the earliest possible moment as it clears the boundary hedge. With the green-and-golden-leaved *Euonymus fortunei* 'Sunspot' behind acting as a light reflector, it makes a picture fresh as the morning itself.

So the garden is built up with a series of studies, each one complete in itself, just as an arrangement would grow from first the background of twigs and leaves, then the flowers.

Imagine a path with a view across a broad expanse of lawn to a flower-packed border beyond. A Japanese cherry at the junction where path meets lawn will, in due course, make a framework which concentrates the attention, turning a view into a vista. There will be days when sunlight patterns the path through blossom-laden branches to form a picture so fine and lovely that it remains fixed in memory. That English version of a Japanese cherry 'Pink Perfection' with flowers that are deep rose in the bud just as the bronze young leaves unfurl would serve the purpose admirably.

That some of the plants which are so useful for cutting are not generally available soon becomes obvious. Fortunately the majority can be successfully grown from seed or cuttings, which is much the cheapest way of stocking a garden anyway. There is a natural tendency for people who share a common interest to seek out the company of fellow enthusiasts. The more experienced gardener-floral artists will maintain well stocked gardens. From exchanging information it is a very small step to swapping divisions, cuttings or seeds. Though this may appear to be a slow, rather laborious way of furnishing a garden, nevertheless it ensures everything planted will be useful. There is a mystique which has built up around the successful propagation of plants. Though there are gardeners who can persuade the most dormant seeds to germinate, and when challenged can cause shovel handles to strike roots, their success is more a result of experience and observation than the proverbial green fingers.

Raising plants from seed is the most natural of processes; all the gardener has to do is provide the ideal conditions for germination. By using a standard compost, either loam or peat based, the seedlings are assured of the best possible start in life. To germinate, most seeds require moisture, oxygen, a sufficiently high temperature to stimulate activity and, eventually, a readily available food supply to maintain healthy balanced growth.

Any compost used, no matter how it is made up, should be free of pests, diseases, and weeds. There should be sufficient moisture for the plants' needs, yet drainage has to be good enough to avoid stagnation. The standard composts sold for the purpose of seed sowing fulfill all these essentials. There are exceptions which serve only to prove the general rule. Standard composts are not suitable for raising seedlings of calcifuge plants: rhododendron, camellia, and others which need acid conditions. These temperamental individuals are well catered for with a specially formulated ericacious mixture which is without lime.

Fill the container, pot or box, with compost, firming lightly with the fingers, then use any object with a smooth flat base to produce a level surface on which to sow the seed. All seeds should be sown thinly, for overcrowded seedlings starved for light and air are far more prone to attack from diseases. Make sure also that each pan or tray is properly labelled with the name and date of sowing. This is most important information for though annuals may germinate in a matter of days, some shrubs and perennial seeds may take a year or more to show growth.

Once the seedlings are large enough to handle they will need to be moved into a larger container before they become drawn, overcrowded, or exhaust the available food supply in the compost. As a committed seed sower, I appreciate the benefits to be derived from stocking a garden from home-raised annuals, perennials, shrubs and even trees more than most people. Though *Magnolia stellata* took seven years to produce its first flower there was more rejoicing over that one than over the dozen blooms on a nearby *Magnolia denudata* bought for gold at a local nursery.

Many herbaceous plants and some shrubs may be increased by simply digging them out, then splitting off any young, strong, well rooted pieces for replanting before discarding the older portion. This method of increasing stock assumes that the plant providing the offshoots is already growing in the garden.

Sometimes the introduction to plant propagation by means of cuttings comes about more by accident than design. Cut stalks left for a week or two with one end stuck into moist Oasis frequently root. Such happy occurrences prove how much easier propagation by means of cuttings is than the inexperienced gardener might first think.

There are three types of stem cuttings. Soft wood, which are available early in the growing season, are made from young, soft

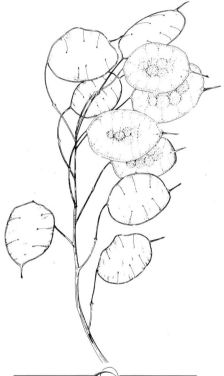

Honesty, Lunaria annua, *is a quick-growing biennial plant with mid-green, coarsely toothed, heart-shaped leaves and scented purple flowers. The fragrant purple flowers are decorative enough, and the silvery pods feature in numerous dried flower collages. Sow seed in nursery beds during May–June. There is a more attractive form, 'Variegata', which has darkly crimson flowers and leaves marbled with a creamy-white variegation.*

shoots before the bark hardens. Because they are so succulent and full of sap they need to be kept in a close and fairly humid atmosphere to prevent them from drying out before roots are formed. Given the right conditions, soft wood cuttings root in ten days to a fortnight. Semi-hardwood cuttings are prepared from shoots midway through the growing season and are the most widely used method of increasing many woody plants: heathers, camellia, small-leaved rhododendron, clematis, and many others. The hardwood cutting is fashioned from fully ripened shoots at the end of the year, during October to early December. This is a useful way of propagating roses and a whole range of popular garden shrubs, for they will root if inserted into a sandy soil outdoors.

For semi-ripe and soft wood cuttings a small frame with bottom heat will give best results. Sharp sand, perlite, or similar inert material makes a good rooting medium. As the confidence bred by success grows, other methods of propagating plants will suggest themselves. Some shrubs will root from sections of stem with a leaf and well developed bud attached. Vines and camellia are most obliging in this respect. There are also plants which have the ability to grow fresh shoots from detached pieces of root. These root sections may be removed at any time from September to mid-May. Any plant with a fleshy root system is worth trying: phlox, romneya, primula, anchusa, poppies and several more have all been introduced to my garden by means of root sections.

There is no aspect of gardening more interesting than that which involves raising new stocks of plants from seed, or by means of cuttings, layers, grafting, and budding. To see the apparently dead husk push up a green shoot or watch a piece of twig casually pushed into compost develop roots and grow new leaves is still to me amazing.

OPPOSITE
Eryngium, the popular herbaceous perennial, provides valuable cut-flower material
BELOW
Vitis coignetiae is one of the most spectacular autumn colouring vines, and easily propagated from stem sections

Rhododendrons, viburnum and shrubs of similar character are very expensive to buy, so when some do need to be included as providers of cut material I automatically layer any of the convenient branches, whether there is a need to increase stock or not. Any young, non-flowering shoot which can easily be pulled down to the ground may be tried as material for propagation. Prepare the soil beforehand by forking in a dressing of coarse sand and peat. Pull down the branch to be layered and where the underside touches the soil make a cut to form a tongue 1–3in (2.5–7.5cm) long. Use a piece of twig to hold the wound open, then bury it 3–4in (7.5–10cm) in the compost and peg it firmly in place. In addition to the peg, I use a large stone to hold down the layer. In about eighteen months it should be well rooted.

For all forms of vegetative propagation access to a stock plant which will provide suitable cutting material is essential. Stealing cuttings is not the way. There are various descriptions used to define plants scarred by thieves ripping off shoots. 'Pockler's pestilence', 'finger blight', and 'pilferer's pox' are three of the printable definitions.

There are several shrubs which because of an ability to thrive in almost any soil and situation are dismissed by the gardening *bon-ton* as 'common', meaning undistinguished. *Aucuba japonica* 'Variegata', in the sense meaning widely planted is, indeed, frequently met with, yet is far from being merely commonplace. How a shrub which belongs to the dogwood order was dubbed 'Variegated Laurel' is one of those idiosyncrasies of the gardening vernacular based more on the practical than on the romantic. The Chinese name, *Tao-yeh Shan-yu*, which means 'Peach leaves Coral' is poetry by comparison. Aucuba are handsome, evergreen, shade-tolerant shrubs which will bring a touch of colour to even the dankest corner. Though *Aucuba japonica* 'Variegata' is the most popular and widely planted form for the cutting border, *Crotonifolia* with larger leaves, marbled and spotted with gold, is very useful.

Mainly because they thrive in the same shade conditions I planted Bergenia 'Abendglut' with the aucuba. The handsome foliage of the bergenia which colours deep wine red in winter, together with the red flowers which show themselves in March, make this a 'must have' perennial. Where space permits include also Bergenia 'Bressingham Ruby', Salmon, and White to give a choice of colours.

Lack of space dictates that only the most useful plants are included in the smaller garden, and camellia with dark-green, highly polished evergreen leaves would qualify on foliage alone. They make such commendable tub plants that in exposed gardens, or where the soil contains lime, this is the best way to grow them. Some years ago I visited a garden where camellia grew with the same luxuriant enthusiasm shown by laurel in my own garden. A small Japanese moon pool some 4ft (1.2m) across, and raised 3ft (0.9m) above ground level formed a centre piece to a minuscule glade. Each morning freshly picked camellia flowers were floated on the still surface of the pool. As the owner of the garden explained, this was so that the beauty of each could be given proper

Aucuba japonica 'Variegata' has been for too long linked in the general gardening public's mind with backyard gardens, soot-grimed park shrubberies, and the landscaping of public toilets. A combination of aucuba foliage with Corsican Hellebore flowers will lift the gloomiest February day to an acceptable level. That this most maligned and ill used shrub will survive in most soils and tolerate even dense shade should at least gain it a better appreciation.

appreciation – one of those pieces of plant artistry that remains colour bright in the memory. Camellia need a cool, humus-rich acid soil and refreshing light shade to be truly content. When doubtful of the hospitality offered by the garden, try first *Camellia japonica* hybrids 'Apollo' with rose-red flowers, 'Donckelarii' red, sometimes marbled-white petals, or the white-bloomed 'Mathotiana Alba'. When grown in tubs, camellia respond to feeding with high potash tomato feed by producing prodigious crops of flowers.

Brunnera macrophylla 'Variegata' and *Arum italicum* 'Pictum' are handsome foliage plants which both cohabit well with camellia in friendly association. The leaves of *Arum italicum* 'Pictum' are arrow-shaped, dark green and conspicuously marbled with white. The brunnera is admirable grown in sun or part shade, the yellow and green variegated foliage topped by sprays of sky-blue flowers in June. There are other evergreens with glossy leaves which are a rarely failing source of background foliage for cutting. *Choisya ternata*, the sweetly fragrant Mexican orange blossom, is one which forms a medium-sized shapely shrub. Anyone handling the leaves quickly discovers they are aromatic when bruised, while the white flowers of late spring and early summer are, as the name implies, reminiscent of orange blossom fragrance. There is a golden-leaved form of *Choisya ternata* well named 'Sundance' which requires shelter from cold winds to give of its bottled sunshine best. Grown as a patio plant in light shade, this delightful shrub provides an excellent foliage complement to other flowers. I like it particularly in the company of *Wisteria sinenses* whose pendent racemes of lilac-blue flowers are so graceful.

Not until recently did I realise why just the mention of choisya immediately calls to mind white lilac, one of the essentially cottage garden plants. Then, I was reminded in conversation with a friend of my schooldays that the two grew together in a narrow border in front of the headmistress's house. Lilac, the *Syringa* of botanists, with those tightly packed, sweetly fragrant panicles of flowers opening in May, is a part of spring's rhythmic pattern in so many gardens. The colour varies from white through primrose-yellow to purple, blue and red in both double and single forms. Lilacs will grow in most well drained soils, yet positively luxuriate in those containing free lime. There are numerous cultivars of *Syringa vulgaris* from which to make a selection. Of the singles offering long-stalked, very cuttable blooms, 'Marechal Foch' bright rose crimson, 'Souvenir de Louis Spaeth' wine red, and 'Vestale' white, are good value. As for the double blooming cultivars, 'Charles Joly' dark red, 'Katherine Havermeyer' purple lavender, and 'Madame Lemoine' purest of white, are first-class and reliable. Lilac is lovely when the blooms are cut by the armful and then arranged in one of the large pewter water jugs which featured in many an isolated country house in pre-bathroom days.

Roses should always be seen in bloom before choosing which varieties to plant in the garden, for the difference in colour between a catalogue illustration and the living flower can be deceptively great. Though the shrub roses may not last very long when

Some 500 years after the birth of Christ an Indian Prince called Dharma visited China to bring instruction to the natives in the duties of religion. There was one occasion when, worn out with prayer and fasting, he fell asleep while meditating. In an attempt to expiate this human weakness Dharma cut off his bushy eyebrows and dropped them on the ground. There they struck root, sprouted leaves, and grew into the first camellia, a decoction of whose leaves has a property of banishing sleep and promoting deep thought. The Chinese call the infusion Ch'a, or Tcha; we call it tea. Camellia japonica which is probably the best known has the beautifully descriptive name of Ch'a Hoa, 'Flower of Tea'.

One of the most subtle-shaded and elegant arrangements I have seen recently was made up of foliage only, with not a single flower of any sort included in its composition. Leaves show such a wide variation in colour, texture, and shape that each one needs to be chosen with the same care and purpose as would be given to selecting a flower. Use all the shades of blue, green, yellow, cream, silver and purple when making up a display, and of a certainty the multi hues of autumn seem to gain special expression when used in conjunction one with the other.

arranged in the house, they have a compelling charm which is so insistent that cutting them to bring the colour and exquisite scent to be enjoyed indoors is always a pleasant, cool-of-the-morning exercise. Indeed, there are some which my flower arranging acquaintances insist are indispensable as they cut bunches of flowers to take home with them from the bushes in my garden: 'Constance Spry' with large, delicately pink, loosely formed blooms which look so beautiful growing with the silver-leaved *Artemesia* 'Powis Castle' or the slightly taller *Artemesia* 'Lambrook Silver'. This is one garden arrangement which is even more attractive when reproduced in a vase. 'Chaucer' is a byblow from 'Constance Spry', with a fuller-petalled flower which is a shade deeper pink. Voluminous would just about describe the shape of this useful variety.

Wandering amongst shrub roses in full bloom, enjoying the quality of the flowers and inhaling the scent they distil, is a mind-beguiling business. Trying to compare flower shape and scent usually leads to a splendid extravagance born of mental intoxication. Compare the double white, very fragrant 'Boule de Neige' with the most shapely but less scented 'Mme Hardy' of similar colour, and choosing between them is difficult. 'La Reine Victoria' has the deep-pink, cup-shaped flowers so often featured in Dutch paintings. That they are intensely fragrant persuades our indulgence.

Then there is the vast array of what are termed the Gallicas, largest group of all and certain to succeed in most soils yet needing a place fully exposed to the sun. Names like 'Charles de Mills', whose rich maroon petals shade purple with age, and 'Surpasse Tout', vigorous in growth with semi-double crimson flowers, form a useful dense hedge as an alternative to the doubtfully efficient 'Queen Elizabeth' or 'Fred Loads'.

The hybrid perpetual roses popular during Victorian times are much in favour amongst the floral art gardening fraternity. 'Mrs

Grey or silver tone down the hotter colours, oranges and scarlets, creating a more harmonious effect when growing in the garden or when used in an arrangement in the home. Also when looking at a border or a flower-filled vase from a distance, very dark-red or purple blooms can give the impression of a hole unless they are backed with lighter-coloured foliage. Velvety-red-flowered dahlias arranged with the silver-leaved artemisia take on a depth and brilliance of colour which would otherwise be missing.

Roses are an essential part of any cut-flower garden. They are one of the few shrubs which provide a near continual supply of blooms for mass arranging all summer through. Cutting great sheaves of HT and floribunda roses in the early morning with the cool of night still in them was one of my duties during the six years I spent working in a large private garden. To be made free of a lovely garden in the cool, fresh intimate quiet of what, in memory, were near perfect summer mornings, added a specially rich pattern to the tapestry flowers have woven through my life.

John Lang' has a strong claim, for the soft-pink flowers are borne on long stalks which make cutting a compliment to their utility. 'Agnes' with pom-pom-shaped yellow flowers is useful for mass effect.

As for the modern bedding floribunda and hybrid tea rose, I can only suggest growing those varieties which have unusual petal colour for arrangement; with suitable foliage they do look remarkably effective. Many a happy afternoon can be spent walking around rose nurseries comparing and selecting the varieties which personal fancy dictates will best grace the garden. What a friend of mine describes as 'immersed in colour and bathed in perfume gardening'.

To see a plant growing wild in a natural setting is the best form of introduction. Just as people in familiar surroundings present their best face, so it is with plants. My first meeting with acanthus was in the region of Metsovon in northern Greece. I was looking for *Lilium chalcedonicum* and the acanthus proved a welcome distraction from what, up to that time, had been a fruitless search. The fine architectural form of acanthus foliage, so tradition has it, suggested the design executed on the capitals of Corinthian columns. According to Vitruvius, a basket covered with a tile was accidentally placed over an acanthus root. The leaves growing up through the basket work were curved back by the tile. Callimachus, a famous architect of the time, noticed the beauty and the potential strength of the curving, deeply segmented leaves and copied them in stone. In the garden both *Acanthus mollis Latifolius* and the more compact *Acanthus spinosus* have proved most effective, bold and handsome foliage plants, infinitely superior to the species I discovered in the Metsovon foothills. The height of *Acanthus mollis* varies from 4 to 5ft (1.2–1.5m) and the stems of purple-mauve flowers open during late summer. *Acanthus spinosus* is my favourite, for the beauty of the finely divided leaves is splendidly Corinthian. Both need a well drained soil and a place in full sun. Flowers should be cut in bud to open in steady succession when included in an arrangement.

My first and most urgent interest in the numerous varieties of *Cynara* had more to do with their flavour when drowned in butter than any comeliness of leaf or flower. They are such imposing herbaceous plants that I am sure aesthetic appreciation soon took precedence over gluttony. The silvery-grey leaves are 3ft (0.9m) long, deeply fretted and divided, and they have a recurving elegance which is maintained when they are cut for arranging. The violet flower heads, like over-sized thistles, should be picked just as they show colour and will then open fully in water. I well remember the wrath of a certain head gardener when he discovered the globe artichokes in the kitchen garden had been almost defoliated. Removing the leaves reduces production of what he described as the 'fruit'. This information, along with a graphic appraisal of my

Arum italicum 'Pictum', with its beautifully marbled leaves, will grow well in a lightly shaded corner. A popular plant amongst floral artists.

This *Cynara cardunculus* is the ornamental counterpart of the deliciously flavoured globe artichoke, *C.scolymus*

own qualities as a trainee gardener, has remained firmly in my memory ever since. Whether the purpose is ornamental or culinary cynara need a well drained and fertile soil to prove their value.

A garden or a flower arrangement should be blending of colours and merging of textures, or the presentation becomes flat and toneless with no depth because of a lack of light and shade contrasts. Cut fern fronds are not usually available in florists' shops but are easy to grow in the garden. They are the most useful providers of graceful background material, as elegant in the garden as in the vase. That ferns are an essential component of a cut-flower garden was proved beyond doubt when I had to design and plant an acre of the sixty-acre garden in my care with plants useful for cutting as flowers, foliage, fruit, and stems. Various members of a nationally famous flower club agreed to advise me on the most suitable and useful plants, and all were in complete agreement that ferns had to be included.

The most useful in general terms proved to be 'Lady Fern', *Athyrium felix-femina*, one of our native ferns. The fronds are elegant, lace textured and soft green. There is a form called 'Victoriae' with long tapering crested, lattice-work-patterned fronds which is particularly interesting.

Ferns have an insidious charm which persuades those devoted to their cultivation into a whole new world of gardening. Plant one and it is very easy to become a collector, for they add grace and a delicacy of form which is uniquely their own. Shield ferns, particularly the soft shield form *Polystichum setiferum* 'Divisilobum', are tolerant of dry conditions and so are very useful. The soft, dull green of the fronds combined with the brown-scaled stems make this one of the most distinctive and beautiful ferns.

Matteuccia struthiopteris, the 'Ostrich Feather Fern', is worth a second mention for the fresh bright-green fronds combine so well with hosta, primula, meconopsis, and a whole range of shrubs including the magnolia previously described. The fertile fronds which are dark brown can be used in dried arrangements. *Matteuccia* in suitably moist soils will grow up to about 20in (50cm) high.

In gardens which can supply a suitably moist corner *Onoclea sensibilis* will yield a free growing ground cover. The long, arching, deeply segmented fronds are a bright pea green and are constantly replaced throughout the summer. In a lime-free soil onoclea makes a brave foil to the cream, yellow, and pink foliage of *Leucothöe fontanesiana* 'Rainbow'. The long arching stems of leucothoe are very useful for cutting. For those who prefer quieter tones, the species *Leucothoe fontanesiana*, with leathery green leaves tinted with bronze purple, makes a pleasant alternative.

Though the *Asplenium* has a texture of leaf which is duplicated to a certain extent in plants other than ferns, the glossy, dark-green, strop-shaped fronds are ornamental and useful for arranging. There is a form of *Asplenium scolopendrium* called 'Crispum' whose leaves look for all the world as if they had been crimped in curling tongs – what, I suppose, could be described as a goffered harts tongue which will grow in any moisture-retentive soil. What asplenium do make a happy match with are the 'Dusty Millers', as my father used to call *Primula auricula*, whose umbels of yellow, purple, or dusky-red flowers open during spring. Yellow 'Dusty Miller', 'Red Dusty Miller', 'Gold of Ophir' and the dark-red 'Mikado' grew with lily of the valley, *Convallaria*, in a narrow, west-facing border along with harts tongue fern – ideal material for table decoration, for they all stand well in water. Be warned, the lily of the valley, given the opportunity, will overrun the garden, so keep the roots confined.

Both hosta and helleborus would almost certainly be included in the majority of flower arrangers' top twenty essential requirement list. Though both are given mention elsewhere for they are such good value all-rounders, only when floral artistry became the vogue did they achieve popularity. Hosta are hardy, will adapt to almost any soil and need only to be left to get on with the business of growing undisturbed. As so often happens when any plant becomes sought after, new varieties are rushed onto the market which are little different in form or quality from the established favourites. 'August Moon' is a golden-leaved cultivar with pale-mauve flowers, while 'Halcyon' is my favourite of the silver-grey-foliaged varieties. In the two-tone leaf colour class *Hosta fortunei* 'Picta' offers variations on shades of yellow and green, or the neatly compact *Hosta undulata medio-variegata* shares a similar colour theme. Yet for me *Hosta ventricosa*, as I saw it growing in the lovely Dell Garden at Bressingham, is the most handsome of all. Especially so when the strikingly variegated leaves are topped by the distinctive deep-blue flowers. In the Dell Garden it grew with the golden variegated grass *Hakonechloa macra* 'Aureola', *Meconopsis betonicifolia*, the blue Himalayan poppy, and *Hemerocallis* 'Hyperion' which has canary-yellow sweetly fragrant flowers – one of these plant compositions seen in soft evening light at the end of a flower-packed day which the passing years will never erase from the memory. Hosta will grow in dry soils with almost the same vigour as they do in moister loam, as they proved in the memorable drought years of the mid-1970s.

Helleborus are so simply distinctive in character that, flower arranging notwithstanding, I would always grow them. Include three species where space permits. A bed of Christmas rose, *Helleborus niger*, growing along a border under the Hessle pear tree in my aunt's garden always provided pure white flowers to float in a bowl as table decoration on New Year's Day. Apart from a year-round application of tea leaves, the plants were left very much to their own devices. Failing tea leaves in sufficient quantity, a mulch of leaf mould and a dusting of bone meal will suffice. Lenten roses, *Helleborus orientalis*, in shades of white, purple, and mauve may not last long after being cut, yet are so intriguingly beautiful that this limitation makes our appreciation all the keener. A group of mixed colours around a white-stemmed *Betula jacquemontii* presents a lovely early spring montage. These two helleborus, *niger* and *orientalis* hybrids, are the 'must haves'. *Helleborus argutifolius* (syn. *corsicus*) with pale apple-green flowers in late winter, topping handsome glossily evergreen leaves, is a 'nice to have'.

Onoclea sensibilis is a completely hardy perennial in spite of the common name of sensitive fern. The fronds do, in fact, turn brown with the first frost – a reasonable precaution rather than an indication of tenderness on the fern's part

The root of *Hellebore* has been famous from time immemorial as a remedy for insanity. From its abundance in the Isle of Anticyra, arose the proverb, Naviga ad Anticyras; 'Take a voyage to Anticyras', which was the advice given by the ancients to those who had lost their reason.

In fact hellebore is such a drastic purgative that it was given only to persons of robust constitution and never to the young or the aged.

Hostas are such ornamental perennials
that no garden should be without them

Helleborus argutifolius (syn. corsicus)
has apple-green flowers in winter

There is also *Helleborus foetidus* whose light-green flowers edged
with dark red look so harmonious when grown in company with
primroses and *Epimedium*. Though the flowers of epimedium, pink
on cream, according to the species being cultivated, do not last well
in water, this is a minor drawback. The heart-shaped leaves are so
attractive that the flowers can be considered more as a seasonal
bonus. Given a moist soil in a cool shady position, *Epimedium x
versicolor* 'Sulphureum', with pale-yellow flowers and tinted foliage
in spring and autumn, makes a charming ground cover 12in (30cm)
high. There is a species sometimes listed as *macrantha*, though more
frequently as *grandiflorum*, introduced from Japan in 1830 which has
given rise to several different forms with deep-pink, white, or dark-
lilac-purple flowers carried on 16in (41cm) high stems above
delicately shaded foliage in April to May.

Most of our conception and appreciation of what are collectively
known as grasses focusses on their value when close mown to form
a lawn, or the ornamental charms of the glistening plumed pampas
grass. There is a grace and elegance to be discovered in the arching,
curved foliage of certain grasses and sedges, a lightness in the
flower plumes which gives a delicacy of texture to the shrub or
herbaceous border. Indeed, the one gains from association with the

other, for grasses possess that quality also discovered in ferns of blending the component parts of a border together. This same characteristic is exhibited to an even greater degree when the plumes are incorporated into a flower arrangement.

There is need to be careful over which grasses to plant for some are so invasive that they rival couch grass in nuisance value. Quaking grass, *Briza media*, with lozenge-shaped, nodding heads is charming in the garden and excellent for drying. Though *Carex* belongs with the sedges, it has a grass-like appearance and so is just as good. *Carex elata* (syn. *stricta*) is lovely with golden striped leaves. The original plant was discovered by that remarkable gardener E. A. Bowles of Middleton House, growing on the Norfolk Broads, which explains the varietal name 'Bowles Golden'. Moist soil in full sun will suit this unusual sedge very well.

The pampas grass is so well known as an autumn flowering plant of considerable presence that I will only offer a warning to beware of seedlings whose flower heads would not disgrace a healthy sheep's fescue. Either see the plant offered for sale in bloom or insist on a named variety – *Cortaderia selloana* 'Pumila' with dense, clotted-cream-coloured plumes carried on 4 to 5ft (120–152cm) high stems is ideally suited for the garden where space is limited. At the other extreme, *Cortaderia selloana* 'Rendatleri' grows 8ft (2.45m) high with plumes which are curiously tinged with pink. 'Sunningdale Silver' is a happy compromise between the two, growing 6ft (1.8m) high with feathery, silvery-white open plumes which are the epitome of elegance. A well flowered 'Sunningdale Silver' against a background of golden conifers all bright in October sunshine makes a pastel-shaded picture.

Though I hesitate to admit to attempting

Gladiolus, though difficult to place in a garden context, do make very useful cut flowers. Plant the corms 4–6in (10–15cm) deep in a well drained soil and a sunny position from early April to mid-May. Gladioli grown for cutting purposes should be planted in double rows 12–15in (30–38cm) apart across the vegetable garden where the soil is prepared with well rotted manure

Grasses are admirable dual-purpose plants in that they are beautiful as garden decoration while serving also as very useful cut material. The elegant curving line and the delicate foliage and flower pattern contrasts with other more ponderous plants.

'lily gilding', a bed of scarlet-flowered, bronze-purple-foliaged 'Bishop of Llandaff' dahlia as a foreground may smack of extravagance, yet succeeds in looking superb.

Helictotrichon sempervirens with blue-grey foliage topped by silver-grey flower stems which show shades of pink and lime green as the slender stems are stirred by the breeze are most effective when grown with dark-blue-flowered *Tradescantia x andersoniana* (syn. *virginiana*) 'Isis' and *Veratrum nigrum*. There is one grass which is so distinctive in appearance as to be almost self-electing for inclusion in the cutting border. *Pennisetum alopecuroides* 'Woodside' grows spikes of bottle-brush flowers on 3ft (91cm) high stems, usually in October. The species sold as *Pennisetum orientale* is on the tender side of hardy as the late Leslie Slinger described it, yet it is such an excellent plant as to be worth persevering with. In bold groups the callistemon-like flower heads of grey suede covered in a sheen of purple hairs are most attractively bizarre. *Coreopsis verticillata* 'Moonbeam' with primrose-yellow flowers is just the right sort of

The curious lime-green and cream-coloured leaves of *Hosta undulata medio-variegata* provide a laughing undertone to the rather prim red-and-purple pendent blooms of Fuchsia 'Mrs Popple'. An ideal small-garden composition copied unashamedly from a friend

companion to the pennisetum. Be advised though, the pennisetums do need cosseting against the cold.

The hybrid crocosmia with sword-shaped leaves and dramatically geometric spikes of vivid flowers are unusual and useful as both garden and indoor decoration. There are four varieties growing in a south-facing border in front of my house: 'The Beacon', 'Jennie Bloom', 'Lucifer', and 'Spitfire'. These bi-generic hybrids are infinitely more reliably hardy than the montbretia and certainly more expressive in brilliance, as the flowers vary from flame red through fiery orange to a most attractive light mahogany depending on the variety. 'Spitfire' at 30in (75cm) is the shortest and the last to flower in September, while 'Lucifer' grows to a most impressive 4ft (120cm) and blossoms during July. Growing intermixed with Japanese anemones in company with the corkscrew hazel, *Corylus avellana* 'Contorta', they are as useful to the flower arranger as cut-and-come-again cake is to the housewife.

The *Anemone x hybrida* (syn. *japonica*) 'White Giant' and *hupehensis* 'September Charm' with single pink flowers embellished with a tuft of gold at the centre are lovely with autumn foliage. As for the corkscrew hazel, I like it best as the catkins form framed against the pulsating orange of a February sunset. The spiralling, convoluted stems are so useful as to be well-nigh essential background material.

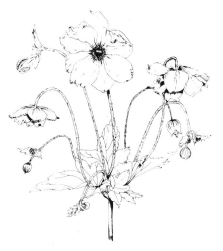

Anemone x hybrida are such useful, late summer and autumn flowering plants that a group for garden decoration and for cutting amply repays ground rent. 'White Giant' (illustrated) looks handsome against purple-foliaged *Cotinus*, while 'September Charm' is more in character alongside the corkscrew hazel. Suits most soils and situations

Brief but Glorious

Annuals which can easily be grown from seed serve many purposes: first, as fillers while the shrubs are making growth, near immediate cuttable material in an otherwise barren plot and most important for the range of colours they offer to brighten summer days outdoors and in.

The taller growing antirrhinum are very good for cutting, and look well grown in groups about the garden. 'Bright Butterflies Improved' is a variety which offers a wide range of colours. Though asters may not, in a cold, wet summer, thrive as they should, I like to grow 'Andrella' as what the gambling fraternity call a 'saver'. The daisy-like single flowers carried on 30in (75cm) stems, open in shades of rose, red, blue and white.

There are some annuals that are unrivalled as cut flowers. Even when measured alongside the better known, commercially promoted iris, chrysanthemum and gladiolus, the annual cosmos 'Sensation' with lovely fern-like filigree foliage decorated with pink, crimson, and white flowers portrays an elegance of form which is delightful to see. Tall at 36in (0.9m), they need to be grown in a sheltered place.

The hyacinth-flowered larkspur are also superb cut flowers which can be sown direct into their flowering positions. The delphinium-like spikes of double or semi-double flowers are displayed on 3ft (0.9m) high stems.

Some time ago I questioned the usefulness of Godetia 'Tall Double Mixed' as a cut flower. The amount of seed sent to me along with instructions on how to use the flowers in arrangements when

Cosmos 'Sensation' from Mexico has rose-pink flowers 3–4in (7–10cm) across, above fern-like foliage. Excellent in pots or borders for cutting. A light soil in full sun suits cosmos best. Avoid a rich soil, and dead head regularly to keep the plants continuously in bloom

they eventually appeared quickly convinced me that godetia are, indeed, an easily grown, long-lasting cut flower.

The 'Bells of Ireland' have never rung quite the right note for me, possibly because green flowers do not appeal for right is, surely, more beautiful than imitation, and there are sufficient green tones in leaves to satisfy me. Flower-arranging acquaintances do, however, assure me that *Moluccella laevis* or 'Bells of Ireland' are well-nigh indispensable. The seed will only germinate when sown in sandy, lime-free compost and kept in a temperature of 75–80°F – something of a prima donna temperament for a flower which looks like a tubular leaf.

Over the years there have always been certain Latin names which I have found difficult to remember. *Salpiglossis* is one of them. Failing memory notwithstanding, *Salpiglossis* 'Splàsh F1' and 'Friendship' which grow to around 24in (61cm) high offer a rich variety of glowing colours with the petals marbled or veined with a contrasting shade.

Salpiglossis, *though they look so delicate, do last well when cut and placed in a vase. The flowers offer unusual colour combinations, reddish chestnut, gold veined with bronze, and a curious peaty brown which is guaranteed to make floral artists eager to have them.*

Both for garden decoration and as providers of a continuous supply of cut flowers, sweet peas are incomparable. By sowing some seed in pots during September, then overwintering the resulting plants in a cold frame, it is possible to begin cutting some flowers in late May. For general use as cut flowers and garden decoration further sowings can be made either outdoors under cloches or into long sweet pea tubes in March. There is one prime requisite for all sweet peas and that is a deep, fertile, humus-rich, moisture-holding yet well drained soil. Demanding they are certainly, but when well grown they pay for the work expended on their cultivation with fragrant armfuls of bright coloured flowers.

11

Sociable Climbers

Climbers are the specialist performers of the plant world which might have been specifically designed for the use of gardeners. Without a covering of vegetation there would be nothing to soften the hard uncompromising outline of stone or brick walls. What means would there be of disguising a featureless fence or hiding ugliness in the shape of garden sheds or concrete garages without climbing plants? A screen of shrubs or trees would, in the course of time, serve to mask unsightly architecture, but this would only be at the expense of occupying most of the available garden space. A climbing plant, taking up an area of ground only large enough to accommodate the root, will cover in some cases many square yards of wall space. Walls and fences offer firm support, shelter, and a variety of aspects and so enable plants to be grown which could not otherwise have been successfully cultivated in the garden proper.

Plants climb in a variety of ways, all of them exhibiting remarkable efficiency in providing a secure means of attaching themselves to the most convenient prop. Some ascend by twining stems, wrapping themselves round the support in a clockwise or anti-clockwise direction. It is interesting that a plant like the honeysuckle which always twines anti-clockwise cannot by any means be persuaded to travel in the reverse direction. The modus operandi, it seems, is an inherited characteristic in twining plants.

Others cling by means of tendrils; sweet peas and vines are two which favour this means of progression. Ivy clings to masonry or tree trunks almost as if welded to them with highly efficient aerial roots. Hook scramblers are the least common, although some roses for the sake of convenience fit into this category, for the thorns on the long pliant stems do serve as grappling hooks when they twine up through a convenient host. The way in which a plant climbs is an important factor in choosing the correct support for the shoots to grow on, over, round or through.

Though walls do provide shelter from buffeting winds and a benign micro-climate which enables a much wider range of plants to be grown than would be possible in the open garden, careful preparation of the soil is essential. The soil immediately adjacent to a wall is generally drier and, if not previously cultivated, less fertile than it is over the rest of the garden. There is no way of turning poor soil into deep, moisture-retentive fertile loam except by working in humus-forming material in the shape of rotted manure, compost, or other organic matter. The improvement is

From An Encyclopaedia of Gardening: *'Flowers which reach from 5 to 7ft in height for covering naked walls, or other upright Deformities, and for shutting out distant objects which it is desirable to exclude'.*
The imagination immediately seizes on the upright deformities: visions of Gothic cow byres, wee houses at the garden end and other architectural memorabilia including static gardeners complete with wheelbarrow. 'Distant objects', and the mind takes wing, could include amusement parks, power stations, and the neighbour's swimming pool.

Abutilon x suntense 'Jermyn's', though not really a climber, will express gratitude for the shelter of a wall by a display of flowers lasting several months

Rhodochiton atrosanguineum is an unusual and beautiful twiner-climber. I first met this attractive plant in southern Mexico and have grown it ever since. Each autumn I save seed, for it seems to be a short-lived perennial. The curiously formed, bell-shaped calyx and long, tubular corolla are that shade of purple associated with ruby wine. As decoration for a picture window, rhodochiton can be guaranteed to provide an interesting topic of conversation. Seed should be sown in a heated place during March

Wisteria frutescens *was the first species to be discovered in the south east of the United States. Mark Catesby introduced it under the name of 'Carolina Kidney Bean'. Once the Chinese* Wisteria sinensis *came into consideration, the Americans lost out to them on all counts.* W.sinensis *is the most sweetly scented flowering in May, and is usually referred to as the Chinese species. The Japanese* Wisteria floribunda *has given rise to numerous cultivars and varieties.*

maintained after planting the climbers by mulching with the same material, supplemented further by watering and feeding. Some ten days before planting work into the soil a dressing of 2oz (50g) per sq yd (sq m) of fine bone meal to provide the superphosphate which is such a prime aid to healthy root development. Though this may seem, as indeed it is, a lot of work, be encouraged by a vision of what is now a bare wall covered in leaf and flower, marrying house and garden so that one becomes an extension of the other.

There was one wall of the old vicarage in the village where I worked briefly after leaving college which was covered in wisteria. In May the racemes of flowers hanging like a deep-lilac curtain filling the air with their fragrance are one of the vivid memories of that period of my life. The other is the taste of apricots picked and eaten from the tree of 'Moorpark' growing on the same wall with the sun's warmth still in them.

One of the major drawbacks to planting *Wisteria floribunda* or *sinensis* is the length of time they take to reach flowering size. There are several hybrids from *W.sinensis* which show a commendable precocity in this respect, 'Prolific' with lilac flowers is one, and 'Black Dragon' with dark-purple double flowers is another. There is a variety of *Wisteria floribunda* named 'Macrobotrys' which in the full vigour of maturity grows pendent racemes of blue-purple, lilac-tinted flowers 30in (75cm) long. To walk under a pergola covered in these plants in full bloom with the flowers hanging through about one's head is a never-to-be-forgotten experience of fragrant beauty. For the first four or five years encourage rapid growth so as to fill the available wall space quickly with a well organised framework of branches. After this, prune all young stems back to within three or four leaves of the base from mid-August onwards to assist in the formation of flowering spurs. Regular liquid feeding with a high-potash fertiliser at this stage will also precipitate flowers.

Shrubs with naturally variegated leaves are not common, apart, of course, from those found in tropical regions, which makes the multi-coloured foliage of *Actinidia kolomikta* something of a rarity, for it comes from the temperate zone of the Far East. It is a climber with long slender branches which will grow 8ft (2.4m) high by as much across when trained on an east-facing wall. The heart-shaped 3–4in (7–10cm) long leaves, given even a modest exposure to sunlight, are made most attractive by a stain of white and pink which begins at the tip and extends gradually inwards. The colour persists until the autumn which makes *Actinidia kolomikta*, particularly in the male form, a most ornamental wall covering. A not too rich soil, well supplied with potash, intensifies the leaf colour.

Some of the loveliest climbing plants are so tantalisingly close to proving themselves hardy outdoors that it is worth reserving the most sheltered corner facing due south that the garden affords. *Campsis radicans*, the trumpet vine, is just such a sun lover which needs a thorough baking to ripen flowering wood. My first *Campsis radicans* grew in a redundant melon pit so exuberantly that it pushed shoots up through the lights to produce terminal clusters of orange-

Solanum crispum autumnale, now known by the cultivar name of 'Glasnevin', is another spectacular climber which needs a warm, sheltered wall. 'Glasnevin' is a semi-evergreen which from midsummer into autumn opens corymbs of rich-purple flowers; the colouring is emphasised most effectively by bright-yellow stamens. Trained over a lichen-covered, grey stone wall it forms a most pleasing effect

flushed scarlet flowers throughout August, September and early October. There is a yellow form named 'Flava' which has flowers the colour of rich Cornish cream. Campsis are real opportunistic self-clinging climbers which can be pruned as necessary in spring.

For many years I struggled to grow clematis on an ill-drained clay and hoarded every frugally offered flower like a latter-day Scrooge counting Krugerrands. In my present garden where the soil is so well drained that heavy mulches are essential to conserve moisture clematis thrive. They are the most endearing and accommodating of plants, for in one context they can be persuaded into expressing a well disciplined formality, while in another they can be enticed into romping over an apple tree like any fruit-scrumping schoolboy. Clematis climb by the stalks of individual leaflets which form the compound leaves, whipping themselves around any conveniently placed support. There are so many cultivars to choose from that only by seeing a wide range of both species, varieties, and cultivars can one be certain of getting the best to suit a particular purpose.

Look first at those varieties whose popularity has been earned in the most testing arena of all, the average garden. Though *Clematis armandii* is not absolutely reliably hardy, it is the pick of the few evergreen clematis species, and a very beautiful climbing plant for a sheltered corner. Seed-raised plants are best ignored as their quality is unpredictable; instead choose named varieties of proven worth, either 'Apple Blossom' with pale-pink flowers or 'Snowdrift' which is purest white.

My introduction to *Clematis alpina* came half-way up the Albergo Formi in the eastern Alps. The slender stems of the clematis had grown up and through a sturdy *Rhododendron hirsutum* and the blend of blue flowers amongst deep pink was very lovely against the

One of the several *Clematis alpina* which I raise from seed each year

snow-covered mountains above. In my present garden *Clematis alpina* 'Columbine', whose flowers are a clear light blue with white stamens, grows through *Spiraea japonica* 'Gold Flame' whose young growths in spring are a deep-golden colour. Another *Clematis alpina* planted in the shade border uses the white-flowered, evergreen *Rh.* (syn. *Azalea*) 'Palustrina' as a support, the cooler combination made even more effective by the under carpeting of *Garryarde Guinevere* primroses.

If I had to make a choice, *Clematis macropetala*, the Chinese version of *Clematis alpina*, introduced to European gardens by William Purdom in 1910, would figure in my top five climbing plants. The dainty, double, nodding blooms are a blend of blue shades, the colour made even more positive by the contrasting white staminoides. There are two other varieties, a delectable white form called 'Snowbird' and another aptly named 'Markham's Pink'

When the flowers of Wisteria hang like a fragrant blue curtain it is a truly majestic sight (*Ripley Castle, near Harrogate*)

OPPOSITE

Actinidia kolomikta covered an east-facing wall with multi-coloured foliage in my last garden. Though the leaves are the most decorative feature, there are tiny inconspicuous flowers. Close investigation of these, one day when I was tying up a branch which had broken free from the wire support, revealed that they are pleasantly fragrant.

with petals of that dusky shade which looks very beautiful when growing against a wall covered in the green and gold foliage of *Hedera helix* 'Goldheart'.

Several years ago, exasperated by the failure of a very large crab apple tree to bear enough fruit to make even a token offer in return for the care expended on its cultivation, I sawed the branches off. A *Clematis montana* grown too large for the half cider barrel it was planted in offered an immediate disguise for my vandalism. Each year since, May has been such a joyful expression of pink, delicately scented flowers that several more trees are at risk from a similar beheading to provide supports for more clematis. Reflecting back over the years, *Clematis montana* in one form or another has proved the most reliable of all the many clematis I have grown. As a disguise for unsightly buildings, clother of nondescript trees, or seasonally colourful embellishment of later flowering wall plants it has few equals, and no superiors. Easy to grow, flatteringly simple to propagate by means of seed or cuttings, *Clematis montana* appears to have only one purpose and that is to please those who offer it hospitality. The type species has white flowers; 'Grandiflora', pure white and single, is also delicately scented. The two pink forms, 'Elizabeth' and the less vigorous, herb-scented, deep-rose-petalled 'Picton's Variety', are worth spending hard-earned gold to obtain. Almost any soil, situation, or aspect is acceptable to this most cheerfully accommodating species.

Rigid self-discipline is essential when confronted with even an abbreviated list of large-flowered hybrid clematis. 'Comtesse de Bouchaud' with pink, mauve-shaded flowers which open in summer provides a colour which needs a carefully contrived background. Whatever else, never choose red brick. Then there is 'Barbara Jackman' which enlivens purple-blue flowers with a bright magenta bar and creamy-yellow stamens in June. The most famous of the Woking Nursery hybrids which bear the family name is, surely, *jackmanii*. The newer, if a seedling introduced in 1878 can be described as new, *C.jackmanii* 'Superba' is the variety most frequently offered by nurseries. One of my most memorable experiences came when I was researching the history of clematis for a television series 'World of Flowers'. To read through the nursery stud book kept by George Jackman listing all the various crosses made of clematis and describing the resulting seedlings was like holding time in my hands. Both *C.jackmanii* and *jackmanii* 'Superba' carry a profuse display of velvet-textured deep-purple flowers in late summer.

Though 'The President', like the *jackmanii* hybrids, was introduced over 100 years ago, the large, striking handsome, purple-blue flowers ensure this a high place in any popularity poll. That it is vigorous and blooms continuously almost from May to September ensures it an ongoing success. Some of the pink and red cultivars fade to a washed-out pink, and should be ignored in favour of one of Walter Pennell's finest hybrids called 'Charissima' with cerise-pink flowers carrying a maroon stripe down the centre of each petal. If a rosy flush over a light clear blue indicates a degree of indecision,

Raising clematis from seed adds a further dimension to the cultivation of this beautiful climbing plant. The species tangutica, orientalis *and others of similar character set seed in such quantity that it is ungrateful not to accept what is so freely offered. The hybrids also produce seed each year, though unlike the species the seedling will not, in all probability, be identical with the parent. I always harvest one or two of the tufted heads from selected parents and sow them. There is always the same sense of excited anticipation as the seedlings come into flower which I find more than rewards my efforts.*

Clematis seed looks larger than it is because of the feathery tuft attached to each one. In order to avoid sowing too deep I carefully mix the seed in moist sand before sowing.

then 'Perle d' Azur' reassures with such huge masses of flowers as to pre-empt criticism. Along with *C.jackmanii* 'Superba', 'Perle d' Azur' is one of the most popular clematis, lovely when grown over a west-facing wall with the self-clinging, white-flowered, climbing *Hydrangea petiolaris*. The final flush of clematis flowers come as the hydrangea leaves take on gold autumn tints.

Clematis tangutica is most untypical of the race with lantern-shaped yellow flowers which are followed in due season by silvery silken-tasselled seed heads. In the White Craggs, Ambleside garden the plants grown from seed sent home by the Lakeland plant collector William Purdom were allowed to grow as he described finding them in Kansu, China, tumbling down a rock face. To see a profusion of sea-green, fern-like foliage, festooned with yellow blooms tumbling down over white limestone was one of the joys to be anticipated on my visits to this most beautiful garden. This is a species which grows very readily from seed sown in standard potting compost, in heat, during March.

The spring flowering *C.montana, alpina* and *macropetala* require little pruning apart from some judicious thinning of the framework branches to keep them in order. Those clematis which, like *jackmanii*, carry all the flowers on current season's growth may be cut back in March to within one bud of where growth began the previous year. This simple, undisguised butchery is satisfyingly uncomplicated to carry out, and a mulch of peat, well rotted compost or manure mixed with a generous dusting of bone meal is of proven benefit applied each spring after pruning.

Rambling and climbing roses share with clematis a place in garden folklore reserved for a few very special plants which are

Hydrangea petiolaris with *Clematis 'Elsa Spath'*. The lavender-purple flowers of this clematis are a feature in June and July, then again during autumn

simple, beautiful, and easy to grow. The two are always linked in my memory, for *Clematis jackmanii* grew through and amongst 'Zepherine Drouhin' roses in the days of my increasing awareness of gardens and gardening. Initially a total inability to tell the difference between the ramblers and climbers of the rose world looked like blighting any prospect of my becoming a real gardener. Having to prune a 'Dorothy Perkins', 'Crimson Shower', 'Alberic Barbier', and 'The Garland' finally resolved the problem. Ramblers are the 'floppers' and 'sprawlers' which can be grown over almost any support from steeply sloping bank to a castle wall including every possible variation between the two extremes. Rambling roses, with *Rosa wichuriana* or, as some would have it, luciae blood – or should that be 'sap' – in their parentage, produce only one brief but glorious display of flowers. 'Crimson Shower' and 'Dorothy Perkins' revealed the truth of what I had been told, for ramblers do only flower on one-year-old wood. Reassured on this point, pruning did indeed become simply a business of cutting out all shoots carrying spent flowers, then tying young bright-green, pliable stems to replace them. 'Albertine' confused me briefly as did several other hybrids by not producing young shoots near ground level. By cutting selected old stems hard back they can be persuaded to do so. The remaining shoots are otherwise cut back to where new growths have developed. Simply a business of cutting out as much old wood, and retaining all the new necessary to maintain a well furnished, peak flowering framework.

Climbing roses, many of them developed as 'sports' from hybrid tea or floribunda bush roses, offered no problems as to how they should be pruned, once I understood the flowering sequence. Most flower on young shoots of the current season's growth, and are therefore pruned in spring. During the first two or three years a main framework of branches needs to be established to cover the available space. The short lateral growths which appear at intervals along this framework are pruned back to two or three buds in March. At intervals young growths will be required as the older parts of the bushes lose vigour. Young shoots selected as replacement should be tied in to supports in autumn as a temporary measure to prevent damage from gales or snowfall. Once the old shoots are cut out in spring, the new vigorous growths are tied in to replace them – a form of self-renewal which will prolong the climbing rose's productive life considerably. There is one golden rule when training a climbing rose: never allow the shoots to grow straight up, always take the stem out sideways, then up. This constricts the sap flow, causing side growths to form all the way along the stems and not just at the tip.

Feeding of both rambler and climbing roses should be an annual routine. By mixing a generous helping of slow-release fertiliser into a mulch of rotted manure, compost, peat, or finely pulverised bark the dual process of soil conditioning and feeding is reduced to one simple operation.

All who garden will have special memories of summer days made brighter by a pageant of roses growing over trellis or pergola,

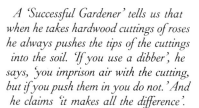

Pruning the climbing and rambling roses was one of those jobs reserved for days when the soil elsewhere in the garden was too wet for walking on. Trying to hold thorny shoots in place while numb fingers secured them to the supports with raffia is one of my most painful memories. Then one of the older gardeners, who was a never failing source of practical information, showed me how the shoots could be held firm for tying with a pitch-fork. Once this trick had been mastered, pruning and re-tying became a much pleasanter occupation.

A 'Successful Gardener' tells us that when he takes hardwood cuttings of roses he always pushes the tips of the cuttings into the soil. 'If you use a dibber', he says, 'you imprison air with the cutting, but if you push them in you do not.' And he claims 'it makes all the difference'.
From Success in the Garden, *published in 1933, price 6d (2½p).*

across a wall or twining themselves up and through the branches of a tree, offering flowers which belong to warm sunny days and gladsome things. 'Casino' needs the shelter of a wall to be persuaded by the extra warmth into producing a goodly crop of deep-yellow, well shaped flowers paling to primrose with age. 'Dreaming Spires' with blooms of golden hue adds the extra quality of fragrance. The very dark-green leaves show the petal colour to good effect. 'Handel' is quite distinctive and one of the most obliging varieties in that it provides a regular supply of young shoots from the base as replacements for old worn-out stems. The deep-cream petals revealed when the high pointed buds open are edged with cherry pink. I grew a 'Handel' rose for several years in a tub with a lattice-work trellis fitted to it. This made a beautiful mobile screen which could be moved as required about the terrace to give shelter or shade according to the prevailing weather conditions.

'Joseph's Coat' is splendid as a pillar rose, for in that sort of position where the varying light tones can have free play at all angles around them, the large flower trusses are seen to full advantage. Not everyone admires the curious colour mixture of a yellow ground tone flushed with orange and cherry red, so view first before buying. 'Mermaid' is a beguiling rose which needs a warm wall to cherish and protect it in the colder areas of northern Britain. The large, single yellow flowers have a delicate, persuasive fragrance; this is one for the people who enjoy a twilight walk around the garden. 'Parade' grew well for me on an east wall where the shoots could be trained up and over an arch. There, the slight tendency shown by the deep carmine-rose flowers to droop their heads was proved to be meritorious. Anyone pausing under the arch looked straight into a massed canopy of flowers filling the air all about them with their delectable scent.

A garden is, if nothing else, a place where time has only a relative existence, having meaning only in reference to the passing seasons. This is the reason why when working with and amongst plants I find that there is not the same frenetic urgency to get things done. Never be in a hurry to replace old, well tried roses with new varieties before early acquaintance has had sufficient time to ripen into a lasting relationship. Each summer finds a horde of fresh introductions on the market, each untried yet with the assurance that in quality it surpasses anything created previously. After twenty years of conducting trials of seedling roses I now make sure that they are an improvement on what has gone before and that their alleged superiority is not just a figment of some advertiser's imagination. 'Pink Perpetue' with double-pink flowers was one I tried over twenty years ago and still find attractive; lovely when grown on a rustic fence, for this in my experience is the best stage of all for a rose to display its true quality. Most roses show a markedly increased resistance to mildew where the air can circulate freely through and around them.

The more vigorous varieties which are so useful for covering a large expanse of bare wall and unsightly buildings are also superb

On manuring the author of Success in the Garden *writes:*

As our roses grow and develop, we shall find it necessary to feed the trees either with a good mulch of manure and soot, or by the application of a good fertiliser. This is BEST administered during STORMS or RAIN.

Handling soot and manure in a rainstorm would also, I think, unhinge the mind.

INSET
Clematis tangutica, hung with yellow Chinese-lantern flowers – a subject of much comment
OPPOSITE
Clematis 'Nelly Moser', and *C.* 'Ville de Lyon' jostle for a share of any appreciation offered

when allowed to grow naturally. 'Alberic Barbier' is one best left to find its own way in life; scrambling eagerly up a convenient tree like a boy let out of school, to hang a screen of creamy-white flowers about the heads of passers by. A splendidly furnished specimen grew over the ha-ha wall in my first garden, and there the foliage was retained all the year round to become a favourite roosting place for small birds.

'Albertine' is the wall rose which excels all others in colour quality and fragrance during the brief June season when this variety is so abundantly in evidence. The richly coloured coppery-pink buds open to salmon-rose-shaded flowers whose fragrance fills the garden. I can well understand why 'Albertine' has held so firm a place in gardeners' affections for so long. There was a fine old specimen trained across the wall of a house where I stayed recently and the perfume drifting through the open windows was purely delightful.

'Dorothy Perkins', of fond memory, grew up the wall of a stone building where the clay pots, canes, and fruit nets were stored in the garden at home. Memories of the cascade of clustered double rose-pink flowers borne in such profusion as to hide the wall behind are, unfortunately, veiled in the grey haze of mildew. What a cause for regret that this much loved rose is so susceptible to an unsightly disease which is difficult to control. 'Maigold' which I grew for eight years on a trellis is so incredibly thorny that it is fortunate that very little pruning is needed to keep it in good order. The bronze-yellow flowers are faintly fragrant. As a barrier against those most persistent penetrators of the supposedly impenetrable, pigs and small boys, 'Maigold' has few equals.

Wordsworth's cottage in Ambleside is always pictured in my mind with the large semi-double flowers of crimson draped across the wall all brightly welcoming in July sunshine. I was briefly distracted from my interest in Wordsworth's habitation in trying to find out the name of the rose – much to the annoyance of the guide showing us round. The rose, as it turned out, was 'Paul's Scarlet' climber, a hardy, very vigorous, late flowering *R.wichuraiana* hybrid which I very much doubt existed when the Wordsworths occupied the house. This is a flower colour which shows up well against a slate-blue or limestone-grey-coloured masonry, and screams in outrage when contrasted with orange brickwork.

OTHER THAN ROSES

Eccremocarpus scaber was the unwitting cause of embarrassment to me in the days when the few botanical names of plants loosely fixed in my memory never matched the plants I wanted to grow. Seed selection from catalogues was at that time a very hit-and-miss affair. For some reason I assumed *Eccremocarpus* to be an annual, so the seedlings when large enough were duly bedded out in a narrow border fronting a wall covered in morello cherries. To my surprise the supposed annual survived the winter and the following spring, grew up through the wires supporting the morello cherries to open

---

From Plant Lore Legends and Lyrics:

The rose was a domestic flower sedulously cultivated by the ancients, but especially by the Romans. It is said to have early flourished at Rhodes and possibly gave its name to that island.

Anacreon gives a poetic account of the origin of the rose, connecting it with the goddess of love and beauty.

Oh whence could such a plant have sprung?
The earth produced an infant flower.
Which spring with blushing tinctures drest,
The gods beheld this brilliant birth,
And hailed the rose, the boon on earth.

Eccremocarpus are from South America so it is hardly surprising they are liable to be killed in a severe winter. Given a well sheltered corner E.scaber (illustrated) will survive to produce a quite remarkable display of nodding orange-red flowers

a succession of flowers throughout the summer and into the autumn. The orange, tubular flowers are borne on slender racemes and for many years I grew only the type species. Over recent years a yellow-flowered *E.scaber aureus* and a carmine-red *E.scaber carmineus* have been introduced. Like the type species all are easily grown from seed and do not, at least in my experience, become climbers until the second year.

Climbers with attractive foliage, particularly those which are evergreen, make an important contribution and deserve special commendation. The several different species and innumerable cultivars of *Hedera* (ivy) afford a most interesting and decorative means of covering a bare wall in a tapestry of coloured foliage. For years, because ivy showed such a rare ability to grow well in the most inhospitable soils and situations, it was planted only in the dankest, darkest corners, there to provide a home for spiders and quarrelsome sparrows while hiding ugliness under a screen of glossy green leaves. Now, in a more enlightened gardening age, ivy is given ample opportunity to prove itself to be amongst the foremost evergreen climbing plants. There could be few places more darkly arid than a north-facing yard backed by three-storey buildings to the west, south, and east. In an effort to mask the stark desert of smoke-grimed masonry the house owner, a keen gardener, planted three varieties of *Hedera helix*, the common ivy. Within five years the trio composed of *Hedera helix* 'Goldheart' (dark-green leaves with a central splash of yellow), H. 'Donerailensis' (dark-green foliage tinged with purple in winter), and *H.helix pedata*, whose bird's foot leaves are white veined, had transformed the lower part of the wall into a garden.

There is no doubt that a growing interest in floral art has

Although ivies will make a shift to grow in most soils be they infertile sand or clinging clay, they do respond to kindly treatment. Prepare the soil by working in a mixture of well rotted organic matter and bone meal, leave time for this to settle, then plant the ivy roots in it. The result at times is dramatically vigorous.

contributed to an increasing use of ivy in garden design. Unfortunately, as so often happens with any plant which suddenly gains in popularity, the proliferation of new varieties is bewildering to the experienced gardener, and must be utterly confusing to the beginner. For the flower arranger and as garden decoration, the variegated Persian ivy is quite outstanding. The large light-green leaves are margined with creamy yellow. Initially the trailing stems need support and directional training. There is no more beautiful covering for a low wall, fence or tree stump than that provided under a mantle of Persian ivy, *Hedera colchica* 'Dentata Variegata'. Unless, of course, you include 'Sulphur Heart' which with typical Irish juxtapositioning has the variegation reversed to a pale-yellow splash in the centre of its leaves. I sometimes think the old name for this variety of 'Paddy's Pride' is the more appropriate.

Fortunately for the gardener's sanity, there are varieties of common ivy, *Hedera helix*, which can be recommended for specific purposes. 'Chester', for example, with cream-marbled leaves is a delightful, self-branching, west wall cover – the perfect backcloth for clematis 'The President'. 'Brigitte' and 'Green Feather', with mid-green foliage, and 'Hahn', variegated with blue-green, white-marbled leaves, are all useful for clothing low walls, pillars, and terracing.

Though foresters would, I am sure, not agree, there is a rugged and rare beauty to be found in the ivy-covered bole of a deciduous tree in midwinter. The deep-green glossy foliage of ivy gains full expression in that situation and season. A curious fact is that ivy seems to need a place sufficiently high up and in the sun in order to flower and fruit. Theophrastus noticed 2,000 years ago that ivy which crept close along the ground never flowered. Ivy does flower when old enough in early winter when little else is in bloom. The nectar is particularly concentrated which makes it a valuable habitat plant, a point to note for conservation-conscious gardeners. Fortunately, ivy is no longer associated with tombstones and graveyards. Instead of describing ivy, as did Hassard writing a century ago, as 'One of the best of graveyard plants', we consider it a most proper plant for growing indoors and out. Should any further inducement be needed, according to Folkard, dreaming of ivy portends 'friendship, happiness, good fortune, honours, riches, and success'.

A PLANT LOOK-ALIKE

Plants do show some surprising variations in form even between members of a single genus. Few astonished me more than when I was told that the climber covering one wall of the vicarage was a hydrangea. Was this a close relation of the blue-flowered pot plants it was my seemingly endless duty to water on hot summer days? Having suffered much already at the hands of older gardeners, my first reaction was disbelief at yet one more attempt at leg pulling. Be that as it may, *Hydrangea peteolaris* as already mentioned in association with clematis 'Perle d' Azur', is a quality, self-clinging

OPPOSITE
Rose 'Albertine' growing over the wall of a house built during the sixteenth century, and well content with the hospitality provided (*Parcevall Hall, near Skipton*)

Hedera helix 'Goldheart' in flower. The leaves on the flowering shoots are larger and of a different shape while still retaining the attractive green-on-gold variegation

Climbing hydrangea reach up to 16yd (15m) climbing by means of aerial roots. The white flowers are borne on lateral shoots which grow out from the main stem, so do not be surprised if young shoots fail to flower. Any cutting back is best done in spring.

climber which will grow well on any wall, even one which faces north. Though self-clinging, the stems will need some support until the habit asserts itself. The heart-shaped leaves which turn lemon yellow in the autumn are nearly hidden in July behind large, flat corymbs of white flowers.

PRIDE OF THE EVENING

Few plants are viewed with the same affectionate regard as that accorded to *Lonicera periclymenum*, 'Woodbine' to some, 'Honeysuckle' to the majority, and 'Pride of the Evening' to my grandmother who lived all her life at the end of a driftway bordered by hedges wreathed in this her favourite flower. The air in the cool of evening as we walked along the grassy track was filled with the most delightful scent from hundreds of creamy-yellow, flushed-purple flowers through all the long golden days of summer into autumn.

There are two named forms of common honeysuckle, *L.periclymenum* 'Serotina', the so-called late Dutch honeysuckle with red-purple flowers, not to be confused with 'Belgica', the early Dutch honeysuckle which also has flowers of the same shade. Twenty years ago I ordered plants of both from five different nurseries, and so far as I could see all were identical with *Lonicera x americana* or *L.caprifolium*, both excellent climbers. *Lonicera x americana* is a very vigorous free blooming climber whose white fading to deep-yellow flowers are heavily tinged with purple on the outside, and distil a glorious scent. *L.caprifolium* is the cottage garden honeysuckle and the earliest to flower, opening long fragrant cream-coloured tubes in June. The orange-red berries set in quantity as an ornamental afterthought. By growing all my *caprifolium* from seed I am certain of getting the best blooming form. Honeysuckle grow and flower freely in partially shaded places, and in the leaf-mould-rich soil along hedgerows or wood edge – not a nutrient-rich soil particularly, just one that is spongy and moist.

The majority of jasmine species are found growing wild in areas loosely described as semi-tropical. There are two species of such proven worth and durability that they would be in many gardeners' top twenty climbing plants. *Jasminum nudiflorum*, 'Winter Jasmine' introduced from western China over a century ago by Robert Fortune, is one of the duo. Though honesty insists that it should be described as a sprawler rather than a climber, the bright yellow flowers open along bare branches to bring cheer to many a winter's day. It is best grown as a wall shrub, for then the shoots which carry the flowers can be pruned hard back in April as the petals fall to encourage an even heavier crop of flowers the following year.

Common white jasmine is a popular name that should not in any way be interpreted as meaning undistinguished

Jasminum officionale

> *'The honeysuckle is so called on account of the honey dew found so plentifully on its foliage', according to Richard Folkard in* Plant Lore, Legends and Lyrics.
> *As the honey dew is produced and deposited on the leaves by greenfly, I suspect Folkard was maligning this lovely climber. The popular name derives, according to* A Dictionary of English Plant Names *'from the pleasurable sucking of honey from the corolla tube' – much more romantic than assuming all honeysuckle are infested with greenfly.*

or ordinary. *Jasminum officinale* has been cultivated in gardens for centuries, so long, in fact, that its country of origin is not known for certain. There is no question as to the plant's vigour, for there have been occasions when I have been prepared to declare it is possible to see common white jasmine growing, though 30ft (9m) or thereabouts seems to be the ultimate height. The sweetly scented white flowers open during summer in terminal clusters on short side shoots. There is a form of *Jasminum officinale* known as 'Affine' with slightly larger flowers which are pink in the bud, yet in spite of what might be termed these embellishments the type species is the one most often met with.

WHAT'S IN A NAME?

When is a 'Virginia Creeper' not a 'Virginia Creeper', and the answer could be any one of the five names botanists have imposed on this well known climber. No wonder Jean Santenil exclaimed 'The only sound to be heard was that of the vain Virginia Creeper at her toilet drying her scarlet leaves'. Even now, though the botanists have finally settled on *Parthenocissus*, the layman still calls the 'Boston Ivy', *P.tricuspidata Veitchii*, virginia creeper, when this popular name properly belongs to *P.quinquefolia*.

Enough of piling confusion on vanity, *Parthenocissus* as they must now be known, natives of Asia and North America, climb to astonishing heights on walls or tree trunks. They attach themselves to whatever support offers with tendrils which either twine or cling by means of adhesive pads. All the species are easily grown, adapting with no obvious signs of discontent to most soils and situations in full sun or shade. *Parthenocissus henryana* is best grown on a west- or east-facing wall, then the beauty of the leaf develops fully for it is not bone hardy. Like a starling's plumage the leaves change colour according to lighting. Dark green shaded bronze with silvery-white veins is the most consistent tonal theme, and in autumn they turn red before falling.

Parthenocissus tricuspidata 'Veitchii', the Boston ivy, covered all the south wall of a bothie I came to know well. The sparrows who quarrelled, roosted, nested, and in general made use of the tangle of vegetation woke me up at 4am. There was a large mulberry tree growing in a small lawn in front of the bothie. In August the fruit, rich, black, and pleasantly acid to the taste came just within reach of my outstretched arm. In the shelter provided by high walls both mulberry and ivy flourished. At the approach of autumn the rich crimson and scarlet leaves of the creeper contrasted with the lime-green and yellow-tinted mulberry foliage.

Parthenocissus quinquefolia, the true virginia creeper from eastern North America, grows comfortably to 16–20yd (13–18m) high when suited by soil and climate. There is a vicarage which I visit each autumn where frontage and outbuildings are covered in the five-fingered elliptic leaflets of virginia creeper. At the first hint of frost the creeper-covered walls are suffused with glowing crimson like a great auto-da-fé in celebration of the season.

In Gardening on Walls by C. Grey-Wilson and Victoria Matthews, common jasmine, J.officinale, is described as native to the Himalaya and southern China. Commonly naturalised also in southern Europe and western Asia. A cosmopolitan climber and beautifully fragrant.

Parthenocissus tricuspidata, *Japanese creeper, will grow up to 22yd (20m) so is one of the largest, and certainly in the full brilliant scarlet of autumn leaf, most spectacular of all climbing plants hardy in Britain.*

Tropaeolum *will grow in most aspects, north, east, south or west-facing so long as its roots are in shade and never get too dry. Propagation is effected by means of either seed or tubers.*

By Adam Cursed

All gardeners must have cursed certain plants, not all of them weeds, for being too invasive. Lily of the valley is one I spend time keeping within prescribed limits in my present garden. Never have I achieved quite the lurid, expressive fluency used by a neighbour of mine when describing *Tropaeolum speciosum*, Scotch Flame Flower. Nearly the whole of his garden has been taken over by what is to most gardeners a lovely climbing plant. The slender stems with their pale-green five-foliate leaves scramble over hedges, shrubs, and ascend 10ft (3m) and more into a variegated holly and golden yew. When the vermilion-scarlet flowers appear the display of colour is quite beyond anything I have seen from this remarkable climber, even in the Levens Hall Garden, Kendal. The bucketful of white roots left on my doorstep one spring came with a warning to plant them only where the outrageous, colonising instincts of the plant could be restrained. The swollen roots were duly installed along a line of four holly trees, one plain green, the rest silver and gold variegated. The brightly coloured tropaeolum flowers look elegantly beautiful spread across such a background. The deep-blue fruits which follow the flowers are a further dividend to those who offer this colourful climber garden room.

'Passion Flower', the evocative *Passiflora caerulea*, is a climber which needs the shelter of a wall to be successfully grown outdoors in colder areas

12

The Link between House and Garden

In climates which afford predicatable amounts of sunshine there is a well established tradition of using a patio, terrace, or courtyard as an extension of the house. The enclosed patio courtyards of southern Spain or the peristylium of ancient Rome offered a most gracious style of outdoor living, with house blending into garden so artistically that there was no clearly discernible line where one ended and the other began. There would be a sense of passing from light to shade, though even this was masked to a degree by the skilful use of containerised trees, shrubs, and other plants. Indeed, the whole success of the conjugation depended then as now on the careful, well considered positioning of the plant-filled window-boxes, hanging baskets, and tubs. The aim in both southern and northern latitudes is to bring the style of the garden right up to the threshold. In a benign climate some shelter must be provided from the sun, so shade from high walls and light-foliaged trees gave comfort from the blazing heat of noon. A fountain often formed a central feature, cooling the air and allowing a gentle conversation of running water to permeate house and garden.

Edward Kemp writing on 'How to Layout a Garden' advises against unnecessary divisions as these interfere with 'that beautiful sense of continuity which does so much in the way of producing size and expression'.

This free-standing patio plant trough can also serve as a window-box. Ivy, pelargoniums and antirrhinums are combined for summer display

Plants in vases, urns, and other containers revelled in the cool moistness. Green foliage absorbing and softening the glare of sunlight added a peculiar quality of reflective serenity to the scene. Such refreshing oases of green-shadowed quiet do exist, for I have taken refuge there: in San Antonio, Tuscany, and so many more places when eyes and mind needed rest and refreshment from blinding white sunlight, and found comfort in green leaves and beautiful flowers.

In more northern latitudes, terrace and patio are designed not so much to provide shade, for grey clouds perform that function with soul-searing efficiency. Instead the aim is to catch and hold warmth. Walls provide shelter from chilling breezes and gather, then reflect the sun's warmth so that even in February it is possible to sit outdoors and enjoy flowers which are persuaded to open so much earlier there than in the open garden.

For the town gardener with limited space in which to grow plants, window-boxes, hanging baskets, and a selection of tubs, urns, and pots are a splendid extension to a minuscule plot. Yet even though there is enough space in my three-quarter acre (one-third hectare) plot to grow a fairly extensive range of plants, I still do what my family describe as 'cluttering up the best sitting out places on the terrace with containers' for growing the more select, difficult, or tender shrubs, alpines, herbaceous perennials, and brightly flowered annuals.

One of the great advantages of containers is that the compost for each can be adjusted precisely to suit the needs of whichever plant is to be grown in it. Pests or diseases can be kept more easily within bounds because the routine maintenance of watering, feeding and dead heading means that the mini gardens and their occupants are under daily observation. Action is offensive rather than defensive, with no pest or disease having a chance to proliferate. Almost an Eden, though not quite, for containers, window-boxes and hanging baskets exposed as they are to sun and wind do dry out very quickly and must be watered frequently.

There are almost as many different shapes and styles of containers, which can be bought and used in the garden and around the house perimeter, as there are plants for growing in them. So many, as I learned to my cost, that it is very easy to end up with such an assortment of pots, boxes and tubs so vastly different in character that all hope of achieving an overall co-ordinated pattern becomes virtually impossible. Now I choose the style of container and type of material it is made from that fits in well with house and garden.

Stone, even carefully tinted reconstituted stone, somehow never matches too well with brick. Oddly enough, shaped concrete pots or vases, coloured to blend with the material used for constructing house and terrace, blend in sympathetically in most cases. Earthenware or terracotta pots look elegant in a formal terrace or patio setting. Wooden boxes or barrels introduce an element of rural simplicity which in the right context can be refreshingly casual.

Containers are the most convenient way of growing hydrangeas in areas of low rainfall and limey soils. Kept moist and well fed they flower profusely. The illustration shows deep-blue-flowered *Hydrangea* 'Klius Superba' with *Vinca major* 'Variegata'. The blue of most *Hydrangea macrophylla* varieties changes to pink when lime is present in the soil or compost. Special chemicals are on offer which can be watered onto the compost to 'blue' the flowers if there is any doubt as to the soil's base state

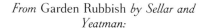

Containers made from plastic or fibre glass have the advantage of being so light that they can be moved without undue effort to provide colour at focal points anywhere in the garden. They are cheaper than containers made from stone, concrete, or iron, and may be used as a reserve to supplement the static displays. By making up the cheaper containers with summer bedding in late April, a month, that is, before the spring display is due to be retired, the plants are already in flower when the time comes to make the exchange at the end of May. The 'off-duty' container emptied of the worn-out plants and with compost refurbished can be replanted with a selection of autumn blooming mini dahlias, michaelmas daisy and the like to carry through until winter drives all but the dedicated children of Adam indoors.

BASKETS, BOXES, AND OTHERS

Free-standing containers are only a part of the mechanism of blending house and garden together. Window-boxes and hanging baskets together with free growing climbing plants also play an important part in covering up merely functional masonry. As one exasperated builder expressed himself when I was concerned that his pointing of the house wall should not damage a patriarchal wisteria growing across it, the wall did have other, admittedly less important, functions than providing support for my plants, and holding up the roof was one. A house front without masking vegetation lacks that air of warmth and welcoming hospitality that flower-covered masonry offers.

Both window-boxes and hanging baskets should be firmly fastened to the wall and secured beyond any doubt or question that they will break free. A large soil-filled container falling even a few feet and striking some unsuspecting passer-by on the head could do them serious injury. This lesson was impressed on me at a very early stage in my professional gardening career. I had just finished planting up a large window-box with wallflowers and pansy and was stooping to gather up my tools when the supporting brackets broke free from the wall. The box had only a few inches to fall before it struck my shoulder, but the weight knocked me flat onto the paving stones. Since then I have checked all supports carefully before putting any weight on them at all. Brackets strong enough to hang a gardener on will usually take the weight of flower-filled box or basket.

Window-boxes need to be well made, of tough and durable material. Large, deep containers obviously hold more compost and therefore do not dry out so quickly and provide a deeper root run, which saves a lot of time which would otherwise be spent on watering and supplementary feeding. Dehydration is a major problem. Window-boxes and hanging baskets are fully exposed to hot sunshine and drying winds so they lose moisture at a phenomenal rate and require watering once or twice a day in dry weather. Whatever the size, shape, and type of container, it must have adequate provision for surplus water to drain away through

From Garden Rubbish *by Sellar and Yeatman:*

Take it from us, it is utterly forbidden to be half-hearted about gardening – You have got to Love your garden whether you like it or not.

To plant up a hanging basket standing comfortably upright, place a large flowerpot or bucket on the bench or patio table. The basket sits firmly on that at a suitable working height. Line it with sphagnum moss or whatever material is ready to hand. The various trailing plants are poked in through the sides and their roots covered in compost as the work proceeds.

Where space is limited, hanging baskets are an expressive extension

holes in the base. Wooden containers should be treated with a wood preservative both inside and out before painting. I also paint all metal bands, brackets and hooks with a liquid which is a combined rust proofing and undercoat.

TAKE CARE OF THE ROOTS

The question of which compost to use for filling the containers was resolved to my personal satisfaction by experiment: a simple system of loam-based John Innes No 3 for long-stay perennials, shrubs, trees and climbers. Aluminium or plastic hoops which add an extra 3in (7.5cm) of depth to a container enable me to top dress and mulch just like, as one visitor put it, 'in a real garden'. The hoops are an idea copied from days when I grew fruit under glass during my early formative years in private gardening, and have served a useful purpose ever since.

The short-stay annuals, tender perennials, and anything whose tenancy is short are planted in peat-based or pulverised bark mixtures. These have the advantage of being light, functional and clean to handle. People living in flats and who have to carry composts upstairs will sensibly opt for using peat- or bark-based mixes for everything.

As to Plants

Working out planting schemes which will be colourful and consistently pleasing to the eye over several months is a most enjoyable part of my gardening year. Some of them work well, others tolerably so; as for the few which turn out less agreeable than expected, like a doctor's mistakes they can be decently buried. Not for anything, no matter how successful a particular combination may have been, would I slavishly try to reproduce it year after year. That for me would take all the adventure and interest away.

Winter Need Not be Our Discontent

Though a certain basic honesty forces the confession that it is by no means easy to find plants which still look attractive though wind blown and frost bitten, the best solution is to rely heavily on foliage interest: what are collectively known as heathers, with special emphasis on forms of *Erica herbacea* which, in addition to having

Choosing the right plants can present problems. Strong bright colours are best in full sunshine but do draw the eye. Pastel shades lighten the dark corners, looking most attractive when patterned with light and shade.

Bright-flowered annuals transform a stone courtyard into a colour-filled garden

The compost will need to be kept moist throughout the autumn and winter, with particular care being taken to ensure that the plants are not dehydrated by the drying winds of March. Do not water at all during frosty weather, and move hanging baskets into shelter if the climate is exceedingly severe.

attractive foliage, crowns good with excellence by producing flowers in late winter as well. In spite of *Erica herbacea*'s well publicised tolerance of lime soils it grows best in an acid compost. Undoubtedly, *Erica carnea* (syn. *herbacea*) 'Foxhollow', whose bright golden-yellow leaves are tinged with pink during winter, lets itself down with a meagre display of lavender flowers. For this reason I now prefer 'Westwood Yellow' with similar foliage and a more generous distribution of bloom. Grown with the dark-green-leaved *Erica herbacea* 'Myretoun Ruby' whose flowers are a most remarkably brilliant shade of ruby red, they project a robust good cheer on even the greyest winter day. Such an arrangement can be further enlivened by planting crocus 'Whitwell Purple' and yellow-petalled *Iris danfordiae*. A similar combination works well in hanging baskets, with a gold- or cream-and-green variegated ivy instead of the golden-leaved erica. The trailing stems of ivy hanging down hide the basket base.

Once the various plants have served their turn in basket, window-box or tub they may be planted out into the garden.

There are several varieties of *Euonymus fortunei* with attractive foliage which because of their neat compact habit are admirably fashioned to form a focal point. 'Emerald Gaiety' with cream-white and green foliage, 'Emerald 'n Gold' whose green-and-gold leaf colour is suffused with pink, or 'Sunspot', with a central splash of yellow, are all useful. In a tub or window-box such dwarf shrubs help give a change in form and level. I have no hesitation in lifting any one of a dozen or more dwarf shrubs out of the garden to do duty in tubs or window-boxes. The gap left in the garden is easily filled with annuals until the chosen shrub is returned none the worse for its experience. *Hebe pinguifolia* 'Pagei' and *Hebe* 'Quick-silver' are two silver-leaved dwarf shrubs which offer an interesting alternative theme to the rest as centrepieces in a winter compilation. Bedded around with coloured primroses or winter flowering viola, they bring just the right note of optimism to many a cheerless winter day. *Hebe* 'Quicksilver' is almost prostrate in habit and has proved most useful for softening the hard edges of tubs or pots. The branching system is such that crocus and *Narcissus bulbocodium romieuxii* planted underneath can push up flowers from amongst the silvery-blue foliage. That they bloom in this sort of situation during January makes them more welcome than the first swallows.

Though there are few days in winter when scent can be fully appreciated abroad in the garden proper, the patio or terrace provides conditions which are far more congenial. I first grew witch hazel, *Hamamelis mollis*, as a tub plant twenty years ago. In due process of time this grew too large and had to be planted out, yet I had seven flowering seasons as a reward. Plant around with snowdrops and *Iris histrioides* 'Major', whose vivid blue petals form a lovely complement to the yellow, sweetly fragrant witch hazel as they open in January.

Only recently I visited a garden where *Mahonia japonica* with handsome, evergreen, pinnate leaves and racemes of lemon-yellow, lily-of-the-valley-scented flowers was being grown in preference to

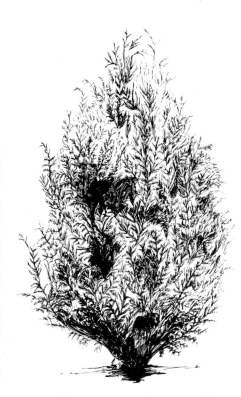

Slow growing conifers, particularly those which have golden foliage, are most excellent, all-year-round terrace shrubs. *Juniperus communis* 'Golden Shower' is an attractive form of a native conifer which has proved very effective. The yellow fades to bronze in winter, so I plant it around with *Iris histrioides* 'Major' whose blue flowers are lovely against the foliage of the conifer

witch hazel. I must admit that, forced to make a choice, I would settle for the mahonia because the foliage is so attractive. An underplanting of *Vinca minor* 'Aureo Variegata' with blue flowers and yellow variegated leaves led to the breaking of a certain commandment about coveting one's neighbours' goods.

SPRING AND THE UNFOLDING YEAR

There is a wealth of material to choose from, yet so often the spirit of adventure, possibly immobilised by the chill of winter, dares attempt nothing more than the merely conventional. Tulips, hyacinths, wallflowers, polyanthus, and pansy do not need a champion for they are beyond any other criticism except that of being safe and traditional. Grow them always, particularly wall-flowers and hyacinths for when in bloom they distil a fragrance which is all springtime. There is a refreshing simplicity to the season which needs to be reflected in the quiet colour tones and uncomplicated bedding schemes used to brighten window-boxes and tubs.

A combination of 'Primrose Bedder' wallflowers which grow to a modest 15in (38cm) high, with Spanish bluebells, *Hyacinthoides hispanica*, is delightful and a triumph of restraint. Plant all *Hyacinthoides* species immediately the bulbs are on sale, for having no protective skin, unlike tulips or narcissus, they do dry out very quickly.

Hyacinths can be persuaded to flower early if the tub or window-box is sited in a sheltered corner. When the summer bedding lingers on in the autumn, hyacinth bulbs are best potted up so that not a day of the growing season is lost. When the time arrives for making up the containers, having the bulbs in growth makes the work much easier. A reconstituted stone urn planted up with *Hyacinthus orientalis* 'Orange Boven', or 'Gypsy Queen' with flowers of that shade of peachy orange, looks most effective with a cream-and-green-leaved *Hedera* 'Glacier'. The ivy is a permanent resident. Kept clipped back from growing into the compost, the shoots are persuaded instead to hang down over the sides.

Aubrietia is another first-class spring flowering edging plant when mixed in with *Arabis* 'Snowflake'. I have used this most ebullient pairing in association with different varieties of tulips in an effort to discover which colour combination suits best. A group of *Tulipa tarda* in bright yellow and white combined with blue aubrietia and white arabis is crisply inviting like a well concocted spring salad.

One of the happiest combinations of all was the idea, not the plants, I unashamedly borrowed from a parks bedding scheme and used in a window-box: just a simple mix of pink-and-white double early tulip 'Peach Blossom' with *Muscaria* 'Heavenly Blue'. The view from the window-box looked out over the packed array of flowers and had a white-blossomed canopy of *Prunus Tai-Haku* as a background.

Because viola are such good value I am at times guilty of over-

Narcissus bulbocodium romieuxii is always the first of all to flower given a reasonably sheltered situation. These early, delicate, hooped-petticoat flowers remind me of an April day when I stood looking across pastures bright yellow with millions of this tiny narcissus to the snow-covered mountains of northern Spain. As the breeze ruffled the blooms to set them all aripple, the spring sunlight threw pale-primrose, then dark-gold shadows across the scene.

Though bulbs never trail, this should in no way prevent their use in window-boxes or hanging baskets. There is no law that I am aware of, which insists a hanging basket has to be placed at eye level or above. A neighbour has one medium-sized basket hanging alongside the bell set in the wall beside a door. Anyone visiting looks down into a floral composition made up of purple crocus, yellow 'Jumblie' narcissus, orange, primrose and cream on green variegated ivy. That the basket offers the same, happy welcome as a smiling face and warm handshake is beyond question.

Pots of all shapes and sizes, also window-boxes were used by the Romans as decoration for roof gardens. Pliny describes earthenware pots used specifically for growing lemon trees which had 'breathing holes for the roots'. Window-boxes, tubs and urns feature in medieval and post-Renaissance paintings. Indeed, anyone touring the art galleries of Holland and Italy today will be astonished, as I was, at how little the containers used today have changed in character from those depicted in the paintings.

Hooks to carry hanging baskets or window-boxes should be fixed firm enough to take the weight of a large gardener

A shallow trough filled with Sempervivums (house leeks) makes an interesting perennial terrace or patio decoration. The varieties need to be carefully selected in order to give the widest variation in leaf colour, from silver through purple to shades of green.

planting them in containers and elsewhere in the garden. Though they flower later by about fourteen days when grown in shade, there is no other noticeable inconvenience caused by lack of direct sunlight. Primrose-type primula show a similar response to shade conditions which provides a useful basis for several very lovely planting arrangements. Primrose-type primula really are the most convenient of spring bedding for they are propagated by division immediately after flowering, just when they need to be removed to make way for the pelargonium and other denizens of summer.

There is another primula, *marginata* by name, which I planted in an old earthenware strawberry pot which had a hole at the top and at intervals up the sides. These are variously sold as crocus bowls, herb pots and whatever. Certainly the three I have do yeoman service throughout the year. The form of *Primula marginata* which has proved most suitable is known as 'Holden Clough'. The grey-green, silver-edged leaves dusted with powdery farina, topped by blue scented flowers, are lovely grown with white crocus. For a window-box on a northerly aspect pale colours help to light up what even on a spring day can be a dark, depressing aspect. Primroses, *Primula vulgaris*, are of that particular shade of yellow best described as luminous, which looks so natural with colonies of *Scilla* 'Spring Beauty' growing up around it.

So, then, to viola which have provided the basis for so many shady side arrangements, a descriptive term which is sinisterly suggestive of a Mafia connection. *Viola* 'Spring Magic Moonlight' has petals of a creamy-yellow shade which are lovely when contrasted with a dwarf rhododendron called 'Blue Tit'. I grow a selection of dwarf rhododendrons, pieris, euonymus and others in pots to use as a solid background in window-boxes and tubs. There is no need to knock the roots out of the pots, so that as the seasons change so do the shrubs without suffering any check to growth. As each outgrows its usefulness fresh stock can be raised from cuttings before the parent is given a permanent place in the garden.

The prime arrangement of those tried so far on a west wall window-box is dwarf narcissus 'Jumblie', which is quite the longest lasting in flower of the genus, and primula 'Garryarde Guinevere' with bronze flushed leaves. There is a special appeal in the bronze, dusky pink, and daffodil gold which perfectly compliments the season.

There is a modern development in the patio decoration theme which could enable those gardeners with only very limited space to enjoy home-grown apples. This is made possible by the introduction of a new strain of apple which grows naturally as a single vertical stem without producing side branches, only fruiting spurs. So in the spring there is the joy of apple blossom, then in autumn the delectable prospect of crisp apples picked straight from the tree. Growth is so moderate that the trees can be comfortably contained in tubs or pots. There are, to date, four varieties. 'Maypole', a crab apple with very dark-red flowers followed in August by red-purple fruits, provides a colour contrast to the 'Golden Hornet' crab apple I have container-grown for several

ABOVE
Work out a colourful planting scheme.
This one is *Celosia cristata* with marigold
and pelargonium

RIGHT
A happy combination between *Tulipa
tarda* and blue *Scilla*

The recently introduced single-stem 'Ballerina' varieties of apple should enable even those with only a balcony to plant an orchard

years, which has near-white flowers and deep-yellow fruits. The other three varieties, 'Waltz', 'Polka' and 'Bolero', are what a young friend of mine calls proper apples: meaning those which he can eat, not just look at. I have only been able to grow apples even on a dwarfing rootstock as patio plants by almost weekly pruning during the growing season. These new 'Ballerina' apples, according to the East Malling Research Station, need at most only a little nipping out of shoots which can be done between finger and thumb. Some tubs, planted with primroses, daffodils, cowslips, even snakes head fritillary and snowdrops should offer all the evocative beauty of an orchard within the limited confines of a patio or terrace.

Though herbs are more a part of the summer scene, the planting is usually carried out in springtime. After years of patient enquiry and experiment with containers of every shape, make and mode of construction, for my purpose, if for no one else's, a large beer barrel cut in half makes a most useful herb garden. Painted white with the iron hoops rust proofed with black they have the same look of neat efficiency as a uniformed staff nurse. Mint, being a ground hog, is best kept in a separate container. A 10 or 12in (26–30cm) clay pot is large enough to supply a family of four. John Innes No 3 compost with extra sand and some lumps of charcoal mixed in suits very well for all herbs. That the barrels are made up more for ornament than utility is a frequent complaint which I must confess is quite justified. A white Yorkshire Rose which grows only 12in (30cm) high, bedded around with a golden-leaved form of lemon-scented thyme, *Thymus x citriodorus* 'Aureum', and a grey-leaved, blue-flowered compact-growing lavender, *Lavendula* 'Munstead Dwarf', is all through the summer a delight to see.

There are golden- and purple-leaved forms of sage more attractive than the grey-green leaved, yet just as useful for flavouring. There was a tradition in the village where I spent my childhood that sage in the garden kept the gate against death. Long years after I read that an Anglo Saxon manuscript stated 'No man dies while sage grows in the garden'. Needless to say, my sage, planted with rosemary, is well cared for. *Salvia officinalis* 'Purpurascens' has dark-red stems and purple leaves, while the variety 'Icterina' has foliage of an attractive old-gold shade. Rosemary keeps its green colouring when cut longer than any other herb, which explains why it is used at weddings as a symbol of everlasting love. A barrel with holes cut in the side offers an interesting way of growing the very fastigiate *Rosemarinus officinalis* 'Miss Jessop' which has lavender-blue flowers. Rooted cuttings planted in the holes grow up to form a backcloth to the sage or whatever else is growing in the tub.

Summer allows a freedom of expression which carries over into the autumn. For this brief season there can be brilliant Mediterranean colour combinations to reflect the July sun. Having ready access to a plentiful supply of sphagnum moss I still prefer the old-fashioned way of lining hanging baskets with a generous thickness of this material. When planted up, the basket should give the impression of a complete ball of foliage and flowers, a feat impossible with the modern, self-watering affairs. Seen from below the plastic container looks precisely what it is – the underside of a plastic container unable to be disguised behind a decent mask of flowers.

Pelargonium, lobelia, petunia and other popular flowers serve their turn of duty year after year. Dangling from lamp posts, the balconies of mayoral bowers and innumerable house frontages throughout the land, these most durable plants serve their purpose well.

Some of the most attractive summer basket and rack plantings of recent years have been composed entirely of the begonia 'Sensation' which is a trailing form bred specially for use in basket, rack and window-box. The colour range includes orange, pink, scarlet, and yellow, and the full double flowers open in succession over many weeks. The *Begonia pendula* 'Chanson' mixed and *Begonia x tuber hybrida* are also excellent value; needing no supplementary planting, they are sufficient in themselves.

A hanging basket, once made up, should last, apart from routine maintenance, watering, feeding, and dead heading, for three months at least. There are several fuchsia varieties which are commendably long flowering and so make very useful hanging basket shrubs. One of my favourite arrangements over many years is a combination of *Fuchsia* 'Marinka', and the sport 'Golden Marinka' whose naturally trailing habit and beautiful leaf colour make it ideally suited for basket work. Though 'Marinka' was first introduced in 1902, there are few modern varieties which are more floriferous. The tube and sepals are rich, lustrous red, the corolla a slightly darker colour. Lovely in combination with variegated ground ivy, *Glechoma hederacea* 'Variegata' and a trailing *Lobelia erimus* 'Blue Cascade'.

In the last ten years there have been some quite remarkable variations in plant fashions. With the generous assistance of the plant geneticist, Busy Lizzie, *Impatiens*, has been transformed from a cottage window plant to one of the most all-round, useful bedding plants. It will grow outdoors during summer in sun or shade. For window-box or basket cultivation it offers a range of flower colours as richly varied and brilliant as the flamenco dancer's skirt. A hanging basket planted round the F1 hybrid impatiens and pale-blue trailing lobelia makes a brave show of vivid flowers. Impatiens baskets are best made up early, while the root ball of the Busy Lizzie is small enough to go through the mesh sides of the basket, which then presents the appearance of a flower ball.

Herbs are both attractive and useful. In foliage colour and flower they are well qualified to compete on aesthetic terms alone for peak viewing on a south-facing terrace. Because regular supplies of mint, as prime favourite, have to be within easy reach of the kitchen, the barrel is kept on an east-facing terrace conveniently close to the back door. Rosemary, sage, parsley and others with a more seasonal demand also need to be readily accessible.

Of all the culinary herbs Rosmarinus is my favourite, and it is well named 'Dew of the Sea'. When I stayed on a farm in Tuscany harvesting orris root I was told the bed linen was thrown over bushes of rosemary to dry after being laundered so gathering fragrance as it aired.

The contents of a herb barrel need regularly rejuvenating, so take cuttings each year of sage, rosemary, and other woody-stemmed plants. Parsley and those raised from seed are sown as part of the normal spring routine.

Almost my favourite summer window-box planting: African marigolds and dark-purple heliotrope

Gazania is one of the best plants for seaside gardens, asking only a full exposure to sun and well drained soil. The curiously striped and zoned daisy-like flowers open in succession all summer. Sow seeds in a heated greenhouse or on a window-sill indoors in early March, then prick off into individual pots during late April

A window-box or tub on a south-facing wall will be subject to extremes of temperature which will test the durability of anything planted in it. The plants used need to be sun-loving for even in temperate Britain temperatures into the 90°F on a south wall during summer are not uncommon. Pelargonium are an obvious choice, for being South Africans they are used to hot sun and drought. They are so widely used in baskets, boxes, and beds of parks departments, that for home garden decoration it is pleasant to have a change from the pelargoniums-with-everything theme. Exceptions can be made in the case of new introductions as with the recently classified 'Floribunda' pelargonium which are still listed under geranium by seedsmen. The 'Sensation' hybrids are different in producing many flower heads earlier and over a longer season, which makes them a very bright prospect indeed for basket, tub, or window-box culture. The flower colour is traditional pelargonium – vivid shades of scarlet, cherry, salmon, and blush pink, so there are several interesting associations to work on. Pelargonium 'Pink Sensation' with *Pinus mugo* 'Mops' as a centrepiece, and a silver-and-green-speckled ivy, *Hedera helix* 'Kolibri', trained so as to mask the container sides, is especially engaging. *Gazania* 'Carnival F1' or 'Chansonette' will certainly respond to being baked under hot sunshine with a wealth of multi-coloured flowers like chrysanthemums in shades of plum, red, yellow, orange, and cream, with all the permutations therefrom. To accentuate the very positive colours of *Gazania*, use *Verbena x hybrida* 'Amethyst' or the sweetly fragrant *Heliotropium x hybridum* 'Marine'. The last named looks very fetching grouped with dwarf double French marigolds like 'Gypsy Sunshine' in a window-box, so that the perfume flushes in through the open window.

By grouping several tubs together on a patio a lot of interesting variations can be worked on a simple basic theme. Dwarf conifers form a central core to some of my own favourite contrived mini-gardens. A *Tsuga canadensis* 'Minima' growing in a reconstituted stone tub like a green waterfall is a permanent feature on the terrace. In spring, tubs are filled with crocus and aubrietia, followed by a mixed planting on one side of *Lithospermum* 'Heavenly Blue' and deep-crimson *Phlox subulata* 'Red Wings'. The midsummer theme is composed of *Ageratum* 'Blue Ribbon', and *Antirrhinum* 'Royal Carpet Pink', or, as this year, *Begonia semperflorens* 'Volcano' with scarlet flowers and bronze foliage.

White-painted containers present such an air of refined elegance when associated with gold or cream and green foliage that they scarcely need flowers except as points of emphasis to give expression to a restrained theme. *Chamaecyparis obtusa* 'Nana Lutea' grown in a container forms a neat pyramid of golden yellow; to contrast with the militarily precise upright habit of the conifer, *Hedera helix* 'Goldchild', trained so as to go down over the sides of the container. Nothing else is permanently planted; pots containing suitable flowers are simply plunged while in bloom, then replaced

Gazania splendens *cultivars will only perform well in warm places, so a south-facing patio or window-box is ideal for them. New self-coloured varieties like the deep gold shaded 'Garden Sun' are particularly useful. Grown with an edging of silver-leaved* Cineraria maritima *'Dwarf Silver', the association is very simply beautiful.*

Fuchsias are indispensable window-box, basket, and tub plants, in bloom continuously throughout the summer

For six years I had responsibility for three large stone vases sited on a York paving terrace below a tennis court. One year in a spirit of real adventure I planted them up with agapanthus and fuchsia 'Mrs Popple'. The combination of deep blue agapanthus flowers with purple and dark-red fuchsia was sensational.

Agapanthus 'Headbourne Hybrids' (righ) have proved themselves so indestructibly hardy over the twenty-five years of our close association that they now spend all four seasons outdoors. The erect stems 24–30in (61–75cm) high carry umbels of flowers in various shades of violet, blue or white. They will thrive in any soil which is moist without being germinate and the resulting seedlings will reach flowering size in two or three years. When planted in tubs I grow agapanthus in John Innes No 3 compost, and liquid feed each month during the growing season with high-potash tomato fertiliser

Begonia semperflorens varieties are most useful multi-purpose plants. In summer bedding, tubs, or window-boxes they are indispensable. It is sometimes overlooked that they also make good house plants

as fancy dictates. In spring there is *Rhododendron obtusum amoenum* with small leaves and darkly orange-red flowers – possibly a selected form this, which like most dwarf rhododendrons is so easily raised from cuttings that those which outgrow their welcome can be quickly replaced with home-grown youngsters. *Geranium cinereum* 'Ballerina' and a *Campanula* 'Dicksons Gold' offered a lilac-pink and pale-blue-on-gold tone one year.

Begonia or fuchsia for colour and length of flowering in shades according to taste have up till now been like sardines and cucumber for lunch, frequently repeated.

There is no doubt, judging from my own experience, that almost anything growing in the main garden can, if only for a year or two, be accommodated with roots confined in a tub as patio or terrace decoration. Climbing roses, clematis, cherries, crab apples, Japanese maples, and all the rest have offered such beauty to the eye and pleasure in their cultivation that even with a garden large enough to indulge most of my whims and fancies I still grow a selection of special or new and unusual plants in pots. Some, like the agapanthus, nerine, and crinum, flower more profusely with the extra care lavished on their cultivation when pot grown. So they should, for any left-over liquid feed is always directed towards them. Without the container-grown shrubs, herbaceous, perennials, annuals, and bulbs, the garden would stop abruptly at the terrace wall, except, of course, for the climbing plants which hide some of the arid masonry.

Of all the seasons autumn is my favourite: wanton profligate, it offers a 'Prodigal Son' experience without the penalties. What is done, mistakes, failures, successes, will soon be erased from all except memory as winter wipes the slate clean.

What, then, is this third season which extends from the descending equinox to the winter solstice? Once the sun crosses the equator on its journey southwards the days shorten appreciably, and yet most gardeners notice changes taking place in the garden which are more subtle than that. Usually, sometime in August, there is a cool crispness to the morning air which signals a barely discernible change in tempo. This maturation process is apparent long before the astrologically designated date of September 21st. The quiet of autumn is different from the intense deadness of a snow-covered winter's day, for there is a vibrant quality to the stillness; a sense of expectancy with none of the foreboding which comes later as the chill deepens.

Work which, for reasons of tidiness, had to be urgently taken in hand a month ago becomes unimportant, for a less well groomed appearance is a part of mist-hung mornings and a scattering of birch leaves across the lawn. Often I catch myself pausing in the middle of whatever work is claiming my attention just to stand and listen to the all-encompassing quiet. There are, of course, sounds which serve only to emphasise the stillness. A cockerel crowing from the barnyard two fields away, or a stanza of song from a robin perched on the crab apple tree are two, often repeated, comforting intrusions – the robin's brief song of autumn like a tinkling of icicles, so different from the springtime melody.

Of course there is work to do, some of it made urgent by the weather when crops are ripe for harvesting. This gathering in of fruits and vegetables is a part of the season's satisfying completeness. Apples gathered in during the Indian summer's daytime warmth, then left to cool overnight outdoors before being taken in for sorting and storing carry satisfaction in every bite.

Pears need to be kept well apart from apples in store, and each time I handle a 'Comice' or 'Hessle' or any other of the dozen or more varieties which grew in the garden at home, the instruction I was given then to 'treat them like eggs only more carefully' comes immediately to mind. Why apples and pears were kept apart was a mystery, for they mixed quite happily in my stomach. Over the years, experience has proved that one hastens the ripening of the other to an alarming degree. Anyone who has never picked fruit on a sunbright, autumn day, whether in orchard or along a blackberry and crab apple-verged lane, has missed one of the most satisfying, peasant-based experiences. Picking mushrooms, foraging for leaf mould, or gathering firewood are all a part of the autumn scene to be relished afresh each year.

There are vegetable crops also to be made safe from the weather. Potatoes to lift, then allowed to dry and harden for an hour before being gathered into hessian or paper sacks. A dark, reasonably dry and frost-proof building is an essential part of every vegetable gardener's equipment. Leave just enough roots in the ground if the soil is slug-free to keep the kitchen supplied until early December. Freshly lifted potatoes have a delicacy of flavour which is lost in store.

The various forms of Michaelmas daisy are as one with dahlias and chrysanthemums in advertising the coming of autumn. The roots are better divided every second year.

Beetroot is devoured by rodents if left in the ground too long, so, to be safe, gather the crop and after twisting off the tops store the roots in sand. Carrots, after years of lifting, cleaning, and clamp building, I now find it best to leave in the plot where they are growing to be used as required. When frost threatens, lift a few extra to tide you over till the soil thaws out.

Stringing onions makes a useful, relaxing, wet-day job and is certainly the most effective way of storing this most important winter vegetable.

Often the weather is the gardener's time keeper, as it is in autumn. Though I am careful to lift half-hardy summer bedding plants long before there is any danger of real frost, dahlias are an altogether different matter for the growth they make in autumn is an essential part of the ripening process. There needs to be a frost severe enough to blacken the foliage without damaging the roots, and this usually happens sometime in October. Once the dahlia tubers and montbretia are out of the borders it is time to tuck the garden up ready for winter.

All the ready-to-use compost needs to be out of the bins prior to being dug into the soil. With all the cleaning, weeding, and clipping down there will be more than enough to fill all the compost bins to overflowing again. This recycling of waste is as old as gardening itself. If for some reason home-grown vegetable, compostable material is in short supply, I make up the difference with straw – after making sure that it has not been sprayed with a herbicide.

There comes an afternoon when the trees along the garden boundary stand etched in bold relief against a sky all pale orange and chill duck-egg blue. The soil as dusk deepens is crisp underfoot and covers are needed on the frames for the first time. Winter has arrived to close the door on one year and open it on another.

A mist-hung September morning with 'Iceberg' roses pretending it is still high summer

13

Indoor Gardening

With the increasing interest in what is, after all, a specialised form of gardening, there has developed a whole new range of growing techniques. Hydroponics, which enables a plant to grow without soil, merely with its roots immersed in a nutrient solution, is an extreme example of specialist cultural technique. There are self-watering containers where the only skill needed is the ability to keep a reservoir topped up with water; osmosis completes the process.

There are other ingenious devices whose degree of sophistication increases, or so it appears, in direct ratio to their cost: gadgets which can calculate whether a compost requires watering or topping up with nutrients; indoor lighting systems to suit all needs, pockets and purposes. As the ultimate in hygienic living, there are labels which, when pushed into the compost, will effectively destroy any pest which sucks, sips, or bites a leaf or tissue.

The genuine, dedicated indoor gardener soon discovers that an understanding of each plant's needs, and daily inspection to spot any trouble before it gets too serious, is the best insurance in favour of a long and healthy life for all house plants.

There comes a day, usually in late November, when being indoors offers an indisputably pleasant alternative to being outside in the garden. Days there will certainly be in plenty before spring returns to complete the winter digging, pruning, and other general routine seasonal work. For the present inside is best side. Growing plants indoors is for me something of an escape to a form of gardening where frost, snow, and bitter wind can do nothing to disturb the slow maturation process of a plant from seed to flower. For those who live in flats the cultivation of house and more temporary florists' pot plants is their only means of access to the therapy of what is best described as 'the soothing quiet of growing things'.

Indoor plants fall into well defined groups. *Monstera, Ficus* or *Yucca* are like the dining room table – a permanent feature in a room. That in time these 'pet' plants become almost heirlooms is part of an inevitable process, they might even be given a pet name. Florists' pot plants, cyclamen, poinsettia and azalea, are treated as lodgers capable of paying rent only when in flower. Bulbs also fall into this category of briefly loved, then decently hidden from sight.

Whether permanent resident or temporary lodger, each will make demands on our skill as gardeners, success or failure depends on our ability to discover and provide for their requirements in precisely the same way as we strive to cultivate the plants growing in the garden outdoors. In just the same way, too, there will be those indoor plants which for no obvious reason will settle in immediately and thrive. Equally certain is the fact that there will be others which in spite of our best endeavours will sicken and die, though it is possible to lessen the risk of losing a plant by making sure before buying that you can provide the right conditions which will make growing it a possibility rather than a questionable probability.

Buying any plant, whether for indoor or outdoor cultivation, should be a leisurely, enjoyable process. Usually, before setting out on a visit to the nursery or garden centre most likely to stock the plants, I have taken time to make myself reasonably familiar with the best compost, lighting conditions, and other points of cultivation. Even so, I double-check and ask for advice from the vendor. When is the best time to repot, what is the most suitable growing temperature, how often will I need to feed and, most important, is the object of my attention a lime-hater or, if the idea is really to impress with my linguistic dexterity, a calcifuge rather than a calcicole?

Have a look around first to see if the plants on sale are well cared for, free from pests and disease. Reject any which are weed-infested or pot-bound or showing similar signs of neglect. Above all, the person selling the plants should be able to supply all the information the customer needs to grow it successfully. If this is not forthcoming, then apologise for wasting their time and take your custom elsewhere. After all, half the pleasure of visiting a nursery or garden centre is the prospect of a good gardening gossip. Indeed, the times when I manage to leave a nursery with only the plants I set out to buy are rare. Inevitably there are others on display which are irresistible, a fact well known at my local nursery.

The greatest single factor which will influence the type of plants chosen must surely be, what sort of growing conditions the various rooms in the house afford. There is no use in trying to grow cyclamen in the overheated, dry air of a modern living-room. Better by far in these sorts of places to invest in a glass case or terrarium and grow a selection of plants in the moist, humid, micro-climate that it provides.

Just as the garden imposes limits on the plants we can grow as opposed to those we would like to include in the design, so there will be similar restrictions indoors. Within these usually fairly flexible boundaries we can give free rein to personal preferences, and what a fascinating adventure this can prove to be. By grouping

General rules for all. Always use water with the chill taken off it, never ice cold, for house plants. Water less frequently in winter and preferably before mid-day. DO NOT leave a plant with its roots standing in water. Keep the foliage dust-free and clean. Though there are exceptions, African violets for example, a fine overhead spray with clean water is marvellously refreshing particularly for evergreen foliage. Feed little and often, but only established plants and never when the compost is dry. Water as required, thoroughly soaking the root ball, then no more until the compost dries on the surface. The automatic daily dribble is worse than useless. On cold nights move the plants out of the window or provide some protection from chill night air. A buoyant, fresh atmosphere is good for plants, cold draughts are harmful. Water liberally in the growing season.

The Swiss cheese plant, *Monstera deliciosa*, is easily identified by its curious leaves

those plants which need similar temperatures and routine care, the labour of watering, feeding, and general looking after is made easier. A group of plants is like a mini rainforest in creating its own micro-climate of moist air against excessive dehydration. That a careful juxtapositioning of selected plants exploits all the combined qualities of flower and foliage is as true indoors as it is when applied in the garden.

One thing I have discovered over the years since my first introduction to house-plant culture is just what a wide variation in temperature some house plants will tolerate. Many will withstand quite cool conditions so long as these remain constant. A room heat which rises to the mid-70sF during late afternoon and evening, then falls to near freezing overnight will scarcely be endured. On the other hand a temperature of 55–60°F with only slight variations will suit a wide range of house plants.

Most plants hate draughts as much as we do. To be subject to a blast of cold air every time a door opens will cause even the iron-constitutioned 'Fat headed Lizzie', or x *Fatshedera lizei* to the more erudite, to show discomfort. Plants will fare best in good, diffused light, though some shade from direct sun at mid-day in summer time may be advisable, cacti and succulents being the exceptions which, providing they are well watered, respond to being cooked with a prodigal display of flowers.

More plants are killed, according to popular legend, by over-watering than by drought. Water as necessary according to the type of compost, peat- or loam-based, temperature, and whether the plant is in active growth when a regular supply of moisture is essential. When merely resting, the compost should be only moist enough to prevent dehydration.

To Feed or Not to Feed

When resting no plant needs or, indeed, can make use of nutriment; otherwise feeding is adjusted according to vigour of growth, type of compost, and whether the plant is being grown for beauty of flower or quality of foliage. The over-zealous feeder of plants, and I am a reformed sinner in this respect, soon discovers that over-feeding is not just ill advised, it can actually kill. An excess of fertiliser sours the compost, kills plant roots, and wastes money.

Similarly, no rules can be laid down as to when a plant needs repotting. Were it simply a case of waiting until the roots fill all the available space, then the whole business would be made commendably easy. The trick is not to wait until the plant is obviously unhappy before repotting, by which time it is often too late. Rather, tip the plant out, look at the roots and if they are forming a web right around the outside of the ball, repot into fresh compost. This should be of a similar composition to the one it is growing in – loam into loam, peat into peat-based mixtures. For loam composts a clay pot is advisable, while for peat-based mixtures a plastic container is most suitable, otherwise all sorts of problems can occur with watering.

Strelitzia reginae produces striking flowers indoors during early summer. It is often grown from seed by those patient enough to wait up to nine years for the first blossom. Full sunlight is essential

Primula marginata is a superb cool-room house plant, shown here in a moss garden with dwarf shrubs. Propagation is simple; I just pull older plants to pieces after flowering

Looking at the collection of *Pleione*, *Paphiopedilum* and *Bletilla* growing on a west-facing window-sill, I can only reflect on how fashions in house plants have changed over recent years. My orchid window is a very pallid imitation of a much grander affair in a friend's sitting-room. Whereas my taste in house plants embraces anything and everything, there only members of the clan orchid are allowed across the threshold. Certainly the breathtaking picture which they present makes a compelling case for specialisation.

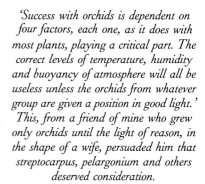

'Success with orchids is dependent on four factors, each one, as it does with most plants, playing a critical part. The correct levels of temperature, humidity and buoyancy of atmosphere will all be useless unless the orchids from whatever group are given a position in good light.'
This, from a friend of mine who grew only orchids until the light of reason, in the shape of a wife, persuaded him that streptocarpus, pelargonium and others deserved consideration.

ORCHIDS

There are over 20,000 different species in the orchid family. Some are so specialised in their cultural requirements that they are difficult to grow even in a greenhouse where levels of temperature, humidity and ventilation are under precise control. Fortunately, there are those like the venus's slipper, *Paphiopedilum*, which do make obligingly easy-to-grow house plants. The orchid which aroused my interest in this fascinating and beautiful family grew on a kitchen window-sill in a farmhouse. The compost this astonishing

The orchid window, late in the season, with only *Phalaenopsis* in bloom. Though the normal flowering season is supposed to be May to June, *lueddemanniana* surprised a friend of mine by producing blooms during October. These orchids are best in a warm, humid greenhouse, and need a resting period during the winter months

plant thrived on was a mixture of molehill loam, sand, and leaf mould in equal parts. Years later I found out the name – *Paphiopedilum insigne*. That it is still my favourite house-plant orchid is a tribute to the flower's insidious charm. The waxy-textured flowers which measure 3–4in (8–10cm) across open during the winter and are a mixture of colours, lime green, yellow, and brown predominating. *Paphiopedilum callosum*, with flowers a range of shades which include pure white striped with purple and green, is another front-runner in my orchids as house plants stakes. The compost is best garden centre mix which on analysis is made up of rock wool, loam, sphagnum moss, crushed bark, sand and a smidgen of leaf mould. One day I shall take courage and try the farmer's compost of molehill soil, leaf mould and sand. Being terrestrial orchids, the *Paphiopedilums* grow best in light shade and a moderate temperature with 55°F the winter minimum. Keep the compost moist, not saturated, except after flowering when watering is reduced to once a week to give the plants a short rest for about a month only.

Though I have grown *Pleione* for thirty years and more, the fragile beauty of the flowers as they open still surprises and delights me. They are not difficult to grow in a blend of loam-based compost. John Innes No 1 potting is the one I use, mixed with rubbed sphagnum moss plus a little lump charcoal. The pseudo bulbs are just gently pushed into the compost until the lower third or thereabouts is buried, the remaining two-thirds being left exposed. Water very carefully until the roots form, usually after four to six weeks, then increase the supply of moisture plus a dilute liquid feed every ten days or so. In the autumn as the leaves shrivel reduce watering so that the compost is kept only just moist enough to prevent shrivelling during the resting period. Repotting is done each year just before flowering. The mauve-pink petals and sepals and pale creamy-yellow disc which combine to form the flowers of *P.formosana* are an essential part of spring on the west-facing orchid window-sill.

Just as in the garden I find it hard to consider plants in isolation, so it is with those grown indoors. Only in suitable association, either contrast or complement, with others can flowers or foliage gain full expression of their qualities. The *Pleione* when in flower look well with the delicate lace-patterned foliage of certain ferns, particularly the venus fern, *Adiantum capillus veneris*. The light-green fronds and delicately formed fan-shaped pinnae (leaves) of the fern complement the orchid flowers precisely. That fern and orchid need similar growing conditions is, indeed, convenient. Foliage is as important in the indoor garden as it is in the shrub border.

There are several easy-going, popular shrubs which can be grown indoors so as to form a perennial backcloth to the seasonal pattern of transitory flowering plants. Rubber plants, those ponderously emphatic, glossy-leaved fugitives from the warmer corners of the globe are prime supporting cast candidates. *Ficus elastica* 'Decora' with large, shiny evergreen leaves is a stoutly positive addition to an indoor garden. Good light, though not direct

The terrestrial orchids have a similar root system to most earth-bound plants. Fine hairs attached to fleshy roots absorb nutrients as the orchid needs them. The epiphytic species have in addition to feeding fibres aerial roots to enable the plant to anchor itself firmly to, and creep along, its support, be it a moss-covered branch, basket, or whatever medium is provided.

There are, just to confuse the issue, single-stemmed orchids, technically known as monopodial, which grow aerial roots only – at which stage the less than enthusiastic beginner gives up all thoughts of gardening and develops an interest in keeping racing pigeons.

sunlight, regular watering and freedom from draughts are easily supplied basic requirements. *Ficus benjamina* has an elegance which the other species lack. Eventually forming quite a tall weeping shrub 4–6ft (1.2–1.8m) high, it can easily be kept within bounds by ruthless pruning. The most effective combination I ever achieved was when a *Clematis indivisa* 'Lobata' with the practice of care and patience was trained to climb up through a *Ficus benjamina*. The weeping fig was planted in a tub set back from a patio door so that the late afternoon and evening sunlight fell upon and through the arching branches. Pure white, yellow-stamened clematis flowers against the dark-green ficus leaves is one of the memories of a room where so many plants grew exceedingly well.

There was a rhododendron, 'Lady Alice Fitzwilliam', whose white flowers filled the room with honeysuckle fragrance. *Acacia dealbata* with panicles of very sweetly scented yellow flowers also flourished in this room which always, in memory, is sun-bright and flower-filled. This combination of *Ficus benjamina, Rhododendron* 'Lady Alice Fitzwilliam' and *Acacia dealbata* has featured in many gardens indoors over the intervening years, for all of them make useful container plants.

BREAD AND BUTTER PLANTS

What, to a committed and experienced cultivator of house plants, may be very basic indeed is to the beginner pristine fresh. This is one of the stimulating and fascinating aspects of gardening, that there are always fresh avenues of investigation left to be explored no matter how proficient we may be.

The plants tried and tested in the rough and tumble of life outside the carefully controlled conditions of a greenhouse form the basis for most indoor gardens. There are advantages to be gained from including several plants which are almost hardy and able to grow in north-facing rooms where the light is less than ideal. This is one reason why the various forms of common ivy are so popular. They also adapt better than most plants to fluctuations in temperature, one of the scourges of the less resilient. Care should be taken that the light intensity is not so low that the variegated-leaved varieties revert to plain green foliage. If this happens just move the plant to better light.

There are some very attractive foliage plants included in the ranks of *Hedera helix*; 'Glache' with a light-cream on green variegation, or 'Domino' with bright-yellow and green marbled leaves. For a jardiniere, 'Ardingley' is self-branching and busy. Grown with primroses and small ferns it makes a most attractive spring compilation. Three others which offer degrees of variegation are 'Goldchild', 'Heisse' and a form of the Canary Island ivy 'Gloire de Marengo'.

Cultivators of house plants show the same poetic invention in their choice of popular names as that shown by country folk in identifying wild flowers. Nowhere is this illustrated better than with *Philodendron scandens*: Heart leaf, sweetheart plant, and the more

There are between 800 and 900 species included in the genus Ficus *(fig), only a small number of them suitable for growing as house plants. Most have attractive foliage, and included in their number are shrubs, climbers, and creepers. Given opportunity, certain* Ficus *will eventually grow to tree size, which in the average living-room can be a little disconcerting.*

Climbing and trailing plants are a very useful extension of what I would describe as sedentary pot plants. The feature common to most is that they cannot grow up without support. They can be trained up to cover a bare wall with pleasant greenery, or grown in pots or on window ledges, shelves, or in a macramé basket they can trail down to provide a living curtain of ornamental foliage.

Philodendron *translated means 'Tree Lover' which indicates that under natural conditions they are climbers, scrambling up some tree or tall shrub to gain access to light and air.*

mundane parlour ivy are just three of this most attractive climber's common names. The climbing stems supported on a sphagnum stick afford a lustrous dark-green background to the whole range of florists' plants, particularly orchids, African violets (Saintpaulia) and epiphyllum, all of them needing something ponderous and tropical to neutralise their flamboyance.

Philodendron is just one of the plants which are positive enough in foliage character to be used as a focal point. The various rooms in a house offer opportunity to those without a garden to work out designs and try various plant associations in a critically selective way. The indoor gardener enjoys one great advantage with all the material growing in pots; changing a whole design from one room to another is a work of minutes. House plants are nothing if not mobile.

When choosing a feature plant which is intended to become, possibly for several years, a focal point, the first consideration must be what sort of conditions the room provides. The temperature may

ABOVE
Anthurium is one of the many plants easily killed by over kindness. It must be kept well moistened with regular misting over the foliage, and out of direct sunlight. Hot, dry conditions will kill very quickly

OPPOSITE
A cymbidium recently added to the orchid window responded to my kindness by growing three flower spikes, one of them with twenty-one perfectly formed florets

Scindapsus aureus (devil's ivy) twining
around a mossed pole gives height to
the indoor garden

be cool, temperate or hot and dry. Consider this in relation to the light intensity, whether it is good, diffused or shady. A good feature plant will grow in the chosen location without requiring constant attention. Though groups of florists' plants such as cyclamen, poinsettia, chrysanthemum, and a legion of others are extravagantly pleasing and exciting, they are a stimulating interlude only. The calm, soothing undertone supplied by the leaf shape and colour of the feature plant is the overriding factor to be taken into account. Just as a few well chosen special plants form the permanent framework against which to paint pictures in the garden, so well chosen feature plants, like a fine piece of furniture, lend a distinctive character to a room. Most of the plants in this category are both popular and well known.

Fatsia japonica, also offered under the earlier name of *Aralia*, like the common ivy is hardy enough to be grown outdoors when it needs more space, as it will do for this is a quick growing shrub. The dark green five- to seven-lobed leaves have a glossy sheen and are much sought after for use in flower arrangements. A plant growing in front of a west-facing window at a stair corner shared all the years of childhood with me – a comforting, friendly presence especially as evening sunlight added a lustre to the highly polished leaves. *X Fatshedera lizei*, that utilitarian and useful product of a union between a *Fatsia* and *Hedera* (ivy), has never quite lived down the comic popular name of 'Fat headed Lizzie'. The large leathery leaves are rendered even more bizarrely attractive by the creamy-white margin in the form *Variegata*. This is a plant which certainly deserves better than being dismissed as comic relief.

Begonia coccinea, popularly known as 'Angel's Wing', impressed me by surviving all the upheaval of first removal, then house renovation. Fortunately, the winter that year was mild but, though the temperature never actually dropped below freezing, the plant must have spent several weeks existing well below the recommended 50°F minimum. The leaves, which are carried on 3ft (0.9m) long, dark-red stems, are dark green tinged at the edges with red. The clusters of coral-red flowers are in evidence from early summer through to autumn. Though by no means a strongly expressive plant, *Begonia coccinea* has the happy knack of combining well with others of widely divergent character. *Asplenium nidus*, the 'Bird's Nest Fern' with dark-green highly polished leaves, is one. *Scindapsus aureus*, 'Devil's Ivy', is another which shares a peculiar affinity with the 'Angel's Wing' begonia – a company of opposites if ever there was one.

Scindapsus aureus is well furnished with vivid-green leaves up to 6in (15cm) long which are splashed with yellow. There are several varieties with differing degrees of variegation. *S.a.* 'Golden Queen' has both stems and leaves suffused with golden yellow, while in *S.aureus* 'Wilcoxii' the green and yellow is laid on in clearly defined zones. There are those who insist that, just as a plant becomes popular, it should suffer a name change adding confusion to difficulty. *Scindapsus* should now be known as *Epipremnum*. By such means are gardeners' lives made complicated, except that genera-

Begonia *species and varieties do make very ornamental indoor garden plants. Some, like* B.coccinea, B.masoniana, *and* B.rex *are notable for their decorative foliage. Others, namely* B. semperflorens cultorum, *and* B.socrotana *hybrids (Hiemalis) are amongst the most brilliant and long flowered of pot plants. All need a humid atmosphere in summer combined with regular watering and feeding when in active growth.*

Ferns make a beautiful companion grouping to the flamboyant begonia flowers.

Chamaedorea elegans (parlour palm) adds a distinctive elegance to the indoor garden arrangement
Where space is limited the parlour palm offers a neat and compact well-ordered appearance over a long period. A useful centrepiece to groups of short-term flowering plants: primroses, begonia, cyclamen, and poinsettia which define the seasons for house-bound gardeners.

tions hence, what is accepted by botanists as *Epipremnum* will still be known amongst gardeners as *Scindapsus*.

The begonia and bird's nest fern will grow in a west- or north-facing room without suffering undue discomfort, which also suits cyclamen, rhododendron, and primrose. Several permutations are therefore possible on a seasonal theme.

While those house plants with large highly polished leaves carry with them a suggestion of moist, humid, dimly lit rainforest, others like the 'Paradise Palm', *Howea forsteriana*, and the 'Parlour Palm', *Chamaedorea elegans*, are evocative of sun-drenched landscapes of blue and gold. Certainly the tall, elegantly arching stems tufted with narrow, leathery leaves do indicate a sun-loving disposition and this is true in the case of parlour palm *Chamaedorea* which thrives in good light and a cool airy situation. *Howea* is the contradiction where appearances deceive, for it has proved to be one of the shade-tolerant plants, which makes it very useful in adding a touch of tropical grace to rooms where the sun rarely penetrates. This grouping of plants which need similar growing conditions and routine maintenance makes them much easier to look after.

A Swiss cheese plant, or *Monstera deliciosa* by any other of its several popular names, would still not appeal to me and yet it is a very good feature plant. The large, leathery dark-green segmented leaves make this curiously constructed piece of vegetation easily identifiable. The plant's habit of growing aerial roots along the stems can be exploited by training them around supports wrapped in sphagnum moss. The divided leaves are an adaptation to reduce the risk of wind damage in the *Monstera's* native land where hurricanes are not uncommon. In spite of this ingenious protection, *Monstera* in my care have shown an intense dislike of draughts and will very promptly die if kept over-watered in winter. They need lots of water in summer and to be kept only just moist in winter. Regular sponging of the leaves is also a promoter of contentment so far as the Swiss cheese plant is concerned.

Though foliage is such an essential part of the garden scene indoor or out, it is the flowering plants which mark the seasonal pattern. This probably explains why I have no liking for chrysanthemums except in late autumn and early winter as house decoration. In colour, pungent scent, and general aspect they are totally out of context at any other time. My memories of chrysanthemum growing are very much pre the 'PotMum' year-round modern concept of the plant. There are few more welcoming sights than that presented by bronze, russet, red and yellow-flowered chrysanthemums grouped around a weeping fig. On a late October day it is as if the glorious festival of autumn in the garden had invaded the house.

Similarly the Italian bell flower, *Campanula isophylla*, is all of summer. Growing in a macramé holder framed in a picture window the star-shaped slightly-cupped blooms in pale blue and white are as refreshing to the eye on a hot August day as a cool drink is to the throat. The flowering season carries on over three months, and I like them best in company with a ground cover of pelargonium 'Hollywood Star' growing in a box fitted to the window-ledge below. The pelargonium flowers are soft rose with a white centre and, like the campanula, they are lovers of good light and long summer days.

Cyclamen were always included in my top five florists' short-term house plants. As happens in so many cases, the cyclamen's universal popularity contributed to its downfall. In seeking to improve on what was already perfect, hybridists have succeeded only in reducing what was once a beautifully proportioned, pastel-shaded flower into something which is gross and ugly. Now I grow my own plants from seed and so can enjoy elegantly proportioned flowers carried on slender stems above attractively marbled leaves. It is important that the compost cyclamen are growing in is allowed to become dry, almost to the wilting point between waterings. Then to make certain the root ball is thoroughly moist I stand the pot in a saucer filled with rain water. Feeding begins at ten-day intervals as the flower buds form.

Why a plant which originates from Mexico and Guatemala is called 'The Swiss cheese plant' is easily explained. The perforated leaves remind some people of Emmental cheese. The fruit which is cone-shaped and covered in rind is edible, though only palatable when full ripe. A personal opinion: it has a savour which closely resembles banana-flavoured, week-old custard.

Chrysanthemums grouped around a variegated weeping fig form an indoor, autumn garden

Euphorbia pulcherrima, the ever recurring poinsettia, are like the 'pot' chrysanthemums a contrived, though admittedly brilliantly colourful, pot plant. The stem length, again like those of the chrysanthemum, can be reduced by treatment with chemicals to make the plant compact. Though the normal flowering season is during the winter, just as with chrysanthemums, by keeping the poinsettia in a dark room for twelve to fourteen hours each day for nine weeks, flowers and the scarlet, white, or creamy-yellow bracts surrounding them can be induced to appear out of season. Comparisons are odious and in most cases unfair; yet I will, nevertheless, make one. Christmas time it was, with the room decorated as befitted the season with several poinsettia included in the array. The table arrangement of Christmas roses floated in a bowl of water had the effect of making all else appear vulgar and the brilliance of the poinsettia become mere tawdry ostentation. Now I grow them around a bird's nest fern *Asplenium* or similar very positive plant with highly polished leaves which reduces the flamboyance of the bracts to an acceptable degree.

Primroses are one of those useful dual-purpose plants which, having served one flowering term indoors, can then be planted out in the garden. More than any other, primroses are for me the very sum and substance of spring, so to have them in bloom indoors during the winter is like being given a glimpse of light in a dark tunnel. A cool, airy room with good light suits them best as it does *Rhododendron simsii*. In fact, this similarity of preferred growing conditions forms the basis for a complete indoor garden, with a 4ft (122cm) high camellia 'Pink Perfection' providing the essential woodland context. The rhododendrons are grouped on the side furthest away from the window with the primroses and a selection of bulbs, snowdrops, crocus, and early daffodils, as a feature on the lighter side. With the forest bark pot-plunging material hidden under a covering of moss, the picture not only gains authenticity but the close grouping provides the sort of humid climate which suits them all. All the various components of this group spend summer outdoors on the north side of the house. With regular feeding and watering they return refreshed and well furnished with flower buds to the greenhouse, and then in due season are moved to a suitable cool, airy porch as the flower season approaches.

Saintpaulia have proved, possibly more than any other plant in my experience, that though a given set of recommended cultivations may be faithfully adhered to, this by no means makes success certain. The best growing temperature is around 65°F. I have noticed that over 80°F flowering and growth stops, particularly if the atmosphere becomes dry in consequence of the high temperature. The African violet grows best in moisture-saturated air, a condition difficult to maintain under average living-room arrangements. Because of the heat and humidity relationship, bathrooms are frequently proposed as being the best place the house offers as a *Saintpaulia* habitat. I grew the best African violets ever, with robust, blemish-free foliage, by cosseting them in a bathroom.

Rhododendron and camellia, though not true house plants in the accepted meaning of the term, are most rewarding. During the summer outdoors I can watch the slow development of the crop of buds which will mature into flowers. That they open in winter's worst month for me, February, is especially pleasing.

African violets are the most popular flowering house plants. There is no set flowering season although, without supplementary lighting, this is confined to the high light intensity months of summer. Given artificial light, Saintpaulia can be kept in bloom all year round. A dilute liquid feed every two weeks when growth is active helps with flower production.

Unfortunately, the light intensity was such that not one plant in the collection of named varieties flowered. Too late I found out that good light for fourteen hours each day is an essential inducement to flower formation. Plants can be encouraged into flower during the shortening days of autumn and winter by providing supplementary, artificial lighting and keeping the temperature at around 65°F. All things considered, African violets show curiously human characteristics. Their leaves discolour when exposed to over-strong sunlight. Yellowish-coloured mottling on the foliage is a result of using cold instead of tepid water to keep the compost moist. Small flowers simply mean the plant is hungry. There is nothing idiosyncratic about that, for my skin turned distinctly blotchy when I fell into the river during a hill ramble last March. Given due regard to their simple needs, the African violets are a deal less demanding guests than the average relation. Bear in mind one important difference between plant and human. Whereas a favourite relation appreciates the spaciousness of a full-sized bed, African violets need to be kept cosily confined in nothing larger than a half pot. For all varieties have a shallow root system and a deep pot would leave too much unused compost to go sourly stagnant and become poisonously lethal.

I was put off growing Cape primrose, *Streptocarpus*, for years by reports of their seeming intransigence. Only when I was given a packet of seed by a despairing seed merchant with instructions to sow it and see for myself, did the truth about the Cape primrose reveal itself. They are more beautiful than the grossly flamboyant *Gloxinia* which until then had held my attention, for the smaller flowers carried on slender stems are graceful and elegant. The light needs to be bright yet away from full sun, with the pot plunged in peat or moist pebbles to ensure a proper degree of humidity. Like the African violets they are best kept moist with rain water, though the tap sort will do if it is lime-free. Be liberal with water during the summer and keep the compost on the moist side of dry in winter. As to feeding, they respond to a weak high-potash tomato feed every ten days during the growing season by producing a seemingly inexhaustible succession of blooms.

The majority of popular house plants do not adapt readily to cultivation in centrally heated rooms. Hot, dry air is to most of them a handicap to gracious living. For those continually frustrated in their efforts to participate in the joyful pursuit of indoor gardening, let me suggest growing those specially adapted plants which originate from the drier, less fertile regions, collectively known as cacti and succulents. They offer unusual shapes and flowers which are often brilliantly coloured. Many will put up with a winter temperature of 50°F so long as the compost they are growing in is kept only just moist enough to prevent the plant dehydrating. My plants grow on a south-facing, upstairs window-sill, protected from frost by double glazing. They are watered twice or three times a week in summer, given a liquid feed in May, June and July, and they respond to my sympathetic understanding with a gratitude of flowers.

Streptocarpus are elegant, long flowering, easy-to-grow house plants. The streptocarpus illustrated has, at the time of writing, been in flower continuously for eight months which makes it a first-class rent payer. Leaves cut into sections 4in (10cm) long will root if placed in a peat sand compost. A temperature of 65°F quickens up root formation.

Aechmea fasciata, or the urn plant with silver-and-green-striped leaves growing from a funnel-shaped centre, is an everyman plant. In summer all that is required is to keep the hollow central tube full of water and the compost evenly moist. After flowering the parent plant dies but only after forming two or more offshoots as a reward to the gardener for patient care.

Vriesia splendens, the 'Flaming Sword' with equally decorative foliage and a sword-shaped flower spike composed of red and yellow bracts, thrives on similar treatment in good light, though shaded from direct sunlight.

The ubiquitous Easter and Christmas cactus, *Rhipsalidopsis gaertneri* and *Schlumbergera truncata*, given proper care will become a permanent picture growing ever larger and more floriferous. The scarlet or red flowers which grow from the flattened stems are tube shaped and command attention by their profusion and brilliant colour. Like all the breed they need copious watering and regular feeding at fourteen-day intervals throughout summer. In winter I reduce the water supply and do not feed at all, except with adequate praise for floral artistry.

Those plants referred to by the majority of gardeners and non-gardeners alike as cactus offer a fascinating field of exploration. Indeed, several times when suffering from Montezuma's revenge while plant hunting in Mexico I found boskages of cactus the only place for private meditation in an otherwise naked landscape. Such opportunities of frequent, intimate study gave me a fresh appreciation of their quality. I have one memory in particular of prickly pear and the towering column of cereus whose funnel-shaped blooms open at night to fill the air with a delectable perfume framed against an orange and scarlet sunrise. Like all popular plants the cacti and succulents are variously identified with an imaginative selection of names. Lithops or pebble cactus from Africa really do resemble smoothly rounded stones. The flowers grow from a groove between the fleshy leaves.

Aporocactus flagelliformis, the trailing green-stemmed rat's tail, is best grown in a macramé holder so that the pink flowers can flaunt their charms each April.

Peanut cactus, the Argentinian *Chamaecereus silvestri*, is neatly fashioned and undemanding, and surprised me by producing large funnel-shaped flowers of a particularly brilliant shade of red. Orchid cactus, or *Epiphyllum x hybridum*, over the long years of our association have proved such durable, easily grown and amicable house plants that each introduction to the menage is promptly given a pet name. The large, silky-textured flowers which open during the summer range in colour from pink, red, yellow to white and a pleasing orange shade. Cuttings made from stem sections root best when left to dry out on the potting shed bench for a day or two.

Just where *Kalanchoe blossfeldiana* fits in the succulent classification I do not know, for the red flowers insist on appearing just when winter drags leaden-footed into laggard spring. By limiting the amount of daylight each plant receives, the blossoming can be induced at any season. Not being particularly enamoured of flowers, or vegetables for that matter, out of season, I just let nature take its course and allow this little Tom Thumb of a plant to flower as and when it pleases.

There is no better way of exciting a child's interest in growing plants than starting them off with a collection of cactus. In shape, character and flower they are so different from other plants as to stimulate a youngster's interest.

Aechmea fasciata grow naturally in the jungle, away from direct sun, and a mist over the leaves in hot weather will please them well. I add just a drop or two of liquid feed to misting water once a month, for they absorb nutrients though their curious leaves

Index

Page numbers in *italic* refer to illustrations

*By sowing a quantity of seed collected from the numerous species
and varieties of lily growing in my own and friends' gardens I
ensure a regular supply of healthy young bulbs to replace any
which die. Seed sown in deep boxes or large pots in leaf mould,
loam, or sand compost will germinate and grow on with only
minimum attention in the way of watering and feeding until the
time comes for them to be transferred to the garden. Seeds of
some species will germinate very quickly, others germinate yet
show no signs of top growth for maybe a year. Never be in a
hurry to discard supposedly infertile seed; it could only be biding
its own time.*

Epimedium was one of those Latin names which I could never easily remember. Think of a drunken fortune teller, my guide and mentor suggested, and in consequence 'happy medium' gained instant recollection.

Gladiolus byzantinus is a perfectly hardy European introduced to Britain in 1629. Given a suitable, light, free draining soil, it will naturalise both by means of seed and underground stolon. The flowers borne aloft on 3ft (91cm) high stems are shaded with various tints of purple, warm coppery brown, and crimson, and magenta with cream stripes on the lower petals. In the south flowering occurs usually in early June. Lovely when grown in company with Thermopsis montana *of the bright straw-yellow, lupin-shaped flower spike.*

The brilliant blue trumpets of *Gentiana sino-ornata* with the 10in
(25cm) high lilac-rose flowerspikes of *Astilbe chinensis* 'Pumila'
– part of September's entourage

Plain green and variegated hollies (the most durable and beautiful of evergreen shrubs) festooned with *Tropaeolum*

A mature Magnolia grandiflora, *when the enormous creamy-white flowers each measuring 8in (20cm) across are full open on a warm August evening, fills the air with a delectable fragrance. The glossy evergreen leaves, which when they first unfurl are reddish brown underneath, are a proper embellishment to the blossom. Magnolia species may all be grown from seed which is a cheap way to acquire what in nursery terms are very expensive plants. Seed should be sown fresh for it soon loses viability. A* Magnolia sieboldii *seedling will be about 3ft (0.9m) high after two years, so growth is not slow by any standard.*